Documents in Contemporary History

General editor
Kevin Jefferys
Faculty of Arts and Education, University of Plymouth

From Beveridge to Blair

MANCHESTER
UNIVERSITY PRESS

Documents in Contemporary History is a series designed for sixth-formers and undergraduates in higher education. It aims to provide both an overview of specialist research on topics in post-1939 British history and a wide-ranging selection of primary source material.

Already published in the series

From Beveridge to Blair
The first fifty years of Britain's
welfare state 1948–98

Edited by Margaret Jones
Research Fellow, Department of Historical Studies, University of Bristol
and Rodney Lowe
Professor of Contemporary History, University of Bristol

Manchester University Press
Manchester and New York
distributed exclusively in the USA by Palgrave

Copyright © Margaret Jones and Rodney Lowe 2002

The right of Margaret Jones and Rodney Lowe to be identified as the editors of this work has been asserted by them in accordance with the Copyright, Designs and Patents Act 1988.

Published by Manchester University Press
Oxford Road, Manchester M13 9NR, UK
and Room 400, 175 Fifth Avenue, New York, NY 10010, USA
www.manchesteruniversitypress.co.uk

Distributed exclusively in the USA by
Palgrave, 175 Fifth Avenue, New York,
NY 10010, USA

Distributed exclusively in Canada by
UBC Press, University of British Columbia, 2029 West Mall,
Vancouver, BC, Canada V6T 1Z2

British Library Cataloguing-in-Publication Data
A catalogue record for this book is available from the British Library

Library of Congress Cataloging-in-Publication Data applied for

ISBN   0 7190 4102 3 *hardback*
        0 7190 4103 1 *paperback*

First published 2002

10 09 08 07 06 05 04 03 02   10 9 8 7 6 5 4 3 2 1

Printed in Great Britain
by Bookcraft (Bath) Ltd, Midsomer Norton

Contents

ACKNOWLEDGEMENTS

Acknowledgements

For permission to reproduce copyright material, the publishers and editors should like to thank the following:

Professor David Donnison (pp. 13–14); the Controller of Her Majesty's Record Office (p. 11, 2.1.1, 2.1.5, 2.2.4, 3.1.1, 3.2.2, 3.3.1–2, 3.3.4–5, 3.5.1–2, 4.1.1–2, 4.1.4–8, 4.2.4, 4.3.3, 4.4.1–2, 5.1.1, 5.2.3, 5.2.5, 5.4.5, 6.1.1, 6.1.3–4, 6.2.2, 6.2.4, 6.3.4, 6.3.6, 6.3.9), for material held in the Public Record Office, London (2.3.1, 3.4.1, 4.1.3, 6.3.3), and for material from the official reports (Hansard) on behalf of Parliament (2.1.2, 2.2.2–3, 2.3.3, 3.2.1, 4.2.3, 4.2.5, 5.1.2, 5.2.7, 5.3.1, 6.2.1); Cambridge University Press (1.1.1); Ann Oakley (1.1.2); the Conservative Party (1.2.1, 1.3.3, 5.1.3, 5.2.1, 5.2.4); Penguin Books Ltd (1.2.2, 4.2.1); Routledge (1.3.1); the Institute of Economic Affairs (1.3.2); Civitas (1.3.4, 1.4.3); the Institute of Public Policy Research (1.4.1–2); Professor Anthony Giddens and Blackwell Publishers (1.4.4); Times Newspapers Ltd (© 1948, 1984, 1963, 1968, 1973) (2.1.3, 5.3.2, 5.4.1–2, 6.3.5); Ashgate Publishing Ltd (2.1.4, 5.2.2, 5.2.6); HarperCollins Publishers Ltd (2.2.1, 3.3.3, 4.3.4, 5.3.3); the Fabian Society (2.3.2, 2.4.1); David Higham Associates (2.3.4, 3.4.2); the Child Poverty Action Group (2.4.3–4); the Joseph Rowntree Foundation (2.4.5, 6.2.3); PFD on behalf of Nigel Lawson (© Nigel Lawson) (3.4.3); Pan Macmillan (5.1.4); *The Guardian* (5.3.5); Des Wilson (5.4.3); David Skinner (5.4.4); the Audit Commission (6.1.2); the Press Association (6.3.2, 6.3.5); *The Independent* (6.3.7–8).

Every reasonable effort has been made to contact all copyright holders, and the publishers and editors regret if any have been overlooked.

We should also like to thank Rebecca Rutherford and Ian Gough, both of whom contributed in their own peculiar ways to the completion of this book.

Abbreviations

BMA	British Medical Association
CPAG	Child Poverty Action Group
DHSS	Department of Health and Social Security
DOE	Department of the Environment
DSS	Department of Social Security
FC	Family Credit
FIS	Family Income Supplement
GP	general practitioner
HCSA	Hospital Consultants and Specialists Association
IEA	Institute of Economic Affairs
IPPR	Institute of Public Policy Research
MP	member of Parliament
NHS	National Health Service
NUPE	National Union of Public Employees
SERPS	State Earnings-Related Pension Scheme
TUC	Trades Union Congress
UN	United Nations
WFTC	Working Families Tax Credit

Chronology of events

Year	Government	Social security	Health	Education	Housing	Pers. social services
1942	**Coalition** (Churchill)	Beveridge Report, *Social Insurance and Allied Services*				
1943				*Educational Reconstruction*		
1944			*A National Health Service*	Butler Education Act	Dudley Report on housing standards; *Control of Land Use*	Lady Allen letter to *The Times*
1945	**Labour** (Attlee)	Family Allowance Act			White Paper, *Housing*	Death of Dennis O'Neill
1946		National Insurance Act	National Health Service Act	Barlow, *Scientific Manpower*	New Towns Act	Curtis, *Care of Children*
1948		National Assistance Act; the Appointed Day; Attlee's broadcast			Town and Country Planning Act	Children Act
1951	**Conservative** (Churchill) (Eden 1955)		Introduction of charges: Bevan's resignation		Macmillan's 'Housing Crusade'	

Year	Government	Social security	Health	Education	Housing	Pers. social services
1956			Guillebaud Report		Higher subsidies for 'high rise'	
1957	(Macmillan)				Rent Act: staged deregulation of rents	
1959		National Insurance Act: introduction of earnings-related pensions		Crowther, *15-18*	Town and Country Planning Act: deregulation of land	Mental Health Act: care in the community
1960						Ingleby, *Children and Young Persons*
1962			Hospital Plan			
1963		IEA, *Choice in Welfare*		Newsom, *Half Our Future*; Robbins, *Higher Education*	Rachman scandal	Children and Young Persons Act: provision for prevention of neglect and abuse
1965	**Labour** (Wilson 1964)	'Rediscovery' of poverty		Circular 10/65 on comprehensive education	Report into 'Rachmanism', *Housing in Greater London*	Founding of the Child Poverty Action Group and Disabled Income Group
1966		Supplementary Benefit Act; National Insurance Act: earnings-related short-term benefits; Rating Act: rate rebate scheme			Foundation of Shelter, pressure group for the homeless	

Year	Government	Social security	Health	Education	Housing	Pers. social services
1967				Plowden, *Children and their Primary Schools*	Shift in policy towards renovation	
1968					Ronan Point collapse	Seebohm Report
1969				First Black Paper		
1970	**Conservative** (Heath)	Family Income Supplement		Circular 10/70 cancelling 10/65; school leaving age raised to 16		Local Authority Social Services Act: implementing Seebohm; Chronically Sick and Disabled Persons Act
1972		Housing Finance Act: rent rebates		*Education: A Framework for Expansion*	Housing Finance Act: subsidy for people not buildings	
1973		Keith Joseph's 'Cycle of Deprivation' speech	National Health Service Act: reorganisation of administrative structure	Employment Training Act: shift of vocational training to industry	Clay Cross commissioner appointed	Death of Maria Colwell
1974	**Labour** (Wilson)			Circular 4/74: compulsory comprehensive education	Council house rent freeze	

Year	Government	Social security	Health	Education	Housing	Pers. social services
1975		Employment Protection Act: maternity benefit; Child Benefit Act; Social Security Act: SERPS	'Pay Beds' controversy	William Tyndale School controversy		
1976	(Callaghan)			Callaghan's Ruskin College speech; Education Act: end of direct grant schools		
1978				Warnock, *Education of Handicapped Children*		Wolfenden, *Future of Voluntary Organisations*
1979	**Conservative** (Thatcher)		Merrison, *NHS*	Education Act: cuts in school meals and transport		
1980		Social Security Act: reform of the supplementary benefit; Social Security (no. 2) Act: abolished the earnings-related rule, implemented 5 per cent cuts, froze child benefit	The Black Report on inequalities in health	Education Act: assisted places scheme; announcement of GCSEs; Circular 4/74 cancelled	'Right to Buy': sale of council houses	

Year	Government	Social security	Health	Education	Housing	Pers. social services
1981						*Growing Older*
1982		Social Security and Housing Benefit Act: sickness benefit replaced by Statutory Sick Pay				Housing Benefit Act	
1983			Griffiths, *Management Enquiry*: the 'managerial revolution'			Mental Health Act: new responsibilities and powers to social workers
1984						*Care in the Community*
1985		Fowler's Social Security review		Swann, *Education of Children from Ethnic Minority Groups*		Death of Jasmine Beckford
1986		Social Security Act: income support, social fund, family credit		City technology colleges		Audit Commission, *Making a Reality of Community Care*
1988				Education Act: 'opt out' and national curriculum	Housing Act: tenants' choice and Housing Action Trusts	Griffiths, *Community Care: Agenda for Action*
1989			*Working for Patients*			Children Act; *Caring for People*

Year	Government	Social security	Health	Education	Housing	Pers. social services
1990	(Major)		NHS and Community Care Act: set up the internal market		'Rough Sleepers Initiative'	NHS and Community Care Act: local authorities to act as 'enablers' not 'providers'
1992				Education Act: publication of results; Further and Higher Education Act: incoporation of further education colleges and polytechnics		
1994		Commission for Social Justice				
1995						Carers (Recognition and Services) Act: assessment for carers
1996				Nursery Education and Grant Maintained Act: vouchers for nursery education		

Year	Government	Social security	Health	Education	Housing	Pers. social services
1997	**Labour** (Blair)			*Excellence in Schools*		*A New Partnership for Care in Old Age*; *Utting, People Like Us*
1998		*A New Contract for Welfare*: blueprint; launch of the New Deal				*Modernising Social Services*

Introduction

The year 1998 marked the fiftieth anniversary of the British welfare state. Its 'creation' on 5 July 1948 was heralded by an official publicity campaign which proclaimed 'this day makes history'; and it has since come to be regarded as the major achievement of Attlee's postwar Labour government, which in turn is regarded as Labour's most effective period in office. Like all welfare states in western Europe, it initially expanded but after the mid-1970s it came under increasing attack, particularly from the Conservative government of Mrs Thatcher. When Tony Blair won a landslide election victory in 1997 even greater than that of Attlee in 1945, however, its future once again looked secure. A New Labour government, it was assumed, would not disown and – more positively – would at least wish to match the welfare achievements of its illustrious predecessor.

The anniversary celebrations in 1998, however, were surprisingly muted. New Labour did publish a blueprint for reform, *New Ambitions for Our Country: A New Contract for Welfare* (Cm 3805), but its opening paragraphs revealed a considerable ambivalence. They read:

> 1. The welfare state was born 50 years ago. At its birth, the vision was broad and encompassed all welfare services, such as education and health as well as social security benefits. We need to capture that original vision. The existing system needs reform. For many people the system is increasing their dependence on benefit, rather than helping them to lead independent and fulfilling lives.
>
> 2. There are three key problems with the existing system:
>
> • inequality and exclusion are worsening, especially among children and pensioners, despite rising spending on social security;

- people face a series of barriers to paid work, including financial disincentives; and
- fraud is taking money out of the system and away from genuine claimants.

The broader vision, alluded to in the first three sentences, was scarcely mentioned thereafter. Instead, attention was focused almost exclusively on the need for reform and in particular the defects of the existing social security system, itemised in the second paragraph. The real cost of social security, it was emphasised, had increased eight-fold since 1948. Rather than reducing inequality and social exclusion, however, it had encouraged dependency and dishonesty. One-fifth of households containing an adult of working age, for example, had no one in work. One in seven benefit claimants found themselves worse off in work and so did not actively seek it. Some £4 billion a year was being lost in fraud. In short, a great deal of taxpayers' money was being spent to intensify the very problem it was supposed to resolve.

What was the 'original vision' of the postwar welfare state which had become overshadowed and overlooked by 1998? To what extent had welfare policy *as a whole* become as defective as the social security system was perceived to be? The purpose of this book is to 'recapture', through a wide range of original sources, the original vision. It will then look at the record of each of the 'core' welfare services to see the extent to which they fulfilled or betrayed their original objectives.

Welfare policy, however, is an extremely contentious and complex subject. Rarely in the past fifty years has there been agreement about what a welfare state actually is, let alone about what its underlying objectives should be. Before individual policies can be examined, therefore, it is important to provide a working definition of Britain's welfare state and to outline its chronological development. That is the purpose of this introduction. Chapter 1 will then cover the major ideological battles which it provoked.

DEFINING THE WELFARE STATE

The establishment of the welfare state

In the preceding section the phrases 'creation' of the welfare state and 'core' services were placed in inverted commas. This was deliberate. Given that there has been little agreement about what welfare states are, there can equally be little agreement about when they were established and what services they include. The choice of a date or a given range of services, in other words, is not value-free and immediately biases analysis in favour of one definition or another.

Linguistics does not help to resolve the dilemma. The term '*wohlfahrstaat*' was coined in Germany, but it was used mainly by conservatives as a term of abuse for the social rights established in the 1920s which overburdened and finally bankrupted the Weimar Republic. Moreover German historians tend to prefer the term '*sozialstaat*' or 'social state', which suggests a 'mixed economy' of welfare (provided by government, voluntary agencies and the market) and permits the evolution of welfare policy to be traced back to Bismarck in the 1880s. '*Wohlfahrstaat*' remains today, like 'welfare' in the USA, essentially a derogatory term and one restricted to a system of centralised, means-tested benefits.

In Britain, there has been considerable sympathy for such reservations. Even the supposed founder of the welfare state, Sir William Beveridge, disliked the 'Santa Claus' – or the 'something for nothing' – connotations of the term. He preferred the 'social service' state, which emphasised not just social rights but also individual responsibilities.[1] In the 1980s, under American influence, the term was also surreptitiously narrowed down to the social security system. *New Ambitions for Our Country*, with its concentration on social security and its stress on individual responsibility, reflected both these sets of reservations.

The question that should perhaps be asked, therefore, is not why were the anniversary celebrations so muted but why were there any celebrations at all? The answer is that 5 July 1948 was the 'Appointed Day' on which five classic pieces of welfare legislation became operative: the National Insurance and National Assistance Acts; the National Health Service Act; the Town and Country Planning Act; and the Children Act. Each had been planned individually. Collectively, however, they became the subject of a major broadcast by Attlee, and in retrospect they can be seen to have represented a watershed in welfare principles and practice within Britain. In relation to individual rights, the Children Act established the overriding policy objective for children in care to be not just employability (as under the Poor Law) but the proper development of each child's individual

---

1   J. Harris, *William Beveridge*, Oxford, 1997, p. 452.

'character and ability'. The Town and Country Planning Act firmly shifted the balance between public and private rights in favour of the former. Its clauses relating to compulsory purchase and a betterment tax contained the power to release private land for building and to ensure that the community as a whole – and not just the fortuitous landowner – benefited from any 'windfall' profit from land sales. The lives of the vast majority of people were also transformed overnight by the National Health Service (NHS), which, by guaranteeing treatment free at the point of access, released women and children in particular from the fear that, for lack of individual or family resources, they would be denied medical help in times of need. It was above all, however, the National Insurance and Assistance Acts which have been deemed in retrospect to have broken radical new ground.

These Acts were broadly based on the 1942 Beveridge Report, which was itself ambivalent about its radicalism. Like the Germans, Beveridge was fully aware of the achievements of earlier government welfare initiatives – in which he had himself been involved. 'The provision for most of the many varieties of need', his Report admitted, 'has already been made in Britain on a scale not surpassed and hardly rivalled in any other country in the world' (Cmd 6404, para. 3). It then boldly proclaimed that 'a revolutionary moment in the world's history is a time for revolutions, not for patching' (para. 7), but immediately qualified this by admitting that 'the scheme here proposed is in some ways a revolution, but in more important ways is a natural development from the past. It is a British revolution' (para. 31).

However, the American historian Peter Baldwin has had no such doubts, arguing that the Report and its implementation can be seen as 'an historical event equivalent in importance and stature to the French or Russian Revolutions'.[2] There are three major justifications for this claim. First, postwar governments adopted Beveridge's 'holistic' approach by accepting, unlike in the 1930s and again in the 1980s, that economic and social policy should be complementary and not antagonistic. Secondly, there was the principle of universalism. To eradicate want, *everyone* was obliged by the National Insurance Act to pay a weekly insurance contribution into a common fund. This eradicated the division between 'first-class' and 'second-class'

2 P. Baldwin, 'Beveridge in the *longue durée*', in J. Hills et al., *Beveridge and Social Security*, Oxford, 1994, p. 40.

citizens, and thus between first-class and second-class services. A measure of national unity or 'social solidarity' was thereby achieved. Finally, there was the principle of comprehensiveness. Each contributor was covered against every eventuality that might lead to an inadvertent loss of income 'from the cradle to the grave'. Everyone, therefore, was able to enjoy a privilege previously available only to the rich: 'social security' or the freedom from the fear of poverty. As one clearly relieved shop assistant proclaimed in 1943: 'it is like marrying a rich husband without having to have a husband'.[3]

Consequently the key historic significance of the Appointed Day, with its broad implementation of the Beveridge Report, was its fusion for the very first time of individual freedom, which had always been the central value of liberal states, with collective security, which had always been the major attraction of authoritarian ones. Ordinary people were no longer just free in theory but, released from the fear of poverty, became free in practice. Faced by mass unemployment and poverty between the wars, liberal democracies had looked feeble compared to fascist and communist regimes. Now they no longer need do so. This was the optimistic vision that, at the start of the Cold War, the British welfare state projected.

Such retrospective analysis reinforces contemporary instincts that the Appointed Day 'made history'. In relation to grand theory the sociologist T.H. Marshall had claimed that, by the establishment of individual social rights, the 1940s were the culmination of a historic movement which had seen the successive establishment of individual civil and political rights in the seventeenth and nineteenth centuries (see 1.1.1). Rather more prosaically, he also best expressed the widespread feeling that the sum of welfare legislation was greater than its individual parts. As he wrote:

> The natural evolution of ideas and institutions led ultimately to the transformation of the system. The transformation, or revolution, consisted in the welding together of the measures of social policy into a whole which, for the first time, acquired thereby a personality of its own and a meaning that had hitherto been only vaguely glimpsed. We adopted the term 'Welfare State' to denote this new entity composed of old elements.[4]

3 J. Jacobs (ed.), *Beveridge, 1940–1992*, London, 1992, p. 24.
4 T.H. Marshall, *Social Policy*, London, 1975, p. 84. His grander theories are expounded in *Citizenship and Social Class*, Cambridge, 1950.

The core policies

The British welfare state, as established in 1948, was thus a mix of universal and comprehensive policies through which government became more positively responsible for the promotion of individual welfare. What precisely, however, did the mix contain? Its 'core' policies have been conventionally equated with the 'five giants on the road to reconstruction' identified in the Beveridge Report: want, disease, ignorance, squalor and idleness (para. 8). Hence they include social security and the personal social services, the health service, education, housing and employment policy. Over time and in international perspective, however, such a range of policies has been exposed as rather narrow.

Richard Titmuss, as professor of social administration at the London School of Economics between 1950 and 1973, was 'the most perceptive critic and the strongest advocate' of Britain's welfare state during its expansion, and as early as 1955 he identified two additional 'major categories of welfare'.[5] The first was 'fiscal welfare', or the granting of tax allowances to individuals to offset the cost of social responsibilities (such as the upbringing of children) or of certain types of behaviour which government wished to encourage (such as interest on mortgages for the purchase of private houses). The second was 'occupational welfare', or tax concessions to firms which provided services for their workforce (such as occupational pensions). Both were welfare services since they 'involved collective interventions to meet certain needs of the individual and/or to serve the wider interests of society'.[6] They were also redistributory since the revenue forgone by government had to be raised by increased taxation elsewhere. There was, however, one fundamental difference from conventional welfare policy: benefits were targeted on and unduly advantaged the better-off. By the 1970s, for example, the cost of mortgage interest tax relief far exceeded that of subsidising council housing.

Titmuss's critique can be taken even further, because his focus on the tax system underlines the fact that individual welfare is affected not just by how policy is targeted but also by how it is financed. There is little obvious gain, let alone redistribution, if recipients of increased benefits have their tax liability increased by an equivalent sum (be the

5   D. Piachaud, *New Statesman*, 13 April 1973, p. 521.
6   R.M. Titmuss, *Essays on the 'Welfare State'*, London, 1958, p. 42.

tax direct, like income tax; indirect, like VAT or duty on petrol; or in the form of national insurance contributions). The incidence of taxation is therefore central to any analysis of a welfare state and the secret history of postwar British welfare policy is in fact the decreasing progressiveness of its financing as a switch has been made – especially in the 1980s – from company to individual, and from direct to indirect ('stealth') taxation.

Titmuss's focus on occupational welfare also highlights another policy area that has been central to other western welfare systems: the labour market. In Australia and New Zealand, for example, the classic means of state intervention has been through arbitration awards by which workers were guaranteed a minimum wage sufficient to meet their social needs. If everyone in consequence could buy all the services they required, there was no need for the state to provide them. More ambitiously, in continental Europe there is a 'corporatist' tradition whereby government, employers and workers combine to ensure the international industrial competitiveness on which full employment, and ultimately the welfare of all, depends. Government and employers guarantee long-term industrial investment, whilst in return trade unions agree to moderate wage claims and accept, when necessary, retraining and relocation. Britain has flirted with such policies through, for example, the National Economic Development Council established by the Conservatives in 1962 and the national minimum wage introduced by New Labour in 1998. Such initiatives were, however, pale shadows of practice abroad.

Both taxation and labour market policy went largely unmentioned in the Beveridge Report, and this omission, for some, makes it a very restricted blueprint for the postwar welfare state. Absent also is any mention of social legislation (in relation to such issues as divorce, abortion and homosexuality), although the liberalisation of such legislation in the 1960s arguably had as great an impact on individual welfare as any of the 'core' services.

The potential range of welfare policy is, therefore, immense; but for a book of this size there has to be some restriction if any policy is to be covered in adequate depth. Consequently it has been decided to concentrate on the 'core' services at the expense of fiscal and occupational welfare, taxation, active labour market policy and social legislation. Moreover one core policy has been omitted: employment policy. This is by no means to minimise its importance, which is summarised below, but rather because it is covered in another volume in this series: Alan Booth, *British Economic Development since 1945* (1995).

The exception of employment policy

One of the radical breakthroughs in the 1940s, which has already been identified, was the recognition that economic and social policy should be complementary and not antagonistic. Beveridge emphasised the need for this when he justified making 'the maintenance of employment' one of the three assumptions on which his plan for social security depended. Administratively, he argued, it provided a check against the development of a 'dependency' culture because the offer of a job could test whether a benefit claimant was genuine or not. Financially, it was vital to the solvency of the social services because it would maximise tax revenue whilst minimising benefit claims. Morally, and most importantly, individual welfare depended on the availability of a rewarding, well-paid job. As he argued:

> Income security ... is so inadequate a provision for human happiness that to put it forward by itself as a sole or principal measure of reconstruction hardly seems worth doing. It should be accompanied by an announced determination to use the powers of the State to whatever extent may prove necessary to ensure for all, not indeed absolute continuity of work, but a reasonable chance of productive employment. (Cmd 6404, para. 440)

Such reasoning was quickly accepted by both major parties, as their election manifestos demonstrated. In 1950, for instance, the Conservative Party insisted that 'we regard the maintenance of full employment as the first aim of a Conservative Government', whilst in the following year the Labour Party retorted: 'Full employment through six years of peace is the greatest of all Labour's achievements. It has never happened before. It has meant a revolution in the lives of our people.'[7]

By the mid-1970s, however, doubts had begun to grow about whether governments could, or indeed should, guarantee full employment. In a famous speech to the Labour Party conference in 1976 the

---

7   F.W.S. Craig (ed.), *British General Election Manifestos 1990–1974*, London, 1975, p. 174.

prime minister, James Callaghan, effectively abandoned the commitment because traditional Keynesian policies were seen to be damaging rather than stimulating the economy. As he admitted:

> We used to think that you could just spend your way out of a recession and increase employment by cutting taxes and boosting government spending. I tell you in all candour, that option no longer exists, and in so far as it ever did exist, it worked by injecting inflation into the economy. And each time that happened the average level of unemployment has risen. Higher inflation was followed by higher unemployment. That is the history of the past twenty years.[8]

Similar reasoning informed the simultaneous attack on the welfare state from within the Conservative Party, which was initially targeted more on economic than social policy; and after Mrs Thatcher's election victory in 1979 the opportunity arose to put the new monetarist policy into practice. Beveridge's warnings then came home to roost. Budget deficits grew, contrary to monetarist principles, because declining economic growth and rising unemployment meant that tax revenue was insufficient to meet the additional cost of unemployment relief. Society also became increasingly divisive, as individual expectations were disappointed whilst – and partly in consequence – the unemployed were consistently condemned, as in the interwar years, as authors of their own fate. Given that jobs could not be offered to test willingness to work, there could be no disproof – or indeed proof – of allegations concerning the growth of a dependency culture within an escalating 'underclass'.

So strong was the new consensus, however, that the commitment to full employment was dropped even from Labour Party policy between 1990 and 1997. It was revived in the 1997 manifesto, but only as a modified commitment to maintain 'a high and stable level of employment'.[9] This revived a form of words, first employed in 1944, to disguise disagreement over the precise definition of 'full employment': the conventional definition then had been any percentage of unemployment below 8.5 per cent, although Keynes had preferred 5 per cent and Beveridge 3 per cent – the latter being the figure which governments finally accepted between 1950 and 1975. Just as there

8 Labour Party, *Report of the 75th Annual Conference*, London, 1976, p. 188.
9 *Because Britain Deserves Better*, London, 1997, p. 11.

was no commitment to a precise target, so there were no concrete suggestions in 1997 of how, in Beveridge's words, 'the power of the state' might be used 'to whatever extent may prove necessary'. The traditional policies of economic planning and demand management were rejected; corporatist policies were eschewed; and monetary policy was immediately handed over to the Bank of England. Were the international economy to go into recession and unemployment in Britain consequently to increase, New Labour appeared as powerless to intervene effectively as Old Labour in 1976.

THE EVOLUTION OF THE WELFARE STATE

Just as the potential range of welfare policy is immense, so too has been the variation of policy over the past fifty years. For this reason, the extracts in the following chapters have – wherever possible – been taken from the two major turning points in the evolution of the welfare state, the mid-1940s and the mid-1970s, and from two further 'sub-periods', the 1960s and the late 1980s.

The first key turning point was the period between the publication of the Beveridge Report in December 1942 and the Appointed Day in 1948. The Report sold 635,000 copies and became almost immediately known to an unprecedented 92 per cent of the population. Such popularity forced a radical change in the political agenda, against the wishes of conservative forces within Churchill's wartime Coalition; and, in the middle of war, some of the more powerful politicians and officials were compelled to concentrate on the planning of peacetime reconstruction. The result was a series of white papers covering all major areas of welfare, which in turn have become a subject of considerable historical controversy. For some they are major statements of the 'original vision' for a postwar welfare state. For others they are merely empty compromises papering over political differences within the Coalition for the duration of the war.[10]

The latter view is the one taken in two other volumes in this series: Kevin Jefferys, *War and Reform: British Politics During the Second World War* (1994) and Harold Smith, *Britain in the Second World War: A Social History* (1996). Is it, however, justified? Policy-makers

---

10 See R. Lowe, 'The Second World War, consensus and the foundation of the welfare state', *Twentieth Century British History*, I, 1990, pp. 152–82; and H. Jones and M. Kandiah, *The Myth of Consensus?*, Basingstoke, 1996.

at the time were faced with very real dilemmas and these were best expressed in the introduction of the 1944 white paper *Control of Land Use*, which dealt with one of the most contentious areas of policy. It read:

> Proposals for controlling land use are bound to raise again issues which for many years have been the subject of keen politi-cal controversy. The Government recognise that no proposals on this subject – on which widely divergent views are held with conviction – can be wholly satisfactory to all shades of opinion. They think it important, however, that a determined effort should now be made to find some practical solution of these problems, so that the physical reconstruction of our towns and countryside after the war may steadily go forward. Moreover, they believe that the collaboration of all Parties in a National Government offers a fresh opportunity for finding some common measure of agreement. (Cmd 6537, p. 2)

This encapsulates the urgency of the practical administrative need to agree consensus policies, both during and after the war, together with the deep-seated ideological divisions, at both a popular and political level, which continued to delay or frustrate their attainment. The fact that ideological divisions continued to thwart a 'common measure of agreement' in this particular policy area, town and country planning, lends weight to the 'pessimist' case.

However, as was argued above, the Appointed Day did represent a radical departure in policy and practice. It thereby demonstrates that a significant measure of permanent reform was achieved; and that it was broadly consensual is illustrated by the response of the Conserva-tive One Nation group, which commented in 1950:

> The wall of social security has been built at last. Here and there stones need shifting or strengthening, here and there we could build better and more economically.... If no dramatic advance is possible for some years ... there is still the not less important administrative task of making the Welfare State work.[11]

By 'social security', moreover, it meant not just cash benefits but also the NHS and education. In addition, the Beveridge Report made so significant an impact that it has remained the reference point for all

11 *One Nation: A Tory Approach to Social Problems*, London, 1950, p. 16.

later welfare reform.[12]

The second major turning point occurred between Labour's abandonment of the commitment to full employment in 1976 and the Conservatives' election victory under Mrs Thatcher in 1979. All western welfare states were subjected to similar pressures at this time. In particular the world economy was disrupted by successive oil crises whilst the demand for welfare expenditure relentlessly increased, fuelled by a combination of rising popular expectations, higher professional standards and the needs of an ageing population. This led in Britain, as elsewhere, to perceptions of a 'fiscal crisis' because increased expenditure could not be met by falling tax revenue, and the only means of funding the resulting budget deficit (government borrowing) was considered inflationary – thus exacerbating the price rises occasioned by the quadrupling of the cost of oil. In Britain, moreover, there were additional factors which undermined the resilience of the welfare state. As Callaghan then remarked: 'There are times, perhaps once in thirty years, when there is a sea change in politics.... There is a shift in what the public wants and what it approves of. I suspect there is now such a sea change – and it is for Mrs Thatcher.'[13]

What was the nature of this sea change? In terms of *policy*, Labour's abandonment of full employment ended the postwar optimism that, given the political will, all problems were soluble. The resulting conflict between economic and social policy placed each welfare service under strain. Aggregate welfare expenditure fell in real terms, for the only time in postwar Britain, in 1977 and 1978; and thereafter the objective of each service was scaled down, just as the term 'welfare state' was surreptitiously equated with cash benefits alone. In terms of *public opinion*, starting with the student revolt of 1968 and culminating with the strikes of public sector unions in the 1978/79 'winter of discontent', increasing suspicion was levelled at both the producers and consumers of welfare. Taxpayers, in consequence, were perceived to be far less ready to fund services especially when they were targeted on 'undeserving' minority groups such as the unemployed, single parents and students. Finally, in terms of *academic analysis*, the 'crisis' spawned a number of hostile critiques of state welfare. These included the first major feminist attack in

12 See, for example, *New Ambitions for Our Country*, Cm 3805, p. 91.
13 B. Donoughue, *Prime Minister*, London, 1987, p. 191.

E. Wilson, *Women and the Welfare State* (1977) and a renewed marxist critique exemplified by I. Gough, *The Political Economy of the Welfare State* (1979). Even more significant, however, were the New Right critiques generated largely in the USA which provided the intellectual underpinning for Conservative demands that the state should be 'rolled back' (see 1.3.4).

The mid-1970s mark for many the critical transition from a period of 'social democratic' consensus, inherited from the war, to one of 'Thatcherite' consensus, to which even New Labour at the time of its 1997 election victory was party; and the contrasting assumptions underlying these two periods can best be captured in relation to David Donnison's classic description of the former. He listed the social democratic assumptions as:

1. The growth of the economy and the population would continue. That, by itself, would not solve any problems; but it provided an optimistic setting for debate. The pursuit of social justice could be carried forward by engines of economic growth which would produce the resources to create a fairer society without anyone suffering on the way.

2. Although inequalities in income would persist, their harsher affects would be gradually softened by a 'social wage' (consisting of social services distributed with greater concern for human needs) and by the growing burden of progressive taxes, taking more from the rich than the poor....

3. Despite fierce conflicts about important issues (comprehensive schools, pensions, rent controls, and so on) the people with middling skills and income – 'middle England' you might call them – would eventually support equalising social policies and programmes of this kind. Trade unions and the Labour movement would usually provide the cutting edge for reform; and the Conservative governments which followed them would accept most of its results.

4. Therefore government and its services, accountable to this central consensus, were the natural vehicle of progress. Among their generally trusted instruments were the doctors, teachers, planners, nurses, social workers and other public service professionals. The pretensions and powers of these professionals should be critically watched, but progressive governments were expected to recruit more....

5. Although economic crises, political accidents and sheer ineptitude would often compel governments temporarily to abandon these aims, over the longer run they would all try to increase industrial investment and improve Britain's lagging productivity, to get unemployed people back into jobs, to free poorer people from means tests by giving them adequate benefits as of right, to give children a better start in life and more equal opportunities for the future, and to provide better care and support for the most vulnerable people and for families living on low or modest incomes. 'Middle England', we assumed, would not tolerate any radical departure from these aims. A government which allowed – let alone encouraged – a return to the high unemployment, the social conflicts and the means tests of the 1930s could not survive.[14]

In direct contrast, the slower rate of economic growth after 1975 meant that redistribution could no longer be effected painlessly. Middle England, in consequence, did not instinctively support progressive taxation and 'equalising social policies'. Moreover it was starting to regard entrepreneurs and the market, rather than trade unions and the state, as respectively providing 'the cutting edge of reform' and being 'the natural vehicle of progress'. Indeed it was increasingly insistent that professional 'pretensions and powers' should not only be watched but radically reduced. In short, the 'ratchet' effect, by which the Conservatives had felt bound to accept the reforms of previous Labour governments, was broken; and, as four successive victories between 1979 and 1992 showed, electoral advantage lay in the proposal not the rejection of conflictive policies. Even the 1930s could be portrayed positively as a period of social order, stable prices and – in southern England at least – rising prosperity.

Within each of these broad periods of 'social democratic' and 'Thatcherite' consensus there was a key time when a determined attempt was made to give full institutional expression to its core values. For social democracy the 1960s were such a time when, throughout western Europe, welfare states expanded rapidly in terms of size, the professionalisation of their services and their objectives. Britain was no exception. This was for two main reasons. First, welfare policy was widely accepted to be a necessary precondition, not an impediment, to economic growth. As Beveridge had argued, interna-

14 D. Donnison, *The Politics of Poverty*, Oxford, 1982, pp. 20–1.

tional competitiveness – and thus full employment – depended on the 'greater efficiency and content' of the workforce which a well-targeted education, health and housing policy could bring (Cmd 6404, para. 448). Government alone had the resources to fund such policies. Secondly, the broad objective of policy was accepted to be not just the eradication of want but also – for the sake of national efficiency if not necessarily 'social justice' – the engineering of a more equal society. So all-pervasive were these views that as late as the Conservative government of 1970–74, Mrs Thatcher (in charge of education policy) and Keith Joseph (responsible for health and social security) were high-spending ministers.

The late 1980s were similarly the key years for Thatcherism with the passage of the Social Security Act (1986), the Housing and Education Acts (1988) and finally the National Health Service and Community Care Act (1990). Each, as will be seen in the succeeding chapters, sought to achieve the twin goals of greater economy and consumer empowerment by ending the centralised, monopolistic delivery of services and encouraging increased competitiveness. The resulting institutional innovations have been termed the 'purchaser–provider' split because, although services continued to be financed (or purchased) by government, they were delivered (or provided) under contract by a range of competing agencies. Whether the principal policy objectives were achieved – and, indeed, whether the power of the state was 'rolled back' (as proclaimed) or simply transmuted into greater regulation and inspection (as symbolised, in education, by the national curriculum and Ofsted) – is a moot point. What is indisputable is that these innovations were accepted, and expanded, by New Labour.

1

The political debate

Welfare policy, as stated in the Introduction, is a contentious issue and one frequently in the forefront of political debate (see 1.4.3). Such debate, for political and administrative reasons, has often focused on policy detail. For electoral success, politicians have to appeal to the 'middle ground' where there is greater interest in the practical benefits than in the ideological purity of policy; and once in government, manifesto pledges have to be delivered – and the legacies of past policies, such as the rights earned by insurance contributions, honoured. Such pressures tend to encourage consensual policies. Consensus, however, has to be built on some basic values; and when consensus breaks down, as in the mid-1970s, the nature of these values becomes explicit. There is an open 'battle of ideas' (1.3.3).

The evolution of postwar welfare policy, as has been seen, fell into two phases. The assumptions underlying the first period of 'social democratic' consensus were well summarised by Donnison (pp. 13–14). The major parties accepted the need for greater state intervention in relation to the management of the economy and to both the financing and delivery of social policies. There were nevertheless tensions over the ultimate objectives of such intervention. The Conservatives have been termed 'reluctant collectivists' because, after the interwar experience of mass unemployment and poverty, they accepted state intervention – but only in so far as it corrected proven market 'failures' and created the conditions for individual freedom (1.2.1–2). Their key instinct still remained that economic growth and political freedom were best assured if individual initiative, either through the market or self-reliance, was maximised. The Labour Party, on the other hand, was far more sceptical about both the economic and moral virtues of the market (1.1.2). It advocated greater state intervention in order to engineer a more equal society (which would be not only just but also, by ensuring talent would not be wasted, more

16

efficient) and to create the conditions for greater altruism. There were thus, as Crosland correctly identified, major ideological differences between the parties (1.1.3). They became ever more apparent as state welfare expanded in the 1960s.

Since the war, there had always been a core of opposition to state intervention, principally in relation to economic policy but also with regard to the delivery of welfare. Arguments first advanced in Hayek's *The Road to Serfdom* (1944) were popularised after the mid-1950s by the Institute of Economic Affairs (IEA), which then became the vehicle for introducing to Britain the rising tide of New Right thinking in the USA (1.3.2, 1.3.4). It was this thinking that informed Keith Joseph's attack on state welfare in the mid-1970s and thus 'Thatcherism' (1.3.3). It also underpinned the institutional changes that the Conservatives finally introduced after 1988. It was not denied that some government finance was needed to ensure minimum, and even rising, levels of subsistence, health and education (1.3.1). The market, however, was promoted as the most efficient means of delivering the requisite services. Driven by competition and the desire to maximise profits, it responded quickly to changing needs and met them most cost-effectively. By permitting choice, it also empowered individuals and encouraged individual responsibility – and thereby political freedom which, either intentionally or unintentionally, was denied by state monopolies. Such monopolies, by contrast, were both slow to change and inefficient, because they faced no competition; and any changes were typically designed to satisfy the needs of the 'producers' rather than the 'consumers' of welfare. American thinkers were even more specific in their condemnation. They claimed that the implementation of policy created 'perverse incentives' and thus a dependency culture, thereby intensifying the very problems it was designed to resolve.

New Right thinking not only changed Conservative Party thinking, it also heavily influenced New Labour (1.4.4). State services were also acknowledged to be remote, insensitive and inefficient; and the professionals responsible for delivering them were duly treated with suspicion. Policy was acknowledged to create 'perverse incentives' (1.4.3); and 'welfare to work' programmes, on the American model, were adopted to reacquaint claimants with the psychological and material benefits of working – as well as to combat fraud. During the anniversary celebrations in 1998, as has been seen, it was still the New Right's critiques of the welfare state rather than any positive vision for its future that characterised New Labour's thinking.

There has, therefore, been a rich debate about the values which should underpin the postwar welfare state. These values have been developed by academics and then filtered to politicians through an ever-increasing number of 'think tanks'. The extracts below exclude the more abstract academic debates. This is for reasons of space and because good synopses already exist, as detailed in the Guide to Further Reading. It is not designed to minimise the importance of such debates, which, as stated in the Introduction, were particularly important in the mid-1970s. The anti-racist, 'green' and feminist (see 1.4.2) critiques then started are likely, after all, to have the greatest effect on the welfare state in its second half-century.

The extracts are divided between the four broad political strategies that have shaped policy: democratic socialism, reluctant collectivism, the New Right, and New Labour.

1.1 DEMOCRATIC SOCIALISM

1.1.1 Marshall and the evolution of social equality

In 1948 the socialist T.H. Marshall delivered a famous lecture which heralded the creation of the welfare state as the natural culmination of a political and economic process by which British citizens had successively gained equal civil, political and finally social rights. This was widely seen to legitimate both its creation and the drive for even greater social equality.

[The period before 1900] was one during which the growth of citizenship, substantial and impressive though it was, had little direct effect on social equality. Civil rights gave legal powers whose use was drastically curtailed by class prejudice and lack of economic opportunity. Political rights gave potential power whose exercise demanded experience, organisation and a change of ideas as to the proper function of government. All these took time to develop. Social rights were at a minimum and were not woven into the fabric of citizenship. The common purpose of state and voluntary effort was to abate the nuisance of poverty without disturbing the pattern of inequality of which poverty was the most obviously unpleasant consequence.

A new period opened at the end of the nineteenth century.... It saw the first big advances in social rights.... But there were other forces at work as well. A rise in money incomes ... altered the economic distance which separated [the] classes.... A system of direct taxation, even more steeply graduated, compressed the whole scale of disposable incomes.... Mass production ... enabled the less well-to-do to enjoy a material civilization which differed less markedly in quality from that of the rich.... All this profoundly altered the setting in which the progress of citizenship took place. Social integration spread from the sphere of sentiment and patriotism into that of material enjoyment.... The diminution of inequality strengthened the demand for its abolition, at least with regard to the essentials of social welfare.

These aspirations have in part been met by ... creating a universal right to real income which is not proportionate to the market value of the claimant. Class-abatement is still the aim of social rights, but it has acquired a new meaning. It is no longer merely an attempt to abate the obvious nuisance of destitution.... It has assumed the guise of action modifying the whole pattern of social equality. It is no longer content to raise the floor-level in the basement of the social edifice.... It has begun to remodel the whole building, and it might even end by converting a skyscraper into a bungalow.

T.H. Marshall, *Citizenship and Social Class and Other Essays*, Cambridge, 1950, pp. 46–7.

1.1.2 Titmuss and the virtues of collective action

Marshall's colleague at the London School of Economics and Britain's first professor of social administration was Richard Titmuss. His research and training of social workers symbolised the entry into welfare policy of academic and politically committed experts, which was attacked by the IEA – his ideological opponents (see 1.3.2). His research, typified by this analysis of the Blood Transfusion Service, emphasised the economic efficiency and the broader moral purpose of collective welfare. This extract captures the idealism associated with the early NHS and anticipates later transatlantic comparisons and the problems inherent in 'internal markets' (see 3.3.4).

In comparing commercialized blood market systems in the United States with a voluntary system functioning as an integral part of the National Health Service in Britain we have considered four sets of criteria. These are basic criteria which economists themselves would apply.... [They] are briefly stated: (1) economic efficiency; (2) administrative efficiency; (3) price – the cost per unit to the patient; (4) purity, potency and safety – or quality per unit.

On all four criteria, the commercialized blood market fails. In terms of economic efficiency it is highly wasteful of blood.... It is administratively inefficient: the so-called mixed pluralism of the American market results in more bureaucratization, avalanches of paper and bills, and much greater administrative, accounting and computer overheads. These wastes, disequilibria and inefficiencies are reflected in the price paid by the patient (or consumer); the cost per unit of blood ... in the United States ... [is] five to fifteen times higher. And, finally, in terms of quality, commercial markets are much more likely to distribute contaminated blood....

What is unique as an instrument of social policy amongst the countries we have surveyed is the National Health Service and the values that it embodies. Attitudes to and relationships with the National Blood Transfusion Service among the general public since 1948 can only be understood in the context of the Health Service. This most unsordid act of social policy in the twentieth century has allowed and encouraged sentiments of altruism, reciprocity and social duty to express themselves; to be made explicit and identifiable in measurable patterns of behaviour by all social groups and classes. In part, this is attributable to the fact that, structurally and functionally, the Health Service is not socially divisive; its universal free access basis has contributed much, we believe, to the social liberties of the subject in allowing people the choice to give or not to give blood for unseen strangers.

Of course, in probing the deeper human motives for giving ... it would be facile to suggest that socialized medicine was wholly responsible. We have not said that at all. What we do suggest, however, is that the ways in which society organizes and structures its social institutions – and particularly its health and welfare systems – can encourage or discourage the altruistic in man; such systems can foster integration or alienation; they can allow ... generosity to strangers ... to spread among and between social groups and generations. This, we further suggest, is an aspect of freedom in the twentieth century which, compared with the emphasis on consumer choice in material acquisitiveness, is insufficiently recognized. It is indeed little understood how modern society, technical, professional, large-scale organized society, allows few opportunities for ordinary people to articulate giving in morally practical terms outside their own network of family and personal friendships.

R.M. Titmuss, *The Gift Relationship*, London, 1970, pp. 205, 225–6.

1.1.3 The ideological divide

The Labour politician who took fullest advantage of postwar social research was Anthony Crosland. His *The Future of Socialism* (1956) became the classic statement of democratic socialism, arguing that a 'classless society' could best be achieved not through the marxist-inspired means of nationalisation but through an attack on such traditional bastions of inequality as selective education and inherited wealth. He was the minister responsible for the acceleration of comprehensive secondary education in the 1960s (see 4.2). Here he identifies the differences of principle between the Labour and Conservative Parties. This demonstrates that although there may have been a political convergence on practical policies after the war, there was no ideological consensus.

It does not follow that because politics are now less bitter ... they are wholly drained of content.

First, the emphasis on social welfare. No one supposes that the Conservatives will now suddenly dismantle the Welfare State, or utterly neglect the claims of the socially under-privileged groups. But equally one can hardly deny a deep difference exists between the two parties about the priority to be accorded to social welfare. This is not because conservatives are necessarily less humanitarian, but because they hold particular views as to the proper role of the state, the desirable level of taxation, and the importance of private as opposed to collective responsibility. Their willingness for social expenditure is circumscribed by these views; and the consequence is a quite different order of priorities.

Secondly, the aim of 'an equitable distribution of wealth', related not to the accident of birth but to individual effort and ability.... The application of this apparently non-controversial principle would ... require a determined attack on large-scale inheritance. This a conservative, though he is willing somewhat to mitigate existing

21

inequalities, cannot countenance; for it offends against his view of the role of the family, the proper level of taxation, the rights of property, the need for large personal savings, and the importance of tradition and community in our national life....

Thirdly, the ideal of the 'classless society'.... This would entail a major reform of the private sector of education (and notably of the 'public' schools). This, again, most conservatives would not countenance; for it would offend against their belief about the rights of the moneyed individual, the importance of social hierarchy, and the value of a national elite....

Fourthly, 'the fundamental equality of all races and peoples'.... A belief in racial equality and the rule of law runs deep in the blood of all active socialists (though not all their working class supporters). The typical conservative, by contrast, ... will constantly subordinate them to deeply felt emotions about national prestige or the British Empire....

Fifthly, there are contrasting views ... about the proper dividing-line between the public and private spheres of responsibility. This difference, which runs like a thread through much of our political debate, manifests itself in innumerable ways – over the proportion of the national income to be devoted to communal services, the division between private and public capital expenditure, and increasingly in the field of what is loosely called town and country planning.... We are gradually waking up to the fact that both our cities and country-side are horribly threatened.... Whether we stave off the threat, or succumb to it, will depend on how far the country is willing to sacrifice private interests and unregulated liberty to social control and government initiative. There will be only too much to divide the socialist from the conservative in this field.

C.A.R. Crosland, *The Conservative Enemy*, London, 1962, pp. 123–4.

1.2 RELUCTANT COLLECTIVISM

1.2.1 One Nationism

The 'One Nation' group of backbenchers was formed in 1950 to develop a positive Conservative policy towards the welfare state. It was by no means uncritical, seeking to reduce economic intervention and rejecting socialist calls for an egalitarian society. Its objective was rather to give everyone an equal opportunity to become unequal. As illustrated here, however, it was determined to reconcile the Party to the permanency of the welfare state and to base it on sound Conservative principles (see also p. 11, 5.1.3). After its survey of contemporary reactions, it significantly dismissed the suggestion of the IEA – later restated by American commentators such as Murray (1.3.4) – that state welfare necessarily created a dependency culture.

Almost everyone today benefits to some extent from one or more social service, irrespective of their income or their approval or disapproval of the system. The social services are a permanent feature of national life and many views are held on them.

At one extreme, their automatic provision is held to corrupt citizen's self-reliance, demoralise family and religious life, and magnify the Government. At the other, the Welfare State is seen as an instrument of an egalitarian social policy. Between these views there are many shades of opinion.

Some see the Welfare State as a fulfilment of a social aim, now at least in outline complete. Others believe it is dynamic, needing change as we go along with new and reformed services replacing those no longer needed. A third group hopes that some of the services are self-liquidating – that they exist for purposes which people ultimately will prefer to provide for themselves. A fourth would have the social services serve as a safety net, providing a standard of life below which no-one should be allowed to fall, but above which they should care for themselves.

Common to all but one extreme of these views is the generally held opinion that the social services tend to make people irresponsible.

We desire to set against these differing but overlapping views some general propositions which we think may be widely acceptable....

The social services for the most part are here to stay: in an increasingly complex society they have come to provide a minimal framework of amenity; our contemporaries and descendants will take them as much for granted as we and our parents take drainage and street lighting....

Within each income class there will always be – just as there always has been – a small feckless minority....

No matter what the system there is bound to be some abuse. There was before the war of the then health insurance; there is now in other than social service activities.

Surely it is not seemly for critics – sometimes secure other than by their efforts and seldom thereby demoralised – to seek to deny some share of security to their fellow citizens. Security, even automatic or unearned, is not necessarily demoralising. It is as much a spring-board for vigour and family devotion as insecurity....

We do not think that the slightly increased freedom of choice given by the social services is such as by itself to create irresponsibility. On the contrary, the pre-requisite to responsibility is freedom. The Welfare State, combined with full employment and high earnings, has added to the freedom of the citizen – and the fact that this freedom can be used well or ill cannot be advanced as an argument against it. If we want a responsible society the first essential is as much freedom as is practicable for all.

One Nation Group, *The Responsible Society*, London, 1959, pp. 31–2, 34.

1.2.2 The market and community case for state welfare

The fullest 'One Nation' defence of the welfare state appeared, surprisingly, in 1992 and was written, even more surprisingly, by a former social security adviser to Mrs Thatcher. David Willetts here emphasises the relative efficiency of the collective provision of certain public goods (such as education) and of social, as opposed to private, insurance. He also describes the social solidarity implicit in the concept of 'one nationism'. Later in his book, Willetts opposed any further erosion of self-sufficiency or voluntary action and rejected socialist plans to engineer greater equality. 'The welfare state', he claimed significantly, 'is not a mechanism for changing society but a mirror reflecting it.'

Nobody is very clear *why* a Conservative should support a welfare state. It seems to fit in with the highmindedness of the Liberals and the egalitarianism of the Labour party. But what is conservative about it? If Conservatives do support it, is this mere political expediency?...

Why have a welfare state: efficiency and community
There are two types of argument for a welfare state. Neither is exclusively conservative, but they both tie in closely with two crucial

elements of conservative philosophy – the belief in markets and the commitment to community.

The market argument for a welfare state is that it contributes to the successful working of a capitalist economy.... [For instance] the development of unemployment benefit and retirement pensions contributes to economic efficiency by making it easier for firms to shed labour and to recruit new workers from a pool. Health care and education both raise the quality of a nation's 'human capital'....

We may have explained the need for some of the fundamental services of a welfare state, but we still need to show why the state has such a big role in financing and organizing them. This is where the next stage of the efficiency argument comes in. If there are voluntary, private schemes they encounter the problem of adverse selection – the tendency to get the bad risks.... Commercial insurers are trying to do the very opposite and only accept what they would regard as the good risks. The logic of this drives the government to intervene and require everyone to take out insurance at the same premium. At this point we ... have, in effect, invented state-run national insurance....

The efficiency argument [can] be stated in an even more rarefied form: it is difficult for a homeless family to be fit, or for a homeless child to do well at school, and this, in the long run, is an economic cost – which makes it rational for us to step in.

Rather than develop even more ingenious economic arguments for the welfare state, there comes a point when we really have to confront a simple moral obligation towards fellow members of our community. Regardless of whether people in need have been reckless or feckless or unlucky and unfortunate there comes a point when the exact explanation of how they became destitute ceases to matter. They have a claim on us simply by virtue of being compatriots. The welfare state is an expression of solidarity with our fellow citizens....

The market and community arguments together explain the remarkable consensus in most advanced Western nations that some sort of welfare state is both necessary and desirable. They explain why a Conservative can support the welfare state and also provide grounds for criticizing particular institutional arrangements if they are not living up to those principles....

Mutual insurance

It is when one turns to the role of the welfare state in redistributing resources that political differences emerge. For socialists the welfare state is perhaps the most powerful tool available to achieve their objective of equality.... And because many people think this must be the rationale for the welfare state, they assume that anti-egalitarian conservatives must also be anti-welfare state.

There is a different view of the working of a welfare state. For the conservative it is an enormous mutual insurance scheme, covering us against ill-health, unemployment and loss of earning power in old age.... We think of the welfare state as redistributing resources to others. But if, instead, we think of our own relationship to the welfare state during our lives, it is clear that what it really does is to reallocate those resources through the different stages of the life cycle. In this way resources are taken from us when we are working, and we are given command over resources when we are being educated, or unemployed, or sick, or retired.

D. Willetts, *Modern Conservatism*, Harmondsworth, 1992, pp. 138–42.

1.3 THE NEW RIGHT

1.3.1 Hayek and the road to serfdom

Hayek provided the principal inspiration for both Mrs Thatcher and the New Right in the USA, and he was duly awarded the Nobel prize for economics in 1974. He particularly opposed any extension of the state's economic powers (be it Keynesian or socialist) and was committed to the defence of 'the freedom in economic affairs without which personal and political freedom have never existed'. This extract from his major book warns that welfare policy, introduced for the best of motives, will similarly undermine freedom if it permits no choice. It repeats the warning issued in his more polemical *The Road to Serfdom* (1944), which reinforced Churchill's misgivings about wartime reconstruction planning in the 1945 election. As a refugee from Nazi Austria, Hayek was particularly sensitive to the abuse of government power.

All modern governments have made provision for the indigent, unfortunate and disabled and have concerned themselves with questions of health and dissemination of knowledge. There is no reason why the volume of these pure service activities should not increase with the general growth of wealth. There are common needs that can be satisfied only by collective action and which can thus be provided for without restricting individual liberty. It can hardly be denied that, as we grow richer, that minimum sustenance which the community has always provided for those not able to look after themselves, and which cannot be provided outside the market, will gradually rise, or that government may, usefully and without doing any harm, assist or even lead in such endeavours. There is little reason why the government should not also play some role, or even take the initiative, in such areas as social insurance and education, or temporarily subsidize certain experimental developments. Our problem here is not so much the aims as the methods of government action....

The reason why many of the new welfare activities of government are a threat to freedom ... is that, though they are presented as mere service activities, they really constitute an exercise of the coercive powers of government and rest on its claiming exclusive rights in certain fields....

In many fields persuasive arguments based on considerations of efficiency and economy can be advanced in favour of the state's taking sole charge of a particular service; but when the state does so, the result is usually that those advantages soon appear illusory but that the character of the services becomes entirely different from that which they would have had if they had been provided by competing agencies. If, instead of administering limited resources put under its control for a specific service, government uses it coercive powers to ensure that men are given what some expert thinks they need; if people can thus no longer exercise any choice in some of the most important matters of their lives, such as health, employment, housing and provision for old age, but must accept the decisions made for them by appointed authority on the basis of its evaluation of their need; if certain services become the exclusive domain of the state, and whole professions – be it medicine, education or insurance – come to exist only as unitary bureaucratic hierarchies, it will no longer be competitive experimentation but solely the decisions of authority that will determine what men shall get....

It would scarcely be an exaggeration to say that the greatest danger to liberty today comes from the men who are most needed and most powerful in modern government, namely, the efficient expert administrators exclusively concerned with what they regard as the public good.

F.A. von Hayek, *The Constitution of Liberty*, London, 1959, pp. 257–8, 261–2.

1.3.2 The IEA and choice in welfare

> The Institute of Economic Affairs was established, as this extract reveals, to reverse the relentless advance of state intervention. Its condemnation of contemporary politicians and academics appeared to confirm Hayek's fears and contributed to the later distrust of 'welfare professionals'. Likewise, its defence of the market influenced the reforms of the 1980s, although its principal proposal to counteract market imperfections – vouchers to provide, above all, the poor with independent purchasing power and thus freedom from state control – was never implemented. The IEA mounted four 'choice in welfare' opinion polls in 1963, 1965, 1970 and 1978 in its challenge to expert opinion.

The Institute set out in 1957 to re-investigate the market as a device for registering individual preferences and allocating resources to satisfy them. These are the twin essential purposes of an economic system wherever scarcity enforces choice ... in 'welfare' as well as in every other productive human action.

The market had been increasingly neglected ... since the 1870s.... Fabian teaching had been used to hobble and almost destroy the developing market in ... government services, none of which has to be supplied by political bureaucracies. Keynesian teaching had been used to extend the control of the state from budgeting for government to budgeting for the nation as a whole, and to tighten its control over banking and finance, and even industry and commerce. And Beveridge's teaching has been used, not least by the Titmuss school of social administrators, to extend the power of national politicians and local officials over the intimate lives of people in health, housing, pensions, education, and in many other ways.

In 1957 it seemed to us that the case against the market had been accepted uncritically and that the case for replacing it by government was a *non sequitur*.

The market is a network of inter-connections coming together as buyers and sellers, in everyday requirements or in welfare. The market is imperfect but it does not follow that government would make a better job of matching supply to demand by being more efficient, more sensitive to individual requirements, more equitable, or even more democratic....

The Institute's early studies ... were met with an almost sceptical response from people in all parties, including ... people then in office in the 1955 to 1964 Conservative Governments. The knowing reaction was that, although the argument was persuasive ... the desirable policies were 'politically' impossible....

For several reasons the 'politically impossible' objection was itself unacceptable. First, it seemed to us to be the natural response of politicians who did not relish opposition and of officials who relished a quiet life.... The beneficiaries from preserving existing policies undisturbed were clearly identifiable and concentrated – from recipients of state benefits in cash or kind to officials who administered the system.... The prospective beneficiaries of reform were in contrast widely dispersed: they were the whole nation of taxpayers, who could hardly miss what they had never known....

Our proposals were 'politically impossible' therefore, not because the *public* did not want them but because the *politicians* would require effort and run risks to demonstrate their advantage in practice....

We had thus ... stumbled on the realisation ... that it was unrealistic to adopt the still prevailing conventional wisdom of political science and public administration ... that politicians were benevolent despots and bureaucrats were 'obedient servants' who lived only to serve the public interest....

Second, the objection seemed faulty because it was arguing in a circle.... If a direction, or re-direction, of research and inquiry were excluded because the reform it indicated were thought 'politically impossible', it would never be put to the test in practice....

Third ... the notion of 'political impossibility' pre-judges the public reception of a new idea.... Politicians do not invariably put the public interest before their own, though they would like intellectual support for whatever policy they promote, and they deploy patronage to elicit a supply of testimonials. Academic supply has responded to the political 'demand' for validation of harmful policies of state welfare, which have damaged not least the people they most sought to help....

The 'politically impossible' objection, in short, was based on opinion without evidence. And since the opinion was that of people who thought they stood to lose from change, it could not be accepted without evidence from the public itself.

R. Harris and A. Seldon, *Over-ruled on Welfare*, London, 1979, pp. 5–12.

1.3.3 Sir Keith Joseph and the origins of 'Thatcherism'

Sir Keith Joseph was the senior Conservative politician who, like Crosland in the Labour Party, was most attuned to academic debate. This led him in 1974 to launch a high-profile series of public speeches redefining Conservatism and questioning the Party's past record in government. This Conference speech at the height of his 'reconversion' demonstrates a clear debt to Hayek and the IEA. It also describes the 'ratchet effect' in postwar policy, confirmed in the third paragraph of Donnison's summary of social democratic assumptions (p. 13). What is also significant is both the confidence of Joseph, as with Marshall in 1948, that history was on his side, and the allusions to the principles of European social democracy which New Labour later adopted.

The high hopes have faded. For Socialists current anxieties are particularly bitter, for it is their panaceas which have failed. Nationalisation has produced neither efficiency nor industrial peace. As incomes and council housing and comprehensivisation have grown, so have crime and homelessness and illiteracy. Fashionable economic policies have led to rocketing inflation and rising unemployment. The reaction of socialists in recent years has been to ... call our present problems 'a crisis of capitalism'. We call it a crisis of Socialist damage to responsible behaviour and to free enterprise....

We are one society. Damage prosperity, damage business confidence, damage enterprise, damage professional integrity, and you damage the poor and the weak most of all. While the philosophies of the two parties are so far apart, the prospects for this country are grisly....

What can we do? Polarisation is no way to run a country....

There will only be a full flow of confidence and investment, jobs, prosperity and the freedom and the social services which they underpin when the two main parties operate a mild pendulum rather than a ratchet as savage and destructive as the labour ratchet. This is the basic problem we face ... in considering the future.

Our understandable approach, both to gaining and keeping office and to seeking stability and predictability, has been the middle way, the middle ground, but the trouble with the middle ground is that we do not choose it. We do not shape it. It is shaped for us by extremists. The more extreme the Left, the more to the Left is the middle ground....

Socialist moderates have destroyed grammar schools, have attacked freedom in medicine, embarked by tax upon tax upon the elimination of businesses and farms and charities. You will say that I am therefore absurdly optimistic to contemplate any common approach to national problems. Yet ... events are our allies in dragging Socialists to the common ground of reality....

It is mad, mad to conduct a vendetta against the free enterprise sector on which all jobs and all prospects and all public services depend. Competition, of course, a framework of laws, against fraud, against pollution, against whatever we think proper; but not vendetta. Where there is common sense there can be common ground. We are only trying to achieve by argument what many European social democrats have long understood – that you cannot make the mixed economy work at all effectively if you cripple the private sector and lose control of the public sector. Social democrats in Europe seem to understand that within a framework of humane laws and services a profit–loss system is the only signalling system to sustain a free, prospering and growing society, and look at the results in Western Europe – far greater prosperity than here, far better social services than here and far less poverty than here....

We are a national party and we have a double task – to win the next election and to win the battle of ideas. We shall succeed because realities are with us and because of the contrast between Socialist rhetoric and Socialist performance.

The Socialists have a vision with elements of nobility about it, but wherever socialism is put into practice, the results are poverty and tyranny.

National Union of Conservative and Unionist Associations, *Verbatim Report: 92nd Conservative Conference*, London, 1975, pp. 31–3.

1.3.4 Charles Murray and the emerging underclass

The work of Charles Murray was a foremost example of American influence on British thinking and policy in the 1980s. His key book, *Losing Ground* (1984), argued that policy changes in the USA during the 1960s actively encouraged 'irresponsible' behaviour – and thus the creation of an underclass. He was invited to Britain in 1989 and 1993 to produce two reports which identified similar policy-induced increases in illegitimacy, crime and unemployment. His initial remedy was a restoration of 'civic' society, which New Labour later embraced; his later targeting of unmarried mothers was immediately endorsed by the Major government.

[1989 report]
During the last half of the 1960s and throughout the 1970s something strange and frightening was happening among poor people in the United States. Poor communities that had mostly consisted of hardworking folks began deteriorating, sometimes falling apart altogether. Drugs, crime, illegitimacy, homelessness, drop-out from the job market, drop-out from school, casual violence – all the measures that were available to social scientists showed large increases, focused in poor communities. As the 1980s began, the growing population of 'the other kind of poor people' could no longer be ignored, and a label for them came into use. In the US, we began to call them the underclass.

For a time, the intellectual wisdom continued to hold that the underclass was just another pejorative attempt to label the poor. But the label has come into use because there was no longer any denying of reality. What once had been a small fraction of the American poor had become a sizeable and worrisome population. An underclass existed, and none of the ordinary kinds of social policy solutions seemed able to stop its growth....

As someone who has been analysing this phenomenon in the United States, I arrived in Britain ... a visitor from a plague area come to see whether the disease was spreading....

Britain does have an underclass.... I am not talking here about an unemployment problem that can be solved by more jobs, nor about a poverty problem that can be solved by higher benefits. Britain has a growing population of work-aged, healthy people who live in a different world from other Britons, who are raising their children to live in it, and whose values are now contaminating the life of entire neighbourhoods....

Questions about causation

... I am recasting a version of the Right's view of why things go wrong that is usually expressed in terms of the decay of moral standards, the perverse incentives of welfare policy and the coddling of criminals. The problem with those arguments as they are usually presented is that they are too mechanistic. I do not believe that women read about the latest change in benefit rules for unwed mothers and use a pocket calculator to decide whether to get pregnant, or that young men decide whether to rob the local building society on the basis of a favourable change in parole policy.

Let us think instead in more common-sense terms. The topic is young people in their late teens and early twenties. The proposition is simply this: young people – not just poor young people, but all young people – try to make sense of the world around them. They behave in ways that reflect what they observe. In the 1960s and 1970s social policy in Britain fundamentally changed what makes sense.... The rules of the game changed fundamentally for low-income young people....

What can Britain learn from the American experience?

... The sad answer is – not much.... Let me emphasise the words – *we do not know how*. It's not the money we lack, but the capability to social-engineer our way out of the situation. Unfortunately, the delusion persists that our social engineering simply has not been clever enough, and that we must strive to become more clever.

Authentic self-government is the key

The alternative I advocate is to have the central government ... get out of the way, giving poor communities (and affluent communities, too) a massive dose of self-government, with vastly greater responsibility for the operation of the institutions that affect their lives – including the criminal justice, educational, housing, and benefit systems in their locality. My premise is that it is unnatural for a neighbourhood to tolerate high levels of crime or illegitimacy or voluntary idleness amongst its youth: that, given the chance, poor communities as well as rich ones will run affairs so that such things happen infrequently....

[1994 report]
What to do?

... It is possible to have a social safety net that protects everyone from cradle to grave, as long as a social contract is accepted. The government will provide protection against the vicissitudes of life as long as you, the individual citizen, take responsibility for the consequences of your own voluntary behaviour. Getting pregnant and having a child is, at the present time, voluntary behaviour.

Many will find even this level of restraint on the welfare state unacceptable. But as you cast about for solutions, I suggest that one must inevitably come up against this rock. The welfare of society requires that women actively avoid getting pregnant if they have no husband, and that women once again demand marriage from a man who would have them bear a child. The only way the active avoidance and the demands are going to occur is if childbearing entails economic penalties for a single woman. It is horribly sexist, I know. It also happens to be true.

IEA, *Charles Murray and the Underclass*, London, 1996, pp. 24–5, 43, 50–1, 126–7.

1.4 NEW LABOUR

1.4.1 The 1994 Commission on Social Justice

The Borrie Commission was established by John Smith, as leader of the Labour Party, to adapt traditional social democratic values to the realities of the 1990s. It identified, as this extract shows, a clear 'third way' between the New Right and the Old Left which could achieve a principled reconciliation with the market economy. Its proposed alliance between economic and social policy, and between all areas of welfare policy, was reminiscent of Beveridge's vision. The recognition that an 'intelligent welfare state' had to acknowledge 'the social revolution in women's life chances' was also testimony to the impact of feminist analysis. The Commission coined the phrase that welfare policy should provide a 'hand-up, not just a hand-out' (p. 8).

There are three options on offer:

Investor's Britain: Investors combine the ethics of community with the dynamics of a market economy.... They believe that the extension of economic opportunity is not only the source of economic prosperity but also the basis of social justice. This demands strong institutions, strong families and strong communities, which enable people and companies to grow, adapt and succeed. Investment in people is the top priority. Investors see security, not fear, as the basis for renewal. They argue we must engage with change – in the home or at work, in local government or in Europe – if we are to extend social justice.

Deregulator's Britain: Deregulators dream of a future in which dynamic entrepreneurs, unshackled by employment laws or social responsibilities, create new businesses and open up new markets.... Theirs is a future of extremes, where the rich get richer and the poor get poorer, and where the rewards for success are matched only by the risks of failure. Economically, it depends on the unceasing drive for competitiveness through ever-cheaper production and the pursuit of short-term profit; socially, upon the reduction of the public services and public spending; politically, on a logic of centralisation, destroying institutions that stand between law-making government and individual decisions in the marketplace.

Leveller's Britain: The Levellers are pessimists, who do not see how we can turn the economy round, and in any case argue that economic renewal should not be the concern of a Commission on Social Justice.... They say our job is to protect the poor from economic decay. The Levellers share many of the aspirations of the Investors, but they have different strategies to achieve these ambitions. They believe that we should try to achieve social justice primarily through the tax and benefits system....

An intelligent welfare state works with rather than against the grain of change:

• Wealth creation and wealth distribution are two sides of the same coin; wealth pays for welfare, but equity is efficient

• Social justice cannot be achieved through the social security system alone; employment, education and housing are at least as important as tax and benefit policy in promoting financial independence

• Labour-market and family policy go together; the social revolution in women's life chances demands a reappraisal of the role of men

35

as workers and fathers as well as that of women as employees and mothers

• Paid work for a fair wage is the most secure route out of poverty. Welfare must be reformed to make work pay ...

• The intelligent welfare state prevents poverty as well as relieving it, above all through the public services which enable people to learn, earn and care

• The welfare state must be shaped by the changing nature of people's lives, rather than people's lives being shaped to fit in with the welfare state; the welfare state must be personalised and flexible, designed to promote individual choice and personal autonomy.

Commission on Social Justice, *Social Justice*, London, 1994, pp. 4, 223.

1.4.2 Incorporating feminist perspectives

The Institute of Public Policy Research (IPPR) was set up in 1998 by academics, business leaders and trade unionists to provide an alternative to free market 'think tanks'. It hosted the Borrie Commission on Social Justice (1.4.1). Its radical views were well expressed in this report which, building on new feminist thinking, challenged the assumptions of 'normal' family life implicit, for example, in the work of Murray (1.3.4). Anna Coote was a research fellow at the IPPR and in 1997 became the adviser to the Women's Unit at the Department of Social Security, where Harriet Harman was secretary of state. Patricia Hewitt became a cabinet minister in 2001.

Guidelines and goals for a family policy
... What are the ground rules on which we base our approach to policy-making?

Families are social, not natural, phenomena
Contrary to the assertions of some, families are not natural phenomena.... They are social phenomena: they change over time: they are susceptible to – and shaped by – economic and political developments.

What counts is the process, not the label
It is important to be clear about the focus of policy-making in this area. What does the 'family' in 'family policy' mean? Drawing on

what we know about the ways in which families are changing, as well
as the causes and consequences of change, it seems sensible to focus
on *what happens* in families, rather than on the label or status
attached to different living arrangements.... [I]t is useful for the purposes of policy-making to think of 'the family' as a process, rather
than an institution....

Children come first
This approach to family policy is based on the premise that we all bear
responsibility for all our children. They are society's most precious
resource and everyone has an obligation to them, whether parents
themselves or not. They are tomorrow's producers, who will pay for
the pensions of today's workers. They are tomorrow's carers, who will
raise the next generation of children and look after today's fit young
adults, when they cease to be so. They are tomorrow's politicians,
who will govern ... society in the 21st century. While they are young,
they cannot defend themselves against neglect, abuse or exploitation,
which may come from within their own families; there is therefore a
social obligation to ensure that they are properly protected.

Family policy should primarily be concerned with the process of
bringing up and caring for children....

Policy must work with, not against, the grain of change
Long-term, cross-national trends in the patterns of family life cannot
be halted, let alone reversed, by the efforts of any government.... It is
vital to acknowledge that change can be painful.... The aim of public
policy-makers should be to understand the nature of change and make
the best of it – not to engage in a futile mission to restore the 'good old
days'. Nostalgia fills the air with resentment, breeds taboo and stifles
political creativity. One sure way to stunt the healthy development of
children growing up in one-parent or reconstituted families is to give
them the impression they are abnormal, or that their families are
incomplete or deviant. Rather than accuse increasingly large numbers
of people living in the 'wrong' kind of family, the aim should be to
make sure that policies are adapted to suit changing practice and ... to
mitigate the painful effects of change....

A European perspective
A family policy designed for the UK must take account of what is
happening in Europe.... In matters of parental leave and child care, in
particular, Britain lags behind most of Western Europe.

Moreover, closer integration of the EC means that individual countries can no longer develop social policy in isolation from each other.

Policy goals

...

• *Every child should have the right to be dependent and to grow up in conditions which enable it to become a dependable adult ...*

• *Families need strong, self-reliant women ...*

• *Changing times require a new sense of responsibility in men ...*

• *Public policy should recognise that the essence of successful family life is neither enforced dependency, nor isolated individualism, but interdependence ...*

• *Policies should be adaptable, to support all kinds of family ...*

A. Coote, H. Harman and P. Hewitt, *The Family Way: A New Approach to Policy-Making,* London, 1991, pp. 33–8.

1.4.3 Frank Field and 'stakeholder' welfare

Frank Field was appointed minister for welfare reform in 1997 because of his track record of responding constructively to New Right critiques. In particular he acknowledged that policy, and especially means testing, could encourage irresponsible behaviour and that people felt alienated by welfare bureaucracies. To restore a commitment to universal welfare, and thus prevent a marginalisation of the poor, he recommended a system of 'stakeholder' welfare. Everyone should contribute to one of a variety of insurance schemes, which (as with the mutual aid societies which lay at the heart of nineteenth-century civic society) allowed contributors to retain a strict control over, and thus an interest in, their welfare entitlements. The Treasury was unwilling to accept the short-term cost of his proposals and he left office in 1998.

Welfare is set once again to become *the* issue of high politics.... The collapse of the Berlin Wall and the cross-party agreement on the priority given to the controlling of inflation have largely removed foreign affairs and the running of the economy from the day-to-day battle of party politics. Welfare is sucked into the centre of this political vacuum.

Welfare would have eventually taken that premier position anyway as the post-war settlement breaks up. The pressures fracturing the old welfare consensus came from a budget which:

- appears out of control
- undermines good government
- is increasingly destructive of honesty, effort, savings and thereby self-improvement....

The self-imposed political innocence of the post-war political settlement, with its unspoken assumption of welfare's neutrality on character, now looks incredibly naive....

Key political assumptions

... The first [is] that the current welfare status quo cannot hold.... In the current arrangements the poor are treated as inferior beings pushed increasingly onto means-tested assistance. Here lies the second assumption. The disengagement from state welfare will continue with the poor being made increasingly vulnerable to second-class status. Only by ... developing and offering a new welfare settlement which appeals strongly to the vast majority might it be possible to secure for the poor full membership of the new welfare settlement.

The third assumption underscores the belief that welfare does not operate in a social vacuum. It influences character for good or ill. Because of the growing dominance of means tests, welfare increasingly acts destructively, penalising effort, attacking savings and taxing honesty. The traditional cry that means tests stigmatise is now a minor issue. They do for some, but this is simply no longer the main issue. Means tests are steadily recruiting a nation of cheats and liars....

Fourthly, any new settlement will be dominated by the emerging values which prize ownership and control. What I have called the growing social autonomy of voters – wishing to do 'their own thing' determined on the basis of free association – will be the touchstone of the new welfare. The old style corporatism of the state-run system ... lies dead in the water. The futility of trying to resurrect the old order is the fifth political assumption.

Frank Field, *Stakeholder Welfare*, London, 1996, pp. 8–9, 11.

1.4.4 Anthony Giddens and the 'third way'

The sociologist Anthony Giddens synthesised New Right critiques in the manner most acceptable to New Labour and subsequently became what has been termed their 'thinker-in-residence'. Acceptance of those critiques is apparent in this extract. The description of Beveridge as 'entirely negative', it could be argued, betrays a certain lack of historical perspective.

Third way politics should accept some of the criticisms that the right makes of [the welfare] state. It is essentially undemocratic, depending ... on a top down distribution of benefits. Its motive force is protection and care, but it does not give enough space to personal liberty. Some forms of welfare institution are bureaucratic, alienating and inefficient, and welfare benefits can create perverse consequences that undermine what they were designed to achieve. However third way politics sees these problems not as a signal to dismantle the welfare state, but as part of the reason to reconstruct it....

When Beveridge wrote his *Report* ... in 1942, he famously declared war on Want, Disease, Ignorance, Squalor and Idleness. In other words, his focus was almost entirely negative. We should speak today of *positive* welfare, to which individuals themselves and other agencies besides government contribute – and which is functional for wealth creation. Welfare is not in essence an economic concept, but a psychic one, concerning as it does well-being. Economic benefits or advantages are therefore virtually never enough on their own to create it.... Welfare institutions must be concerned with fostering psychological as well as economic benefits....

The guideline is investment in *human capital* wherever possible, rather than the direct provision of economic maintenance. In place of the welfare state we should put the *social investment state*, operating in the context of a positive welfare society....

Positive welfare would replace each of Beveridge's negatives with a positive: in place of Want, autonomy; not Disease but active health; instead of Ignorance, education, as a continuing part of life; rather than Squalor, well-being; and in place of Idleness, initiative.

A. Giddens, *The Third Way*, Cambridge, 1998, pp. 111–28.

2

Social security

From the Beveridge Report to the advent of New Labour, the social security system has been at the heart of the welfare state; and after 1979, as has been seen, a sustained attempt was even made to make the two terms synonymous. Social security has also remained throughout the period at the heart of comparative international analysis. There are two main reasons for this. First, it is by far the most expensive welfare policy. In Britain it has conventionally cost twice as much as any other social service and in the 1960s it overtook defence as the largest item of government expenditure. Secondly, since it consists solely of cash benefits, its cost is easily quantifiable.

There are three types of cash benefits. The first, and by far the most costly, is national insurance benefits (which include pensions and benefits covering a range of contingencies such as unemployment, sickness, widowhood, maternity and industrial injury). They are also called 'transfer benefits' because the government essentially acts as a savings bank. It obliges everyone in work to pay contributions (supplemented by payments from employers and government) and then pays benefits – or *transfers* this money back – to them when, for whatever reason, they have no earned income. A major advantage of national insurance is that contributions establish an individual's explicit right to benefit. It also encourages financial realism. Any rise in benefit, which is inevitably popular, has to be paid for by an increase in contributions, which equally inevitably is unpopular.

Secondly, there are tax-financed universal benefits (such as family allowances/child benefit). As benefits to which people are automatically and equally entitled as British citizens, they were seen to symbolise the new ethos of the welfare state. However, they became the focus of the battle between the 'universalists' and the 'selectivists' (2.3) and, in consequence, their relative use and cost declined over the period.

41

Thirdly, there are means-tested benefits which steadily increased in range and cost over the period, although it had been the express purpose of the Beveridge Report to eradicate them. They took two forms. There was a national minimum benefit to which everyone was entitled when their income fell below an agreed level. This 'safety net' was called successively National Assistance (1948–66), Supplementary Benefit (1966–86) and Income Support. Its rate was, in effect, the official poverty line. There was also an ever-increasing number of additional means-tested benefits, such as free school meals or rent rebates, designed to target scarce resources on the most needy (2.3.2). The principal problem with all such benefits is that they are progressively withdrawn as a claimant's income increases. This can result in people being financially worse off in work (the 'poverty trap') and thus the encouragement of a 'dependency' culture.

Because social security remained such a central service, its development epitomised each of the stages through which the welfare state evolved. As argued in the Introduction, the historical significance of the Appointed Day – and the pioneering reputation of Britain's welfare state – was to a large part a consequence of the adoption by the National Insurance and Assistance Acts of Beveridge's principles of comprehensiveness and universality (see also 2.1.1 and 2.1.3). By the 1960s, however, the implementation of these principles appeared increasingly outdated. In particular 'flat-rate' subsistence benefits, designed simply to relieve destitution, conflicted with the increasing demand in an affluent society that those on benefit should be able to maintain their accustomed living standards. Consequently, there was a switch to the continental European practice of earnings-related contributions and benefits (2.1.3). Such a switch, by perpetuating income differentials outside the workplace, might appear to contradict the contemporary demand for greater equality. This was not necessarily the case, because some of the extra revenue generated by earnings-related contributions could be redistributed to the less well-off. This explicitly happened with pensions (2.1.4). Such redistribution, however, was relatively late and limited; and, combined with the apparent failings of National Assistance, this confirmed the impression of many commentators that Britain was fast losing its role as a welfare pioneer (2.4.1).

After the mid-1970s, it was not the conservatism but the perceived generosity of the social security system that came under a twin attack. First there was a demand for a return to the Beveridge principle that, should people wish to maintain their accustomed living standard, they should rely on private insurance (see 2.1.1, para. 9). This led, for example, to a major revision of pensions policy (2.2.4). Secondly there was a growing conviction that, although many claimants – and especially pensioners – were genuine, others were not. This conviction was based on the resurrection of the Victorian distinction between the 'deserving' and 'undeserving' poor (2.2.1). It was also given some credence by the increasing complexity of the social security system and specific disincentives to work such as the 'poverty trap'. This led to the demonisation of – and the targeting of benefit cuts on – certain groups of claimants, such as the unemployed and single mothers. After 1986, there were also institutional reforms of varying effectiveness to simplify the system in order to ensure that those in genuine need received help, whilst the work incentives of others were not impaired (2.2.3–4). These were objects pursued with renewed vigour by New Labour in its New Deal and tax reform initiatives (2.2.6–7).

Despite the cost and high political profile, the number of people officially classified as poor relentlessly increased throughout the period. This was in part, admittedly, because the definition of poverty changed. In the 1950s an 'absolute' definition was used, with the poverty line being determined by the cost of a fixed number of 'necessities' such as food, clothing and rent. This was the basis for Beveridge's subsistence benefits, as reflected by the initial level of National Assistance. After 1959, government gradually moved to a 'relative' definition whereby the poor, by the current criteria of the European Union, are 'persons whose resources ... are so limited as to exclude them from the minimum acceptable way of life in the member state in which they live'. Poverty, in this sense, can be measured in two ways: by the number of people whose income falls below the official means-tested benefit level (which has been regularly adjusted since 1959 to reflect rising living standards) or below a fixed percentage of average income (typically 50 per cent). Absolute poverty was largely eradicated in Britain in the 1950s. Relative poverty by the former measure, however, rose from 2 million in 1953 to 7 million in 1979 and then to 12.5 million in 1992. By the second measure it rose even higher from 5 million in 1979 to 13.7 million in 1993. It was the perceived failure of the social security system to halt this relentless rise in poverty, and even its complicity in encouraging it, which cast a shadow over the anniversary celebrations in 1998.

The following documents are accordingly divided into four

sections: the expansion of social security, 'modernising' social security, controversy: universalism versus selectivity, and the poor.

2.1 THE EXPANSION OF SOCIAL SECURITY

2.1.1 The Beveridge vision

These two extracts capture the boldness of vision in the Beveridge Report as well as the author's identification with the issues which were to dominate policy after 1979, such as the need to minimise cost, ensure responsiveness to individual need and encourage self-reliance.

Three guiding principles of recommendations
7. The first principle is that any proposals for the future ... should not be restricted by consideration of sectional interests.... Now, when the war is abolishing landmarks of every kind, is the opportunity for using experience in a clear field. A revolutionary moment in the world's history is a time for revolutions, not for patching.

8. The second principle is that organisation of social insurance should be treated as one part only of a comprehensive policy of social progress. Social security fully developed may provide income security; it is an attack upon Want. But Want is only one of five giants on the road to reconstruction and in some ways the easiest to attack. The others are Disease, Ignorance, Squalor and Idleness.

9. The third principle is that social security must be achieved by co-operation between the State and the individual. The State should offer security for service and contribution. The State in organising security should not stifle incentive, opportunity, responsibility; in establishing a national minimum, it should leave room and encouragement for voluntary action by each individual to provide more than the minimum for himself and his family.

...

303 *Six Principles of Social Insurance:* The social insurance scheme set out below as the chief method of social security embodies six fundamental principles:
Flat rate of subsistence benefit
Flat rate of contribution
Unification of administrative responsibility

44

Adequacy of benefit
Comprehensiveness
Classification

304 *Flat Rate of Subsistence Benefit:* The first fundamental principle of the social insurance scheme is provision of a flat rate of insurance benefit, irrespective of the amount of the earnings which have been interrupted…. This principle follows from the recognition of the place and importance of voluntary insurance in social security and distinguishes the scheme proposed for Britain from … most other countries….

305 *Flat Rate Contribution:* The second fundamental principle of the scheme is that the compulsory contribution required of each insured person or his employer is a flat rate, irrespective of his means. All insured persons, rich or poor, will pay the same contributions for the same security; those with larger means will pay more only to the extent that as tax-payers they pay more to the National Exchequer and so to the State share of the Social Insurance Fund….

306 *Unification of Administrative Responsibility:* The third fundamental principle is the unification of administrative responsibility in the interest of efficiency and economy. For each insured person there will be a single weekly contribution in respect of all his benefits. There will be in each locality a Social Security Office able to deal with claims of every kind and all sides of security…. All contributions will be paid into a single Social Insurance Fund and all benefits and other insurance payments will be paid from that fund.

307 *Adequacy of Benefit:* The fourth fundamental principle is adequacy of benefit in amount and in time. The flat rate benefit proposed is intended in itself to be sufficient without further resources to provide the minimum income needed for subsistence in all normal cases. It gives room and a basis for additional voluntary provision, but does not assume that in any case. The benefits are adequate also in time, that is to say except for contingencies of a temporary nature, they will continue indefinitely without a means test, so long as the need continues….

308 *Comprehensiveness:* The fifth fundamental principle is that social insurance should be comprehensive, in respect both of persons covered and of their needs. It should not leave either to national assistance or to voluntary insurance any risk so general or so uniform that social insurance can be justified. For national assistance involves a means test which may discourage voluntary insurance or personal

saving. And voluntary insurance can never be sure of covering the ground....

309 *Classification:* The sixth fundamental principle is that social insurance, while unified and comprehensive, must take account of the different ways of life of different sections of the community; of those dependent on earnings by employment under contract of service, of those earning in other ways, of those rendering vital unpaid service as housewives, of those not yet of age to earn and of those past earning. The term 'classification' is used here to denote adjustment of insurance to the differing circumstances of each of these classes and to the many varieties of need and circumstance within each insurance class.

Social Insurance and Allied Services, The Beveridge Report, Cmd 6404, 1942, Part I, pp. 6–7, Part V, pp. 121–2.

2.1.2 Abolishing the Poor Law

In 1947 Bevan introduced the second reading of the National Assistance Bill and enthusiastically explained how the financial resources of national government could be married with the responsiveness of local government to end the indignity of the Poor Law. Like Beveridge, he expected these services to be required by an ever decreasing number of people. The difference between the hopes and the eventual reality can be seen in 2.4.1.

Family allowances are in operation; increased old age pensions are being paid; a full scheme of National Insurance is on the statute book, and will come into operation in July next; the National Health Service is on the statute book, and will come into operation on the same date.... However, there will still remain, after all these things have been done, 400,000 persons on outdoor relief, and 50,000 in institutions. There thus remain, after we have bitten into the main body of the Poor Law, these residual categories which have to be provided for. This Bill ... must be seen as the coping stone on the structure of the social services of Great Britain....

The Government approach the problem from the angle that they wish to see the whole residual problem in two special categories. They wish to consider assistance by way of monetary help made a national responsibility and welfare a local responsibility.... It is proposed that we shall transfer to the Assistance Board, the responsibility for providing the financial help ... to assist people in peculiar and special circumstances. There will be a number of persons who will not be eligible for insurance benefit. There will be some who will not be eligible for unemployment benefit, and there will be persons who will be the subject of sudden affliction like fires and floods and circumstances of that kind....

The National Assistance Board shall have the responsibility of providing help of that sort for persons in need of help.... The National Assistance Board, since it has been created, has established itself as a humane system of administration....

There are a number of persons for whom special provision will have to be made. There are, for example, the blind....

We propose to place upon the Assistance Board the duty of providing maintenance of the blind and upon local authorities a duty to make special schemes for their training and welfare....

The National Assistance Board will provide its service on the basis of a determination of needs which we propose to bring up to date....

In calculating the personal resources of applicants there will be the usual disregard of superannuation and war pensions ... as regards other capital, we propose to raise the existing £25 to £50. That is ... a person must have £75 of savings before any deduction can be made in the amount of assistance to be given.... The owner-occupier will have disregarded his house and the effects of the household....

There is another category of persons for whom we shall have an even larger measure of responsibility than we have had in the past, and these are old persons. By 1970, old persons – that is persons reaching pensionable age – will be one in five of the total population. It is a staggering figure; indeed, it can be said that ... the proper care and welfare of the aged is the peculiar problem of modern society. We have ... gone a long way towards it by making provision for increased old age pensions....

We have decided to make a great departure in the treatment of old people. The workhouse is to go. Although many people have tried to humanise it, it was in many respects a very evil institution. We have determined that the right approach to this problem is to give the welfare authorities ... the power to establish special homes.... What we are really thinking about is a type of old people who are still able to look after themselves ... but who are unable to do the housework, the laundry, cook meals and things of that sort.... We have to think of a type of place where these services can be rendered to the old people, and, at the same time, leave them the maximum of privacy and independence....

If we have an institution too large, we might have a reproduction of the workhouse atmosphere, with the workhouse master and all the regimentation and the rules that have to be obeyed....

It is the essence of the scheme ... that old people who avail themselves of these institutions should be of mixed income groups, because it will at once destroy the character of these places if we have merely the indigent living there....

Where an individual has not the resources to enable him to pay normal charges for the accommodation, he goes to the National Assistance Board, and it is the Board that must put him in a position to pay the minimum charges of the hotel....

There must be no distinction between those able to pay the full charges themselves and those who are helped to pay the minimum charges by the National Assistance Board....

These are in the main provisions of the Bill.... It is a very agreeable thing, that despite all our difficulties, hardships and the diminution of our resources, we are able to turn our attention to this work.... The conditions in which the poor lived in the past were harsh and inhumane. Poverty was treated as though it were a crime. Those of us who have been associated with boards of guardians will know how frightfully difficult it was to administer the Poor Law in a humane fashion.

Parliamentary Debates, vol. 444, 24 November 1947, cols 1603–13.

2.1.3 The Appointed Day

In welcoming Attlee's broadcast on the Appointed Day, *The Times* provided a perceptive summary of the revolutionary significance of the new legislation. It also sounded a warning for the future, particularly in relation to means testing and excessive egalitarianism.

Today the British people join together in a single national friendly society for mutual support during the common misfortunes of life. The coming into force of the National Insurance Acts completes the work begun by the friendly societies in the nineteenth century and carried further by compulsory social insurance in the twentieth. The National Assistance Act winds up half a millennium of social history by finally burying the Poor Law....

The new social security system is, as the PRIME MINISTER said in his broadcast last night, the most comprehensive of its kind ever introduced into any country. It is essentially the culmination of half a century of piecemeal social reform now carried to its logical conclusion. All parties in the State, as MR. ATTLEE rightly emphasized, have borne their part in building up this great structure.... For all their inevitable, and mostly constructive, compromises, the new services attempt to embody certain principles which today can be fittingly recalled. They treat the individual as a citizen, not as a 'pauper', an object of charity, or a member of a particular social class. 'Workmen's' gives way to 'national' insurance....

The social security service compels, the health service allows, every citizen to come in, on the grounds alike of expediency and of principle. The bulk of the middle classes could not and would not be shut out. Had an income limit been imposed ... it would have been extremely awkward in services no longer reserved for one easily identifiable class. It was desired, moreover, to strengthen the bonds of human solidarity in a complex society by making all citizens without exception 'stand on equal terms' in insurance, pooling their risks, and giving every citizen in his weekly contribution stamp a personal reminder of his obligation to his fellows. The same emotion inspired the treatment of those injured in industry on the same footing as the casualties of war. Taken together with the contemporary developments in housing, education, wage policy, food, and local welfare services, the new scheme brings the nation close to guaranteeing to every family, although with possibly too few means tests, a tolerable national minimum of income, goods and services in all circumstances of life....

The nation is now in sight, too, of exhausting the possibilities of the socialist Benthamism, which in different guises has furnished first the Liberal and Labour movements, then the Conservatives, and finally the public at large with a working social philosophy. It is already time to ask what comes next. What kind of society is the next generation to build on the floor of the national minimum? Having attended to the elementary needs which all citizens have in common, what scope is society going to allow for the real difference of ability, aptitude, temperament, initiative, wants, tastes, habits and culture which give individuals their individuality, and impart savour and richness to life above the minimum? Can the next generation ... reap the benefits of a social service State while avoiding the perils of a Santa Claus State?

The Times, 5 July 1948.

2.1.4 Going earnings-related

In its 1964 manifesto, the Labour Party promised to modernise the social security system by transferring it from one paying flat-rate benefits (and thus aimed, allegedly unsuccessfully, at eradicating want) to one paying earnings-related benefits (which would enable people to maintain their accustomed living standards). This was in accordance with European practice and the demands of an increasingly affluent society. The promise was limited, partly as a result of the perceived weakness of the British economy. The final paragraph reveals that taxpayers' money was not to be used to realise the redistributory potential of the scheme. The Income Guarantee promised in (ii) was also never introduced.

Social security benefits – retirement and widow's pension, sickness and unemployment pay – have been allowed to fall below minimum levels of human need. Consequently one in four of National Insurance pensioners are today depending upon means-tested National Assistance benefits. Labour will reconstruct our social security system:

(i) Existing National Insurance benefits will be raised and thereafter linked to average earnings so that as earnings rise so too will benefits.

(ii) For those already retired and for widows, an Incomes Guarantee will be introduced. This will lay down a new national minimum benefit. Those whose incomes fall below the new minimum will receive as of right, and without recourse to National Assistance, an income supplement.

A new wage-related scheme covering retirement, sickness and unemployment will be grafted on to the existing flat rate National Insurance scheme. The objective is half-pay benefits for the worker on average pay. Those who are married will get more than half pay, as will the lower paid worker. Since benefits will be graded, so too will contributions, which will take the form of a percentage contribution on earnings. Provision will be made for 'contracting out' good private schemes along the lines laid down in the Government's graded pension scheme....

Labour recognises that the nation cannot have first-rate social security on the cheap. That is why we insist that the new wage-related benefits must be self-supporting and must be financed, in the main by graded contributions from employers and employees. For the same reason we stress again, that with the exception of the early introduction of the Income Guarantee, the key factor in determining the speed at which new and better levels of benefit can be introduced, will be the rate at which the British economy can advance.

'Let's Go with Labour for the New Britain: Labour Party Manifesto 1964' in F.W.S. Craig (ed.), *British General Election Manifestos 1900–1974*, London, 1975, pp. 265–6.

2.1.5 Equality and pensions

Radicalism was reintroduced into welfare policy by the 1974–76 Labour government and particularly by Barbara Castle at the Department of Health and Social Security (DHSS). She sought to bring the welfare provision up to European standards, principally by improving the level, security and redistributory nature of pensions. This was to be achieved by the stricter regulation of private 'contracted-out' pensions and the more generous funding, particularly for women, of the residual state earnings-related pension scheme (SERPS).

Foreword
The proposals set out in this White Paper will fulfil the Government's pledge to bring to an end the massive dependence on means-tested supplementary benefit which is the sad hallmark of old age today. The new scheme will provide better pensions in retirement, widowhood and chronic ill-health. It will bring security at the end of working life to many millions who at present lack the advantages and cover of a good occupational scheme.

In return for wholly earnings-related contributions the scheme will provide earnings-related pensions fully protected against inflation at all times. Moreover we have designed our proposals to help particularly the lower paid.

Chapter 1

1. For 10 years successive Governments have considered plans for pensions reform. One element of the problem to be tackled has always been clear. That is the failure of the present combination of a mainly flat-rate national insurance pension and of occupational pensions of sharply varying quality and limited coverage to guarantee all pensioners more than a low standard of living, or to prevent large numbers of them from having to rely on means-tested supplementary benefits....

2. There is a second factor which has become of overriding significance in recent years – inflation. If people are to face retirement without continual anxiety about money, they must have a guarantee that the value of their pension rights will be maintained both while they are being built up during working life and after the pension has been put into payment....

Dependence on supplementary benefit
3. Of about 8 million retirement pensioners, some 2 million – or about 25% – also receive supplementary pension. Widows form the poorest group among them and in their case the proportion receiving a supplementary pension is 60%. In addition it is estimated that there may be a further million old people entitled to some supplementary pension ... who do not claim it. These figures reflect the paradox that the British social assistance programme is one of the best in the world, while British contributory benefits have fallen behind those of most other advanced industrial nations.

4. It is wrong that such large numbers of pensioners should have to rely on supplementary benefit. Men and women understandably resent the fact that after a lifetime's work and service in the community they have to rely on this type of assistance in order to keep themselves out of poverty. Furthermore, every claim for such benefits requires detailed personal investigation of the particular circumstances of an individual or family group.... The staff of the Supplementary Benefits Commission cope well with this very difficult task, but it is not one which can be satisfactorily undertaken for massive numbers of people. There will always be a few whose exceptional circumstances will put them in need of a 'safety net' provision. It is quite another matter when millions of people need supplementary benefit after a normal working life....

The Government's answer
10. The new scheme will:- ...

(iii) ensure that during working life the pension rights built up, both in the state and contracted out schemes, will retain their relationship to earnings levels generally and that pensions in payment are fully protected against inflation;

(iv) guarantee a woman the same pension as a man with the same earnings record;

(v) provide the first full pensions after 20 years of paying the new contributions, rather than after a working life-time of 40 years or more;

(vi) cover death and long-term sickness by widowhood and invalidity pensions on terms similar to those for retirement; and

(vii) ensure the tests which have to be satisfied by contracted out schemes are such as to secure adequate provision for the members of those schemes and their widows.

Better Pensions. Fully Protected Against Inflation. Proposals for a New Pensions Scheme, Cmnd 5713, 1974, pp. iii, 1–4.

2.2 'MODERNISING' SOCIAL SECURITY

2.2.1 Thatcherite principles

In the account of her premiership, Mrs Thatcher provided a characteristically trenchant summary of the principles underlying Conservative social policy in the 1980s and its indebtedness to both Victorian and American ideas. Modernisation initially meant contraction.

Socialism had failed. And it was the poorer, weaker members of society who had suffered worst as a result of that failure. More than that, however, socialism ... had played on the worst aspects of human nature. It had literally demoralised communities and families, offering dependency in place of independence as well as subjecting traditional values to sustained derision....

The root cause of our contemporary social problems ... was that the state had been doing too much. A Conservative social policy had to recognise this. Society was made up of individuals and communities. If individuals were discouraged and communities disorientated by the state stepping in to take decisions which should properly be made by people, families and neighbourhoods then society's problems would grow not diminish....

> After discussing what she had meant by denying that there was such a thing as society, she continued to explain her beliefs on the importance of individual responsibility and the desired parameters for state welfare.

I was an individualist in the sense that I believed that individuals are ultimately accountable for their actions and must behave like it. But I always refused to accept that there was some kind of conflict between this kind of individualism and social responsibility. I was reinforced in this view by the writings of conservative thinkers in the United States on the growth of an 'underclass' and the development of a dependency culture. If irresponsible behaviour does not involve penalty of some kind, irresponsibility will for a large number of people become the norm. More important still, the attitudes will be passed on to their children, setting them off in the wrong direction.

I had a great regard for the Victorians for many reasons.... I never felt uneasy about praising 'Victorian values' or – the phrase I originally used – 'Victorian virtues'.... They distinguished between the 'deserving' and the 'undeserving poor'. Both groups should be given help; but it must be help of very different kinds if public spending is not just going to reinforce the dependency culture. The problem with our welfare state was that ...we had failed to remember that distinction and so we provided the same 'help' to those who had genuinely fallen into difficulties and needed some support till they could get out of them, as to those who had simply lost the will or habit of work and self-improvement. The purpose of help must not be to allow people to live a half-life, but to restore their self-discipline and through that their self-esteem.

M. Thatcher, *The Downing Street Years*, London, 1993, pp. 625–7.

2.2.2 Breaking the benefit–earnings link

Major changes in social security policy have typically been effected by technical changes to the small print of legislation.

> One of the first such changes enacted after 1979 was the ending of the link between 'long-term' benefits, such as pensions, and earnings – a device introduced by Labour in 1975 to engineer greater equality in society.

The House will appreciate that we have honoured our commitment which we gave in the election to raise pensions in November in line with prices.... But, as the House now knows, in the light of experience in the last 3 years and other factors, we have been driven to the conclusion that the statutory obligation to uprate long-term benefits each year in line with either prices or earnings, whichever is the higher, is not sustainable in the long-term.

Much has been written about the so-called 'ratchet effect'. In years when earnings exceed prices, the real value of pensions increases. When prices exceed earnings and when the living standards of the working population fall the real value of the pension is maintained. It has been pointed out that the result over a number of years is that the proportion of national income absorbed by pensions, and, correspondingly, the proportion absorbed by contributions necessary to pay those pensions, must inevitably rise, throwing an ever heavier and heavier burden on the working population.

I remind the House that between 1970 and 1974 pensions in fact kept closely in line with earnings, though there was no statutory requirement that they should do so. Conversely, in 1976 and 1978, both years in which the statutory obligation was in force, the increase paid fell short of what the Labour Party had led people to expect. The guarantee that really matters is the guarantee against rising prices. I shall therefore be introducing legislation shortly to amend the provision relating to the uprating of benefit, so as to provide that pensions and long-term benefits, should be increased at least in line with the movement of prices.

I should like to make it clear, however, that it remains the Government's firm intention that pensioners and other long-term beneficiaries can confidently look forward to sharing in the increased standard of living of the country as a whole.

Patrick Jenkin, secretary of state for social services, *Parliamentary Debates*, vol. 968, 13 June 1979, cols 438–9.

2.2.3 The 1985 Social Security Review

In 1985 Norman Fowler as secretary of state for health and social security announced the first comprehensive review of policy since Beveridge. It consciously repeated Beveridge's holistic approach and his emphasis on administrative efficiency. It also stressed the contemporary agreement on the need for reform, looking back to the 'targeting' debate and forward to the forging of a closer link between benefit and work.

The Government are carrying out a review that should have been carried out years ago. It should have been conducted long before now, 40 years after Beveridge.... What is significant is that there is now a consensus that change is needed. There is a consensus for three main reasons. The first is the sheer scale of the social security system. By any standards, it is an enormous undertaking, now consuming nearly one third of all public spending and ... dealing with well over three quarters of the population as either contributors or beneficiaries. We have some 30 different benefits with their own rules of entitlement and payment. That, I presume, is why policy reviews in the past have been narrowly focused on one benefit or one small part of the machine. The aim in our review has been to pull all the strands together into a consistent plan. It has been demonstrated that there is ... a consensus on one point – that virtually everybody regards the present system as too complicated and too difficult for people to understand and for the staff to work....

Much of the complication in the social security system flows from the piecemeal development and augmentation of the system over the past 40 years. If we are to rid it of as much complication as possible, we shall have to decide what is really needed now. That means a reshaping of the system, not a tinkering at the edges.... There is no point in having a review if every part of the structure is regarded as sacrosanct. I am prepared to be held to my commitment to meet social need; I am not prepared to be a prisoner of the existing structure....

Secondly, when we talk about need, we should be absolutely clear what we mean. Beveridge was talking about poverty against a very different background. There have been enormous increases in the material prosperity of this country since then.... No-one can doubt that need exists in this country, and one of our aims must be to target the help available more effectively to meet that need. There are also changes in balance between different groups within the population in need. For example, I think that few would disagree with my diagnosis that one of the areas which today gives most concern is the position of poor families with children....

Thirdly, social security is not somehow isolated from the rest of Government policy. In approaching our review of social security I have sought to avoid the straitjacket of focusing only on the social security system. I have been concerned with how social security relates not just to our social policy and objectives, but to our economic objectives and employment policies. I do not define social objectives merely as greater spending on social security or higher rates of unemployment benefit. I am much more concerned to see people taken off social security benefits and able to support themselves through productive employment....

The Government has shown their commitment to the welfare state, but we want a modern welfare state. We want a modern social security system which uses today's methods to meet today's needs....

Parliamentary Debates, vol. 77, 22 April 1985, cols 637–9.

2.2.4 The 1986 reforms

The Fowler Review led to the 1986 Social Security Act, the principles of which were outlined in a white paper from which this extract is taken. It reveals three major aims. The first was an ending of the perceived advantages given by Labour to those with state as opposed to private occupational pensions (see 2.1.4). This led to a major expansion in, and mis-selling of, private pensions. The second aim was the ending of work disincentives, the unemployment and poverty traps, created by the Conservatives themselves in their piecemeal reforms of 1971 – the introduction of the means-tested Family Income Supplement (FIS) to provide extra financial assistance to low-paid working families. Finally, the reforms aimed at administrative simplification through the separation of standard and exceptional means-tested benefits (renamed Income Support and the Social Fund). Although the Social Fund was to deal with an unpredictable amount of need it was, in the competing interests of economy, cash-limited.

Provision for retirement

1.16 Instead of replacing SERPS, the Government propose to modify the scheme so that costs in the next century are substantially reduced.... The changes to SERPS are that:

• Occupational schemes contracted out of the state scheme should be responsible for inflation-proofing guaranteed minimum pensions ... thus reducing the cost now borne by all national insurance contributors of full inflation-proofing.

• SERPS pensions should be based on a lifetime's earnings, not on the best twenty years as now. This brings state and occupational pensions more into line....

• SERPS pensions should be calculated on 20 per cent of earnings rather than 25 per cent.

• Widows and widowers over 65 should be allowed to inherit half their spouse's SERPS rights, rather than the full amount as now. This change again brings SERPS more into line with what happens in occupational schemes....

1.18 However, policy on SERPS is only one part of the Government's pensions strategy. Our central aim remains to see an extension of individual pensions provision – while at the same time widening choice for the individual and increasing competition among providers of pensions.... Six points of this strategy deserve emphasis.

First, we will enable employers to set up new occupational schemes....

Second, there will be a financial incentive to encourage more contracting out....

Third, for the first time everyone will have the right to a personal pension. These are individual pensions – separate from employers' schemes – where a person builds up a fund which he himself owns....

Fourth, legislation will make it possible for new financial bodies to provide pensions....

Fifth, for the first time, all occupational scheme members will have the right to pay an additional voluntary contribution to boost their income in retirement....

Sixth, steps will be taken to provide investor protection for members of occupational schemes and holders of personal pensions....

1.20 Taken together this strategy provides major new opportunities for the expansion of occupational and personal pension coverage.... For the first time everyone will have the freedom to choose the kind of pension that he wants on top of that provided by the state....

Provision for children

1.22 Low-income families with children are among those with the greatest needs today.... Families with children – including one parent families – now make up over half of people on low incomes.... The need is to help working families as well as those who are unemployed....

1.23 The unemployment and poverty trap effects are an additional and major complication in family support policies.... In spite of good intentions, the FIS has not solved these problems.... Families can find themselves worse off working than unemployed....

1.24 The aim of the White Paper proposals is to help families whether they are in or out of work....

First, extra help will go to families in receipt of income support which replaces supplementary benefit. A family premium will be paid on top of the basic income support rate and in addition to the rates for individual children....

Second, FIS will be replaced by the new family credit scheme. This will provide help to working families that is more closely matched to the help available for non-working families. It will aim to ensure that families are better off in work than out of work....

Third, both family credit and housing benefit will be based on *net* income.... This will end the present position where a reduction in benefit as earnings rise can actually leave people worse off.

1.25 Taken together these proposals will direct significant extra help to low-income families while at the same time tackling some of the indefensible distortions in the benefit system....

Income-related benefits

1.28 ... The central feature of the reform of income-related benefits is to replace the present supplementary benefit scheme with a much simpler scheme of income support – with special needs being dealt with separately in a social fund. This tackles the chief problem in the supplementary benefit system itself: the enormous superstructure of extra payments....

1.29 Successive reforms first of the national assistance and then of supplementary benefit have been bedevilled by the attempt to make provision on a detailed basis for the special needs of individuals as well as providing steady weekly income for very large numbers of people. It is the attempt to make the scheme shoulder this double role which has led to the failings of the present supplementary benefit scheme. The Government's proposals for the first time separate the scheme into two separate functions. Weekly payments through the income support scheme are to be on as clear and simple a footing as possible and paid as a right.... There are to be basic personal allowances depending on age, with premiums for clearly and easily identifiable groups who need extra help: pensioners, disabled people and one parent families, and the premium for all families with children....

Social Fund
1.32 ... There will be a minority, as there are now, who have special needs or who run into particular difficulties which cannot simply be catered for by income support.... The Government have decided on a fresh approach – a fund operated with a budget administered by specially trained staff. The creation of the social fund will enable local offices to respond flexibly and promptly to the needs of claimants which the income support scheme cannot meet....

Reform of Social Security: Programme for Action, Cmnd 9691, 1985, Chapter 1, pp. 1–8.

2.2.5 Rethinking Labour policy

In the aftermath of the Conservative electoral victory in 1992, Bryan Gould – who was to compete for the leadership of the Labour Party in July – reflected on the need to adapt Labour's welfare policy to the 'Thatcherite revolution'. Services had to be responsive to individual need. The engineering of greater equality, to which he was still committed, could only be achieved (as in Sweden) through the labour market.

There was an irredeemably old-fashioned 'welfarist' flavour to our proposals that did not appeal to many who were meant to benefit....
We must ... understand that people are no longer content to be identified in policy terms by their membership of socio-economic groups. They rightly insist on being treated as individuals. We have failed to recognise that most people are now accustomed to exercising choice, however limited their purchasing power. They like the sense of power and freedom that choice gives them. They are no longer prepared to 'like it or lump it' with publicly delivered services....

Labour has failed to adjust to these changes because our traditional preoccupation with the delivery of public services means we have identified more with the producers than with the consumers. And our proper anxiety to complement the market with collectively delivered provision has blinded us to the obvious point that the only real purpose of any provision is the satisfaction of individual needs, and that a failure in these terms will be judged harshly....

Resources should be used to equip people to act in their own interests rather than to pauperise them by treating them as dependents. So, for example, instead of concentrating resources on child benefit, it may be more sensible to increase provision for child care, so women may enter the job market.

Labour's concern should be with the initial distribution of wealth, rather than with a *post hoc* redistribution. We should aim to increase people's ability to participate in, and gain the rewards of, wealth creation, rather than limit ourselves to what is, at best, the palliative of redistributive taxation.

Bryan Gould, 'The Labour Party: which way now?', *New Statesman and Society,* 15 May 1992.

2.2.6 The New Deal, 1998

In 1998 the chancellor of the exchequer, Gordon Brown (who was to assume the dominant role in welfare reform), launched the first major initiative in Labour's 'welfare to work' programme. This was focused less on engineering greater social equality than on using the welfare system to encourage people back to paid work and thereby end the perceived dependency culture. The initiative thus owed a considerable debt to Thatcherite ideas and, as its title suggests, to American thinking.

Today marks the start of a New Deal for Britain's young. A new beginning in the war against poverty, and the first step in the modernisation of the welfare state in Britain. It's the Labour Government's 1998 New Year's resolution for Britain – to help our long-term unemployed back to work and to give them the skills they need.

Here today from Dundee and Tayside we launch the first of twelve pilot programmes offering jobs and training to every young person six months out of work.

From April, every long-term unemployed young man or woman under the age of 25 will be offered the new deal options of work or training.

A total of 3 billion pounds is being invested in jobs.

It is not just the young who will benefit from the New Deal. From June, employers will be offered a 75 pounds a week subsidy to take on the long-term unemployed.

During 1998 lone parents with their youngest child at school will be offered help to find work.

And from this year too disabled men and women, denied the right to work for too long – will be given new opportunities to work.

The old deal – of paying people a few pounds in benefit and then forgetting about them – failed the unemployed and failed Britain.

Today begins the long haul towards full employment in the years to come.

From now on in Britain, young people will have new opportunities and a new contribution they can make under the new deal. Rights go hand in hand with responsibilities; from today there will be no option of simply staying at home on full benefit doing nothing.

So it is something for something, not something for nothing....

The scheme offers four routes into work and helps each young person pick the route that suits their needs – a job, full-time education, a job in the voluntary sector or a role in the environmental task force....

I want all of you to feel part of what I believe is a national crusade to clear once and for all the social divisions that are entrenched in our society because of unemployment.

And this is just the start. The government believes in helping thousands more from welfare to work in the years to come as part of the long haul towards our goal of full employment.

That is why we are prepared to extend the New Deal from the under 25s to the over 25s and are prepared to invest more in the long-term unemployed, lone parents and disabled men and women who want the right to work, to make this ambition a reality.

And we will do more. The New Deal is our first step towards a new welfare state and I want men and women who have been unemployed and written off by many to be able to say they now have a new chance to make the best of themselves and to make a contribution, not just to their families, but to the progress of Britain.

Speech by Gordon Brown, chancellor of the exchequer, 'Launch of the New Deal', 5 January 1998, http//www.hm-treasury.gov.uk/press/1998/p2_98.html.

2.2.7 The Working Families Tax Credit

In his 1998 budget, Gordon Brown announced a further initiative designed to achieve the major objectives of policy since the 1960s: the greater integration of the tax and benefits system. It was designed to end both the disincentives to work and the stigma of receiving legitimate benefit, and thereby to address the concerns raised in *New Ambitions for Our Country*. Working Families Tax Credit (WFTC) replaced the old system of Family Credit (FC) in October 1999.

The labour market challenge

2.05 There is increasing polarisation between working and non-working families – about 3.5 million households with at least one adult member of working age have no-one in work – or 18 per cent – compared to 9 per cent in 1979. Non-working women are increasingly partnered with workless men, whereas women with working partners, especially in families with young children, have experienced rapidly rising employment rates. The priority must therefore be to help those without work into work.

2.06 Five million adults and 2.7 million children live in workless households, which account for a growing proportion of those in poverty. The proportion of children living in families without a full-time employee has risen from 16 per cent in 1970 to 33 per cent in 1995. The Government believes that the best way to tackle poverty is to get people into jobs. It is therefore important to improve skills and employability. But it is also necessary to address many of the features of the tax and benefit system that fail to reward work and allow people to ascend the earnings ladder:

• the unemployment trap which can result in in-work incomes being little higher than those available out of work;

• the failure of in-work support to recognise in-work costs associated with child-care;

• the poverty trap which arises when people in work cannot improve their income by working longer hours or for higher pay. At present ¾ million working families face marginal tax and benefit withdrawal rates of over 70 per cent....

2.09 The WFTC is designed to make work pay for families, guaranteeing them a minimum income, above and beyond the level of the minimum wage. Its clear link with employment should demonstrate the rewards of work over welfare and help ensure that people move off welfare into work. As a tax credit rather than a welfare benefit, it should reduce the stigma associated with claiming in-work support, and encourage higher take-up. FC has only ever been taken up by around 70 per cent of those in work who are entitled to it. With the WFTC, the onus will be on the Government to ensure that as many families as are entitled receive the credit.

2.10 The WFTC represents an important step towards greater integration of the tax and benefit systems. It will reduce the wasteful overlap between tax and social security systems: at present, almost 500,000 families pay income tax to the Inland Revenue while receiving FC from the DSS [Department of Social Security].

Budget 98. The Modernisation of Britain's Tax and Benefit System, Number Three: The Working Families Tax Credit and Work Incentives, London, 1998, pp. 6–7.

2.3 CONTROVERSY: UNIVERSALISM VERSUS SELECTIVITY

2.3.1 Choice in welfare, 1963

As identified in Chapter 1, a major ideological battle was ever-present in postwar policy over whether benefits should be universal or selective. The publication by the IEA, a right-wing pressure group, of the opinion survey *Choice in Welfare* in 1963 forced the first serious debate in Whitehall since 1948. Here leading civil servants in the Treasury reject the IEA proposals on practical and, more surprisingly, on principled grounds.

We agree with the Institute of Economic Affairs' claim that not enough is known about public attitudes to the tax system and the social services. These matters are worth further research but to be of value it would have to be carefully planned.

The objectives of the report

7. In the introduction the report states that 'politicians of all parties have overwhelmingly adopted the view that the only policy acceptable to the public is the extension of State services at continually rising standards to increasing numbers of beneficiaries'. The purpose of the survey was to submit this proposition to the test and the conclusion reached is that there is far more interest in freedom of choice in the social services than has been assumed.

8. The report is not concerned with making recommendations ... although it does contain some discussion of means and refers, for example, to the difficulty of using the income tax system to remit taxation to people who 'opt out'. Also, for the purpose of the questionnaire, considerable use was made of Professor Milton Friedman's plan for vouchers to be used in settlement of private bills to be granted to those who chose not to use public services....

11. The present welfare policy may be said to be founded on the principle of universality; with certain exceptions individual contributions are not affected by whether the contributor chooses to use state services or not. Three main justifications for the principle of universality need to be examined:

(1) the maintenance of standards;
(2) the redistribution of incomes;
(3) the sense of national unity.

12. Only the first of these is explicitly discussed in the report. It is rightly pointed out that the maintenance of standards is not incompatible with choice in welfare. The state may prescribe minimum standards in the private sector and enforce them by systems of registration and inspection. On the question of redistribution the report is vague. It is not made clear whether the authors would regard a reduction in the redistribution brought about by the present system as desirable or not.... We have asked ourselves whether more choice in welfare could be compatible with the maintenance of present redistribution. The answer seems to be that it could – for example a system of grants to parents choosing private schools could in principle be financed by increases in income tax falling more than proportionately on the higher income groups who may be expected to make most use of these grants. On the other hand, it seems quite possible that policies intended to give more choice in welfare would have the effect of reducing the redistributive effects of the present system....

14. Thirdly there is the question of national solidarity – an aim to

which great attention was paid when the lines of the welfare state were laid down in the 1940s. There are two schools of thought on this point.... The first school, to which we may assume the authors of the report belong, would feel that the need for universal provision is weakened by the reduction in primary poverty and the increased wealth of the average working man. The other would stress the continuing prevalence of inequality in our society and would fear that a policy of choice in welfare would tend to perpetuate or even exacerbate this inequality.

15. Whatever one's attitude on this last issue, one must acknowledge that the public sector will be bound to provide for the poorest section of the community.... To limit such provision to a small minority would result in considerable economies in public expenditure. At the same time it would institutionalise divisions within the community; and many people would strongly object to this.

16. There is a further point of importance; the present welfare services are designed to ensure that the education, health and minimum pension needs of every citizen are provided for whether or not he wishes to spend his own money on these things. The justification is that society benefits by refusing to allow some of its members to suffer from the consequences of a mistaken order of priorities or lack of foresight. Even if the Institute of Economic Affairs are right in assuming that some or a substantial proportion of our society would fully provide for their welfare needs if left to themselves, there remain strong arguments for keeping state provision for the others....

'Choice in welfare', Commentary by a Treasury Group, Public Record Office, T227/1788, pp. 1–5.

2.3.2 Defending universalism

Brian Abel-Smith, the professor of social administration at the London School of Economics and a policy adviser in the 1966–70 Labour government, here provides a characteristic defence of universalism whilst admitting that selectivity – for all its weaknesses – has increased under both Conservative and Labour governments.

On two points there is common ground between the extremist Institute of Economic Affairs selectivists and ... the 'high priests of universality'. The first is the recognition that poverty in Britain is widespread, which carries with it the implication that poverty should be reduced if not abolished. The second is the acceptance of the need to increase spending on health, education and similar services. But while the universalists want to see an increase in collective spending, the selectivists want to see more private spending....

Selectivists attribute the low standard of our social services to the extent of collective provision on a universal basis. If only state help were restricted to those that needed it, they argue, more help could be given, at lower cost. Thus tax levels could be reduced and, goaded by sharper financial incentives, workers and employers alike would rush to give us both more exports and more growth.

The selectivists write ... as if universal services were on the increase and selective services on the decrease, though the reverse is actually the case. The only new universal benefit introduced by the Labour Government is redundancy payments, while it has extended the field of selective benefits by introducing rate rebates, the mortgage option scheme and free family planning services for poor families....

Poor families are already caged in a veritable labyrinth of means tests. Most of us have only one income return each year to the Inland Revenue.... But depending on its size, circumstances and location a poor family is expected to undergo six or more means tests – for rent rebates, rate rebates, free school meals, welfare foods, uniform grants and educational maintenance allowances.... For these different purposes, different statements of income covering different periods must be provided at different times of the year and on different forms....

An application for a selective benefit which is only available to the poor involves an admission of poverty.... In a society which places great emphasis on monetary rewards an admission of poverty is an admission of failure.... Thus a means test for a poverty benefit is regarded in a quite different light to a means test for income tax assessment or a means test for a parental contribution to a university award.... Whatever may be said about the principles underlying existing means tests for the poor, it is at least clear that the services available on these terms are grossly underutilised.... In the vast majority of cases when the father of a poor family is in full time work, the family does not receive the full complement of free welfare milk, spectacles, appliances, dentistry, prescriptions to which it is entitled.... A further problem ... is associated with these local means tests. There are enormous variations in the amount of help different authorities are prepared to grant to similar families....

Even the most ardent advocate of selective benefits would surely concede that no further selective benefits should be introduced until the existing benefits are rationalised, publicised and administered with sufficient confidentiality and dignity to be used by virtually all those for whom they are intended....

To sum up. Selectivity in the form of means tested benefits for poor families is already playing too large a role. Our need today is not for more means tested benefits but for less.

B. Abel-Smith, 'Conclusion: the need for social planning', in *Social Services For All?*, Fabian Tract 385, London, 1968, pp. 112–13, 122.

2.3.3 Targeting

> The Treasury had traditionally favoured selectivity in order to reduce public expenditure. Here the Labour chancellor, Jim Callaghan, publicly defends it in the guise of 'targeting' and, in so doing, contradicts some of Abel-Smith's arguments.

I agree ... that we need a continuing debate on the manner and way in which we are to channel the available resources in the public sector. It is clear to me that a great deal more help can be given if assistance is concentrated where it is genuinely needed, but it would need to be concentrated in such a way that the humiliating measures of the past were not revived nor essential services denied, and it is for this reason that I ruled out any attempt to reintroduce prescription charges.

Nevertheless I take note that there are many fields in which income testing now exists and some of them are of recent origin. There is no particular shame in that. Parents with a child at university pay according to their income. Tenants on many council house estates pay differential rates according to their incomes. More than 1 million people receive rebates of their rates according to their incomes. We have a vast task to rebuild the slums, to build new schools, to replace unfit homes and to expand the roads and hospitals. The financial requirement is of such an order that we shall need a continuous examination in order to ensure that our methods will give those in real need the benefit that they should have.

Parliamentary Debates, vol. 751, 24 July 1967, cols 98–9.

2.3.4 The introduction of child benefit, 1976

One of the most radical acts of the 1974–76 Labour government was to withdraw the child tax allowance (which mainly advantaged men) and to increase the family allowance (paid in cash, usually to women) by an equivalent amount. The purpose was to increase the value of a universal benefit, to be renamed child benefit, so that it could meet Beveridge's principle of 'adequacy'. This extract from the diary of Barbara Castle, the secretary of state for health and social security, illustrates the administrative and political infighting which differences of policy objectives could provoke.

Monday 29 March, 1976

In the afternoon I had a traumatic meeting with Joel [Barnett, chief secretary to the Treasury] over the rate of child benefit. Brian Abel-Smith and officials have produced an excellent briefing showing that the right level of benefit at which no-one will be worse off, including one-parent families and larger families, is about £2.60 a week. Anything below that would require the payment of a special premium to those groups at enormous administrative complication and cost. The figure which would take us back to 1971 levels of family support would be £2.85. I told officials my fall-back figure would probably have to be £2.70 a week.... When we arrived at the Treasury ... Joel ... asked me to suggest my figure for child benefit. Quietly I spelt out my analysis of the minimum need for family support, particularly in view of the continuing price increases.... I would not, I said, be unrealistic and expect us to go back to the level of family support obtaining in 1955 (about £10 per week for a family of 3 children and on a standard rate of income tax) but it did seem to me reasonable that, in launching this major aspect of our social policy, we should get back to 1971, i.e., a rate worth £7 for three children. They watched avidly as I said slowly: 'And this gives us a rate of £2.85 per week'; Joel exploded with laughter at his officials' dismay.... 'And what would this sumptuous figure cost?' 'We don't know' said Plaitzky, tearing his hair, 'the Secretary of State has gone right through the top of our table'. 'It would cost £217 million', I said sweetly, 'only slightly above the £200 million which is the top end of the amount earmarked in the Contingency Fund for this purpose'. 'Nothing is earmarked', said Joel desperately. 'Don't you realise that the claims on the Contingency Fund already exceed it several times?' He then tried to exert some control over the situation by spelling out the figure *he* had in mind: £2.40 plus a premium of 22 pence a week for one-parent and large families to ensure they did not actually lose. It was my turn to give an incredulous laugh. The Treasury wasn't actually suggesting, was it, I asked, that we should spend Civil Service Manpower, which we had been asked to cut, on paying out little extra driblets of money for a few families because we were in the process of making them poorer.

Joel then went into one of the now fashionable diatribes against universal benefits. Here we were with our backs to the wall and I was proposing an across-the-board increase in family support which would give help to families who did not need it. He waxed eloquent about the wickedness of universal benefits – the need for greater selectivity. It is moments like this that I despair of this Government, dominated as it is by people who don't believe in the policy on which we fought the election.... 'I really don't know why you don't join the Tory Party', I told Joel coldly, 'because the policy of *our* party is to extend the payment of benefits as of right on the basis of the functional need – then to take back from those who don't need them the value of those benefits in taxation'. Joel merely said testily that I was talking sentimental nonsense. It is this kind of attitude that makes me fight for my own departmental corner ruthlessly. Not only am I and others on the left in Cabinet excluded from the centres of real power ... but I am expected to accept meekly the reinterpretations of party doctrine which the Treasury ... just imposes on us....

The atmosphere was beginning to get quite nasty, but once again I was saved by the Treasury overreaching itself. Miss Jennifer Forsyth started asserting that there would be no administrative difficulties at all about operating a selective premium. I thereupon brought in Tony Crocker who ... wiped the floor with her. Lance Errington ... clinched it by pointing out that every one-parent and large family would have to have *two* books in order to get another miserly 22 pence per week. Collapse of Treasury party....

Epilogue
There were even greater setbacks over child benefit. Although when I left the Government Cabinet had been about to agree the rate at which it would be introduced in 1977, silence fell until 25 May when David Ennals announced that the scheme had been postponed indefinitely. Instead, family allowances of £1 a week would be introduced for the first child. The excuse given was that the trade unions had shied away from the cut in their members' take-home pay which the loss of child tax allowance would mean, even though the family as a whole would benefit. Labour back-benchers, particularly the women MPs, were furious and I persuaded the TUC [Trades Union Congress] Liaison Committee to set up a working party to argue things out. The TU members of the working party ... proved devoted allies of child benefit and faced with their determination the Government was forced to accept a compromise under which the scheme was phased in over 3 years. By the time the general election came child benefit had been fully introduced at a rate of £4 a week with the promise of more to come and the Government was glad to claim it as the cornerstone of its policy for the family.

B. Castle, *The Castle Diaries 1974–1976*, London, 1980, pp. 708–9, 737.

2.4 THE POOR

2.4.1 The reality of poverty in the 1950s

Many social workers, such as Audrey Harvey who had worked in the East End of London since 1955, soon became aware that the welfare state had not eliminated poverty. Here she demonstrates how some of Beveridge's aims had not been realised, thereby challenging complacency about the superiority of the British welfare system.

What is wrong?
That we have a divided society, which is rapidly becoming more sharply so, is painfully obvious....
    This may be partly due to loss of contact between people of different education and employment, different resources and ways of living; partly, too, to an over-estimation – encouraged by both the big

political parties – of the extent to which working people have benefited by the reforms. At any rate reaction has set in, bringing with it pressure to chip bits off the services; while among the armchair critics of the Welfare State it is axiomatic that 'they' – meaning roughly the working class – 'get too much done for them nowadays' while 'we' have to foot the bill.

This idea overlooks the fact that only about 4 per cent of the population do not use the State services at all and do not draw family allowances, pensions or insurance benefits or apply for grants for further education of their children at the State-subsidised universities. It neglects the fact, too, that it is chiefly the middle classes who have benefited from the provision of free medical services and entitlement to a full retirement pension after only ten years of contributions....

But while it is obvious that taxation, and particularly indirect taxation, often hits the poor harder than the well-to-do – as do National Insurance contributions – these are not the only payments which State-dependent families may have to make for essential services....

There are assessed charges for the home help service and the school meals service unless inability can be proved; and assessed charges for the care of children in children's homes and day nurseries; and for badly-off people not receiving assistance, there is the whole range of health service charges, from £3 for a surgical boot to £2 for a doctor's report needed for an accident claim. Again and again 'they' are still forced to plead poverty....

Something for nothing?

This is not to suggest that the principle of paying for certain special services is necessarily a wrong one or that it is resented. The outstanding quality of the people I have met in the course of my job is independence. There is a pronounced loathing among families of low income of anything that smacks of charity, and the number of those trying to get something for nothing is, in actual experience, very small indeed. This is also the experience of the National Assistance Board. Its report for 1957 stated that only 65 men on assistance were prosecuted for neglecting to work when able to do so, and that there were only 750 prosecutions for fraud out of a total of over 1½ million people (excluding dependents) then receiving assistance....

Going on assistance

... In 1958 the National Assistance Board had to make 1,119,000 weekly allowances to supplement inadequate pension and benefit rates, and this represented no less than 68 per cent of all allowances in payment.

We know, therefore, that over a million people in this Welfare State were living below subsistence level for this reason alone, and were granted assistance. We also know that for 780,000 of all assisted people the minimum rates of assistance were considered by the Board to be insufficient ... since this was the number of discretionary allowances made ... for extra fuel, special diet and other requirements, in addition to which 152,000 single payments for shoes, clothing and bedding had to be provided for people in the most extreme need.

These figures do not precisely tally with the axiom that 'poverty has been abolished'. But if we can feel little complacency about the numbers of the poor or the extent of their relief ... we can feel even less about the incalculable number in bitter need who did not even apply for help....

Why is there so much aversion from seeking its help?... Even if the officers are kind and tactful, as they often are, the applicant is, in fact, pleading poverty; and since that poverty must be checked, he must be visited at home and asked questions which, to the sensitive, are often embarrassing, and which may involve relatives and other people living in the house.

The price of application is, therefore, a surrender of personal privacy and a strong deterrent is the fear that, even when this price is paid, assistance may not be forthcoming....

We have been deluded into thinking not only that we have already achieved a Welfare State ... but that it is second to none. Our National Health Service is still unrivalled, but in other matters we are falling behind. The Scandinavian countries are ahead of us in providing better old people's homes and up-to-date hospitals; New Zealand enables young families to buy their own houses by advancing Family Allowances. France does not invariably deny a family allowance to the first child of a family as we do; Germany gives better insurance coverage in illness and is spending half as much again on social security as we are....

A. Harvey, *Casualties of the Welfare State,* Fabian Tract 321, London, 1960, pp. 4–8, 31–2.

2.4.2 The 'rediscovery' of poverty in the 1960s

The impressionistic evidence of social workers was statistically confirmed by the research of Brian Abel-Smith and Peter Townsend at the London School of Economics. They revolutionised the measurement of poverty by analysing national data sets of family income (the Family Expenditure Survey) and identifying the number of people whose income fell below the official poverty line (the current level of means-tested national assistance). They estimated that there were 2 million people in poverty in 1953/54 and 7.5 million in 1960. A large number of children were included; and their report led directly to the creation of the Child Poverty Action Group (CPAG) in 1965.

The limited objective of the work upon which this report is based was to find out from data collected in government income and expenditure surveys in two post-war years as much as possible about the levels of living and the social characteristics of the poorest section of the population in the United Kingdom....

This is not the place for a searching discussion of reforms in social security. All that we wish to point out is that there is a two-fold implication for social policy of the evidence in this report – not only that a substantial minority of the population in addition to those living on national assistance live at or below national assistance standards, but also that a substantial minority of the population are not receiving national assistance and yet appear to qualify for it. The legitimacy of the system is therefore called into question.

Possibly the novel finding is the extent of poverty among children. For a decade it has been generally assumed that such poverty as exists is found overwhelmingly among the aged. Unfortunately it has not been possible to estimate ... exactly how many persons over minimum pensionable age were to be found among the 7½ million persons with low income in 1960. However, such data as we have suggest that the number may be around 3 million. There were thus more people who were not aged than were aged among poor households of 1960. We have estimated earlier that there were about 2½ million children in low income households in 1960. Thus quantitatively the problem of poverty among children is more than two-thirds of the size of poverty among the aged. This fact has not been given due emphasis in the policies of the political parties....

The evidence of substantial numbers of the population living below national assistance level, and also of substantial numbers seeming to be eligible for national assistance but not receiving it, calls for a radical review of the whole social security scheme. Moreover, the fact that nearly a third of the poor were children suggests the need for a readjustment of priorities in plans for extensions and developments.

B. Abel-Smith and P. Townsend, *The Poor and the Poorest*, London, 1965, pp. 57, 65–6.

2.4.3 Low-income families in the 1970s

In the 1970s there was a reversion to 'lifestyle' analysis to convey to an affluent public the 'feel of poverty'. The classic surveys were Peter Townsend, *Poverty in the United Kingdom* (1979) and the *Breadline Britain* surveys of 1984 and 1990. Here a CPAG investigator provides an account of a poverty culture remarkably similar to that prevailing before 1939. Virginia Bottomley was to be the Conservative secretary of state for health between 1992 and 1997.

With the help of 25 families Virginia Bottomley was able to report on the lifestyles of poor families in London in 1971.... Virginia Bottomley wrote:

The supplementary benefit level is commonly recognised as the official poverty line.

Those living on or below the poverty line endure a continuous uncertainty about where the next pound is coming from. Their income is distinguished by lack of security and considerable versatility. Income frequently fluctuates; only three of the sample experienced no change in their employment situation in the last year.

Such a precarious financial position made budgeting difficult. Half the families had no savings at all and only one family had more than ten pounds. The lack of money or assets to fall back on made their situation even more acute when earnings dropped. There was the inclination to save; individuals frequently began to put money away (or even cigarette coupons) but found they had to draw on it to meet some unexpected expenses, like shoes. Four mothers were members of a Christmas Club; only one was able to leave her money there until

Christmas....

Five families were behind with the rent, owing between £3 and £104. Similar figures were owed on personal loans and hire purchase agreements....

At least six families relied heavily on their relatives, especially for food.... 'My mother-in-law always brings a piece of meat and some fruit at the week-end'....

Two families without recourse to credit or regular gifts had, on occasion, resorted to petty thieving. 'I'm the only one in my family who's got nothing and none of them help me so I go out and get it for myself'. Four mothers sold possessions to pay off debts or buy food....

The families' major budgetary problem is due to a combination of low income, increasing cost of food and the fact that there is virtually an irreducible minimum expenditure necessarily spent on food. It is self-evident that expenditure on other categories has to be reduced proportionately....

Most housewives conscientiously shopped around for bargains and travelled considerable distances to a supermarket or the market; but even though they spent such a large proportion on food and many went to great lengths to be thrifty, they still complained that it was impossible to feed their families adequately.

One single mother of three children who earned £14 a week as a home-help, picked up discarded fruit and vegetables after the market; another bought 56 lbs of potatoes at a time from the wholesale market, wheeling them the two miles home in a pram. Another said, 'We can't afford two proper meals a day'.

Families living at this level found that after they paid rent and bought food, there was no money left for clothes; mothers were concerned to avoid visible signs of poverty in their children's appearance: 'I may be poor but you won't find better dressed kids than mine round here', said one, but many were not so fortunate....

Most families found it hard to stretch their money to cover household equipment. One woman regularly searched the rubbish dumps near her home for old furniture, cutlery and china. About half the larger pieces of furniture, or machines such as fridges, and chairs were bought on hire-purchase; the rest were second-hand, gifts or found, but very few were cash sales. Two families did not have enough chairs to seat the whole family, and carpets were often threadbare.

Holidays and children's parties are annual events taken for granted by some sections of the population, but which these families can afford only once or twice a decade....

Asked about children's birthdays during the last year, four families had another family to a party. Two either did not want one or had no friends. Eleven had no money to spare on a party.

Frank Field, *Poverty: The Facts,* CPAG Poverty Pamphlet 21, London, 1975, pp. 34–6.

2.4.4 Living on social security

This extract from another CPAG pamphlet pinpoints the practical failure of the 1986 Social Security Act, implemented in 1988, and the growing sense of social exclusion.

Despite two wide-ranging reforms of social assistance (one implemented in 1980 and the other in 1988), the current system still fails, in many ways, to assist the very people it was set up to help. Indeed the people we interviewed felt very much that this had been the case and described in detail the adverse effects the 1988 changes had had on them.

The social security changes

The interviews highlighted a number of effects of recent social security policies:

• Most people interviewed felt that income support did not provide an adequate standard of living. Many felt worse off over the last few years and, in many cases, specifically cited the 1988 changes as being the main cause.

• It was usually impossible for claimants to budget effectively from week to week. This problem had grown worse since 1988, when they had had to start paying water rates and the 20 per cent of the general rates/poll tax and had found benefit increases did not adequately compensate for this....

• Budgeting was made much harder by the removal of most lump sum grants and the introduction of loans. Once again, benefit levels did not take account of this change. Far from increasing independence and promoting budgeting skills, the removal of most grants was generally associated with increased debt, doing without essential items and/or forced (and resented) dependence on help from family or friends.

• Families with children, people with disabilities and elderly people were all suffering. This indicated that the introduction of additional 'premiums' for groups with special expenses did not achieve its aim of targeting help on those seen by the government as most in need, although it did mean that claimants automatically received money for extra needs....

• Although the 1988 changes were designed to make benefits simpler and easier to understand, people reported continuing difficulties.... For some, an internalised sense of stigma attached to being on benefit was exacerbated by stigmatising treatment from officialdom....

Indirect effects of poverty

The people we interviewed were affected by lack of money in many ways. They discussed their struggles to counteract the psychological pressures and stresses of poverty, and the difficulties these could produce in relationships with friends and within the family. They explained how shortage of cash could curtail their participation in social and community activities.

Both studies highlighted the additional problems caused by poor housing and a run down environment with a lack of local facilities (for example, cheap shops, good transport and play provision for children). These produced practical problems resulting in money worries, but also drastically affected people's quality of life. In addition, some lone parents felt strongly that lack of childcare facilities meant that they could not get into work and off benefit.

In summary, the accounts of living in poverty presented in this book bear witness to the continuing failure of social policies aimed at people in poverty. Above all, they present unequivocal evidence that the income support system is failing to meet the needs of the very people it was designed to help.

R. Cohen, J. Coxall, G. Craig and A. Sadiq-Sangster, *Hardship Britain: Being Poor in the 1990s*, London, 1992, pp. 104–7.

2.4.5 Poverty and social exclusion

A major survey in 1999 reviewed the relentless increase in poverty over the past twenty years and identified the main victims. It was based on a questionnaire, in which respondents were asked to comment on whether they felt deprived of a given range of 'goods, services and activities which the majority of the population define as being necessities of modern life'. Such a measure of relative deprivation was felt by some critics not to be an acceptable measure of poverty, particularly given the levels of absolute destitution in other parts of the world.

Adult poverty in Britain
Who is poor?
... 22 per cent of male respondents were poor compared with 29 per cent of female respondents – confirming that poverty is more common for women....

For all respondents the average proportion of people who are poor is 25.6 per cent. There are some groups where the proportion is more than double this average rate:

• non-retired *people who are not working* because they are unemployed (77 per cent) or sick/disabled (61 per cent);

• *those on income support* (70 per cent);

• *lone parents* (62 per cent);

• *local authority tenants* (61 per cent) and *housing association tenants* (57 per cent).

Although the number of respondents in the non-white ethnic groups is very small, the results indicate a much higher poverty rate for non-white ethnic groups especially among the Bangladeshi and Black ethnic groups.

Divorced or separated people are more likely to be poor (46 per cent) and there are also higher proportions of poor people in households of certain types:

• those with *3+ children* (46 per cent);

• those with *youngest child aged 0–4* (41 per cent) or *aged 5–11* (35 per cent);

• households *with one adult* (38 per cent).

Younger people are also more likely to be poor:

• *16 to 24-year-olds* (34 per cent);

• *25 to 34-year-olds* (38 per cent).

A slightly greater proportion of *those finishing education below age 16* are poor (30 per cent) and those staying on to age 19 or above are much less likely to be poor (17 per cent)....

What is notable is that even when controlling for all other factors, those on Income Support are much more likely to be in poverty – suggesting that raising the Income Support levels may be a well-targeted way of relieving poverty.

Child poverty in Britain
How many children fall below the child poverty threshold?
A similar range of statistical techniques to those used for adults ... have been used to determine a threshold for childhood necessities deprivation. This statistical analysis suggests that a child should be considered to be deprived if lacking any one or more of the items in the list because their parents cannot afford them. A third of children – 34 per cent – are poor or 'necessity-deprived', by this definition. However, since a large proportion of children lacked one item in particular (a 'holiday away from home once a year'), it seems sensible also to use a more restrictive deprivation threshold of two or more items. Eighteen per cent of children are poor by this definition.

Which children are poor?
Ethnicity
Although there was widespread agreement between white and non-white parents as to what are the necessities for children, the parents of non-white children are more likely to be unable to afford them.

Over one-half of non-white children are deprived of at least one item and over one-third of at least two. Further analysis confirms the findings of other studies and suggests a number of possible reasons for this.... First, non-white children are more likely to be in larger families, in terms of the numbers of adults and children. Second, they are more likely to be in households with incomes in the lowest quintile. Finally, non-white children are more likely to live in jobless households....

Why are children poor?
 • Children in households where one or more adults receive Income Support or Jobseekers allowance are over 3 times as likely to be deprived.
 • Children in lone parent households are not significantly more likely to be deprived than those in a couple household when other

characteristics are taken into account. Therefore, although a child in a lone parent family has a significantly higher risk of being deprived of necessities ... this is nothing to do with lone parenthood in itself. Rather it is because lone-parents are more likely to be living in local authority rented housing and in receipt of Income Support.

The growth of poverty in Britain
Between 1983 and 1990, the number of *households* who lacked three or more socially perceived necessities increased by almost 50 per cent. In 1983, 14 per cent of households were living in poverty, and by 1990 this figure was 21 per cent. Poverty continued to increase during the 1990s and by 1999 the number of households living in poverty on this definition had again increased to over 24 per cent, approximately 1 in 4 households....

This represented about half a million extra people living in poverty on average each year between 1983 and 1990, and a smaller but continuing increase in the 1990s. This dramatic rise in poverty ... occurred while the majority of the British population became richer.

D. Gordon et al., *Poverty and Social Exclusion in Britain,* Joseph Rowntree Foundation, York, 2000, pp. 23–6, 35–9, 52.

3

Health care

Since its establishment in 1948, the National Health Service has been so closely identified with the welfare state that the two terms have often been considered synonymous. There are two principal reasons for its popularity. First, it removed from ordinary people one of their greatest historic fears: that they or a member of their family would suffer ill-health, or die, because they simply could not afford proper medical care. Secondly, by guaranteeing to everyone in times of need *free* and equal access to *optimum* care, it represented the idealism of the welfare state – far more so, for example, than social security where only *minimum* benefits were provided in return for insurance contributions.

Despite its popularity, however, the NHS has always been dogged by controversy. There is the fundamental question of power. Who should ultimately decide how the NHS is run and how the health budget spent? Should it be government (responsible to the taxpayer for the expenditure of public money) or doctors (with their professional expertise and insistence on the clinical freedom to treat patients as they think best)? This question has led to frequent confrontations, as in 1948 when 90 per cent of doctors voted not to join the NHS only three months before its inauguration and in 1965 when general practitioners (GPs) almost resigned *en masse*. This struggle has been intensified by a battle over scarce resources. The guarantee of 'optimum' health care is in fact a chimera because medical advance and rising public expectations mean that more money can always be spent than can be allocated to health care (3.2.3). How, therefore, are priorities to be established? This dilemma was again present from the start of the NHS and led to a bitter conflict within the Attlee government which ultimately resulted in the resignation in 1951 of the founder of the NHS, Aneurin Bevan (3.4.1).

The power battle is further reflected over how to structure what is, in effect, one of the largest organisations in Europe. The various solutions that have been attempted illustrate the different phases through which the welfare state has evolved (3.3). Initially there was a tripartite division: 14 regional boards oversaw 380 hospital management committees which ran individual hospitals, or groups of hospitals; executive committees were responsible for the delivery of primary care by GPs, dentists, opticians and pharmacists; and local government remained responsible for public health issues (such as pollution) as well as a range of miscellaneous medical services (such as maternity and child welfare clinics, health visitors, health education, vaccination and immunisation). Central government determined the size of overall budget but its allocation and administration was in effect made by appointees on the regional boards and executive committees, who were mainly doctors.

In the 1960s there was a determined attempt to make this structure work and, in particular, an attempt to modernise the hospital system through a ten-year Hospital Plan introduced by Enoch Powell, as minister of health, in 1962. The tripartite division of services, however, was deemed to impede their effective delivery and a new unified structure was introduced by Keith Joseph, as the responsible Conservative minister, in 1974 (3.3.1). This concentrated all medical care within the NHS while local government was given prime responsibility for social work, with its closely related role of caring for the social needs of people within their own homes. The expansionary phase of the NHS concluded in 1976 with the attempt, under the Resources Allocation Working Party, to correct the regional imbalance of facilities inherited from the interwar period.

Since the mid-1970s, the NHS has been at the heart of attempts to reform or dismantle the welfare state. As a monopoly, its economic efficiency came under close scrutiny. The militancy of its staff (with junior doctors and consultants threatening to strike in the mid-1970s, whilst nurses and ancillary workers actually did so) also raised questions about how far, as 'producers' of welfare, they were running the system in their own interests and not those of the patient. Both these concerns led to proposals for the privatisation of the NHS (3.4.3). They were rejected, but in 1983 a new managerial ethos was introduced from the private sector and, when this failed, 'internal' markets were introduced in 1990 in the shape of 'fund-holding' GPs and hospital trusts (3.3.2–4). To maximise patient care, GPs were to use their allocated budgets to strike the best deal between competing hospitals;

and to safeguard further the 'consumer' interest, patient's charters, health targets and even hospital league tables were introduced. These changes all represented a major centralisation of power, which was taken to its logical conclusion by New Labour in three initiatives: the National Institute of Clinical Excellence (to determine clinical guidelines for all medical conditions); National Service Frameworks (to specify the path which all treatments must follow); and a Commission for Health Improvement (to inspect each hospital every three years). Whether these reforms represent a final 'defeat' of the medical profession by government will be determined by the success of the profession in 'capturing' these bodies and thereby influencing their decisions.

Any analysis of the NHS must ultimately be concerned not with its structure but its impact on health (3.5). This raises two major issues. First, the NHS – like all western medical systems – has been dominated by the hospital sector to the extent that it has been frequently referred to as a national hospital rather than a national *health* service. This illustrates the failure of the initial intention to concentrate on the prevention as much as the cure of disease (3.1). Secondly, the NHS is but one influence on health outcomes. Others include related government policies (such as housing, to minimise overcrowding and associated diseases such as tuberculosis, and adequate benefit payments, to ensure adequate diets) and individual behaviour (such as the minimisation of risk through exercise and abstinence from smoking). Statistics for health outcomes must provide the ultimate test of the relative success of the NHS, but these other factors must never be ignored.

To cover these issues this chapter is divided into five sections: the vision, allocating scarce resources, restructuring the NHS, controversies, and health outcomes.

3.1 THE VISION

3.1.1 Wartime plans

In 1944 Churchill's Coalition government published a white paper which underlined the comprehensiveness of the proposed new service, its particular value to previously disadvantaged groups such as women and children, and the need for preventive medicine to secure 'maximum' health. It evaded many of the future 'power' issues, but stressed historic continuities to appease vested interests. See Harold Smith's volume in this series (*Britain in the Second World War: A Social History*, 1996, Ch. 10) for documents on the controversy caused by the white paper.

Scope of a National Health Service
What the new service must offer
The new service is designed to provide, for everyone who wishes to use it, a full range of health care. No-one will be compelled to use it. Those who prefer to make their own arrangements for medical attention must be free to do so. But to all who use the service it must offer, as and when required, the care of a family doctor, the skill of a consultant, laboratory services, treatment in hospital, the advice and treatment available in specialised clinics (maternity and child welfare centres, tuberculosis dispensaries and the like), dental and ophthalmic treatment, drugs and surgical appliances, midwifery, home nursing and all other services essential to health. Moreover, all these branches of medical care must be so planned and related to one another that everyone who uses the new service is assured of ready access to whichever of its branches he or she needs.

The new health service in all its branches will be free to all. Apart from possible charges where certain appliances are provided....

Deficiencies in the existing services
A great deal of what is required is already provided.... The problem of creating a National Health Service is not that of destroying services that are obsolete and bad and starting afresh but of building on foundations laid by much hard work over many years and making better what is already good.

Yet there are many gaps in the existing services and much expansion and reorganisation are necessary to weld them into a comprehensive National Service. Despite the progress made it is far from true that everyone can get all the kinds of medical service which he requires. Nor is the care of health wholly divorced from ability to pay for it. To take one very important example, the first requirement is a personal or family doctor, available for consultation on all problems. The National Health Insurance scheme makes this provision for a large number of people but not for wives or children and dependents – and it does not normally afford the consultant and specialist services which the general practitioner needs behind him. For extreme need the Poor Law still exists. For ... something like half the population, the first-line service of a personal, medical adviser depends on private arrangements.

So, too, in the hospital services ... it is not yet true that everyone can be sure of the right hospital and specialist facilities which he needs, when he needs them.

Again many existing services are provided ... by local authorities. But these services have grown up piecemeal to meet different needs at different times, and so they are usually conducted as separate and independent services. There is no sufficient link either between these services themselves or between them and general medical practice and the hospitals.

Need for a new attitude

Perhaps the most important point of all is the need for a new attitude towards health care. Personal health still tends to be regarded as something to be treated when at fault, or perhaps preserved from getting at fault, but seldom as something to be positively improved and promoted.... While the health standards of the people have enormously improved, and while there are gratifying reductions in the ravages of preventable disease, the plain fact remains that there are many men, women and children who could be enjoying a sense of health and physical efficiency which they do not in fact enjoy; there is much subnormal health still, which need not be, with a corresponding cost in efficiency and personal happiness.

Ministry of Health and Department of Health for Scotland, *A National Health Service: The White Paper Proposals in Brief*, London, 1944, pp. 3–5.

3.2 ALLOCATING SCARCE RESOURCES

3.2.1 Bevan on finance

The NHS almost uniquely was financed by taxation, thereby avoiding the inequities inherent in health systems based on private insurance (as in the USA) and social insurance (as in most European countries). The decision led to charges of extravagance and the early imposition of small revenue-raising charges, which led to Bevan's resignation in 1951 (see 3.4.1). Here, during the tenth anniversary celebrations of the NHS, Bevan justifies his exceptional decision.

Two main conceptions underlay the National Health Service. The first was to provide a comprehensive, free, health service for all the people of the country at a time of need. The second ... was the redistribution of national income by a special method of financing the Health Service....

I rejected the insurance principle as being wholly inapplicable in a scheme of this kind. We really cannot perform a second-class operation on a patient if he is not quite paid up....

Next, and equally important, was the fact that we had found group insurance to be highly undesirable, whether in respect of occupation or in respect of vertical groupings of the community.... Hon. Members with experience of industrial areas will know that additional medical benefits which were available to the better-off members of the working class were denied to those who needed them most.

Miners, steel workers, textile workers were unable to obtain additional benefits from the National Health Insurance whereas the better-off members of the 20 million insured were able to get them because the incidence of sickness and unemployment was less among those than amongst the others. So we found group insurance, occupational insurance, to be highly undesirable. Occupational insurance is particularly undesirable, because medical benefits for the workers engaged would follow the fortunes of their industry and the funds available would expand and contract with the sales or lack of sales of their products.

For all these reasons ... we rejected the principle of insurance and decided that the best way to finance the scheme, the fairest and most equitable way, would be to obtain the finance from the Exchequer funds by general taxation, and those who had the most would pay the most. It is a very good principle. What more pleasure can a millionaire have than to know that his taxes will help the sick?... The redistributive aspect of the scheme was one which attracted me almost as much as the therapeutical.

Parliamentary Debates, vol. 592, 30 July 1958, cols 1383, 1388–9.

3.2.2 The Guillebaud 'economy' report, 1956

On returning to office in 1951, the Conservatives were committed to root out extravagance, but the chancellor and minister of health (Butler and Macleod) were sympathetic to the NHS and employed a like-minded economist, Claude Guillebaud, supported by two left-wing assistants, Titmuss and Abel-Smith, to chair the investigating committee. Its report, whilst questioning some of the NHS's underlying assumptions such as 'adequacy', duly exonerated it and cleared the way for its fuller development in the 1960s.

Our final comment

720. We were asked ... 'to advise how, in view of the burden on the Exchequer, a rising charge upon it can be avoided, while providing for the maintenance of an adequate service'.

We concluded that in practice there is no objective and attainable standard of 'adequacy' in the health field, and that the Government must decide each year what amount of national resources may be allocated to the National Health Service, having regard to the competing claims of other social services and national commitments. Once the resources have been allocated, the aim must be to provide the best service within the limits of the allocation.

We also concluded ... that no major change is needed in the general administrative structure of the National Health Service to secure a more efficient and economical organisation.

721. ... We have found no opportunity for making recommendations which would either produce new sources of income or reduce in a substantial degree the annual cost of the Service. In some instances – and particularly with regard to the level of hospital capital expenditure – we have found it necessary, in the interests of the future efficiency of the Service, to make recommendations which will tend to increase the extra cost....

723. It certainly should not be concluded that we have found the present organisation and administration of the National Health Service to be free from defects. In particular there is much need to integrate more closely the hospital, family practitioner and local health services, and also the welfare services provided by the local authorities under the National Assistance Act. We also believe that the hospital service has been somewhat slow to adopt certain methods and techniques of management which have proved their worth in other large-scale undertakings....

724. These weaknesses apart, and allowing for the manifold shortcomings and imperfections inherent in the working of any human

institution, we have reached the general conclusion that the service's record of performance since the Appointed Day has been one of very real achievement.... The rising cost of the service in real terms during the years 1948–1954 was less than many people imagined; and moreover many of the services provided were substantially expanded during the period.... We would mention in particular the up-grading of many hospitals, the expansion of hospital in-patient and out-patient treatment, the increase in the number and the better distribution of consultants, the development of the health visiting, home help and ambulance services, and the improved care of the aged.

725. The administrative organisation of the hospital service ... may be a novel one; but the experience of the last seven years does not suggest that the organisation has failed to cope with its heavy responsibilities or to control, with greater regard for economy than is commonly credited, the large sums of Exchequer money which have been devoted annually to the Health Service.... Any charge that there is widespread extravagance in the National Health Service, whether in respect of spending money or the use of manpower, is not borne out by our evidence.

Report of the Committee of Enquiry into the Cost of the National Health Service, The Guillebaud Report, Cmd 9663, 1956, pp. 239–40.

3.2.3 Enoch Powell on the fundamental dilemma

Powell, as an economic liberal who had resigned from the government in 1958 over excessive public expenditure, was an interesting choice as Conservative minister of health between 1960 and 1963. He favoured private medicine in principle but in practice recognised that the NHS could not be privatised and so was determined to ensure its efficiency through adequate capital investment. Here he summarises the problem faced by all governments in seeking to balance supply and demand in the absence of a price mechanism, with an interesting allusion to future education reform.

Medical care under the National Health Service is rendered free to the consumer at the point of consumption.... Consequently supply and demand are not kept in balance by price. Since, therefore, resources are limited, both theoretically and in practice at any given time, while demand is unlimited, supply had to be rationed by means other than price....

Common thought and parlance tend to conceal or deny the fact that demand for all practical purposes *is* unlimited. The vulgar assumption is that there is a definable amount of medical care 'needed', and that if that 'need' was met, no more would be demanded. This is absurd. Every advance in medical science creates new needs that did not exist until the means of meeting them came into existence, or at least into the realm of the possible....

The infinity of demand

There is a characteristic of medical care that makes its public provision exceptionally problematic. The demand for it is not only potentially unlimited; it is also by nature not capable of being limited in a precise and intelligible way. This can be made clear by comparison with, for instance, education. The potential demand for education is unlimited, just like the demand for medical care. Nevertheless it is possible to define a specific quantity and quality of education to be provided by laying down, for instance, the ages between which children are to attend school, the subjects they are to be taught, the size of classes, and the qualifications of the teachers....

No similar criteria are available in relation to medical care. On the contrary, the need for any criteria at all is strenuously repudiated in the popular mythology of the National Health Service.... In order to produce some sort of objective limitation it would be necessary to confine the supply of medical care to those suffering from certain conditions, such as epidemic diseases (as was done at the outset of public medicine), or to certain categories of patient, such as children (as is done with the free supply of certain spectacles and dental appliances).

The National Health Service, then, must and does apply covert rationing devices in order to limit demand to the actual amount of supply.

Controlling the supply

That supply is, in theory, determined by the government.... The reality is substantially otherwise and much more complex. It differs in the two halves of the service, hospital and non-hospital.

In the hospital service the Minister, on behalf of the state, does in form decide from year to year, or more often, how much money each hospital board shall be permitted to spend. In practice, as the political odium of being seen to reduce expenditure could not be faced, the decision is how much increase, if any, to make on each board's present rate of expenditure....

In contrast, the Minister has no direct control over expenditure outside the hospitals. Over most of the country the local health executive councils stand ready to enter into contract with general medical practitioners, and to pay ... for all the treatment that dentists and opticians supply. No upper limit is imposed by the Minister. Likewise he pays automatically (through the executive councils) for whatever medicines, short of gross and demonstrable abuse, that are prescribed by the medical practitioners for their patients. In this half of the service, therefore, there is properly speaking no budget, but only an estimate of what will get itself spent. The commitment is, in Treasury jargon, 'open-ended'....

E. Powell, *Medicine and Politics: 1975 and After*, London, 1976, pp. 26–30.

3.3 RESTRUCTURING THE NHS

3.3.1 The 1974 reorganisation

The Conservative government sought in 1974 to correct all the perceived weakness in Bevan's administrative structure by removing the tripartite division of services; resolving the tension between the centre and locality; achieving 'joined up' government by linking the NHS to other relevant services such as social work; and re-prioritising prevention. The reorganisation was based on a 1972 white paper and the resulting 1973 National Health Service Act. It represented a peak in political commitment to the NHS in its 'classic' form but resulted in an administrative structure of such Byzantine complexity that it had to be reformed itself within ten years.

The reorganised service: the main features
I. Unification
1. The National Health Service should be a single service. Its separate parts are intended to complement one another, and not to function as self-sufficient entities. In practice, however, the administration we now have throws barriers in the efforts to organise a proper balance

of services – hospital and community – throughout the country. The administrative unification of these services will make a firmer reality of the concept of a single service....

9. ... [P]lans for unification ... offer the prospects of real benefits, not only to the individual and the family, but to the public in general. They provide for a single administering body locally, which will draw its funds from one source, and will take a wide unbiased and constructive view of its priorities across the whole range of needs, served by the general practitioner and other community health services and by the hospitals....

11. These features will enable the authorities, within the general framework of national policy, to provide sensitive, constantly improving service in their areas, giving proper attention to care as well as cure, and a much needed impetus to the prevention of illness and the promotion of health.

IV. NHS authorities and their functions
Regional and area levels of management
28. The Government has decided that effective organisation of the health services in England requires two levels – regional and area – in addition to the central Department. At each of these levels there will be a unified administration covering the whole span of the NHS. The old administrative divisions between community and hospital services will completely disappear. Since each area health authority will serve the same population within the same boundaries as its matching local authority, the purpose will be that formal divisions between the health, the education and the personal social services will be bridged by the arrangements for collaboration....

Regional administrative tier
32. In theory, the regional organisation ... could take the form of regional offices of the central Department. In practice, they would be much less effective than separate regional authorities.

33. To place the whole job on the central Department and its regional offices would result in over-centralisation and delay: it would draw the Department into many matters that should be resolved locally or regionally; and it would distract the Department's attention from the policy tasks which must be done centrally and which are its proper concern.

34. There is also a positive case for separate regional authorities.... Each regional authority will be a body of local people knowledgeable

about their region's needs. They will have close relationships with the University, which has a key part to play in the region's work through its teaching and research activities, and will be able to develop a continuing and constructive dialogue with their areas....

The job to be done: nationally, regionally, locally
37. ... The planning function in the NHS will be exercised at three levels: area, region and central Department. Each has its own distinctive role. The central Department will settle national health policies, objectives and priorities. The regional health authority (RHA) will have a regional planning responsibility which will include settling priorities when there are competing claims between areas. But the fundamental unit in the planning process will be the area. Area health authorities, plans for the communities within the area – the 'districts' – will strongly influence the way in which local, regional and national priorities are carried into effect in the area, and how they are harmonised with local authority plans.

National Health Service Reorganisation: England, Cmnd 5055, 1972, pp. 1–2, 7–8.

3.3.2 The managerial revolution

In 1983 Roy Griffiths, the deputy chairman and managing director of Sainsbury's, was asked to resolve the chaos into which the 1974 reforms had plunged the NHS. His retrospective review is the most vivid account of the managerial revolution which swept through all public services in the 1980s, its reception by welfare professionals, and its particular consequences for the NHS.

[I was asked] in January 1983 ... to head a team of four business men to give advice on the effective use and management of manpower and related resources in the National Health Service. We were asked not to make any recommendations which would require legislation. The background to the setting up of the Inquiry was the tremendous parliamentary questioning on the waste and inefficiency in the Service. We were not at the outset asked to write a report.... Once we became involved, however, the noise level in the NHS reached almost unprecedented heights and Margaret Thatcher ... requested that we should write something.... Since I and the other members were all working full-time for our respective companies we compromised by writing a 23 page letter to the Secretary of State simply saying ... what we would do....

I quote:-

'we believe that a small, strong general management body is necessary at the centre ... to ensure that responsibility is pushed as far down the line as possible, i.e. to the point where action can be taken effectively. At present devolution of responsibility is far too slow because the necessary direction and dynamic to achieve this is currently lacking.

Recommendations for action

The Secretary of State should set up within the DHSS ... a Health Services Supervisory Board and a full-time NHS Management Board.

Units of management

District Chairmen should:-

• plan for all day-to-day decisions to be taken in the main hospitals and other Units of Management. If decisions are to be taken elsewhere than in the Unit, Chairmen should require justification.

• involve the clinicians more closely in the management process, consistent with clinical freedom for clinical practice. Clinicians should participate fully in the decisions about priorities in the use of resources.

Property

The Chairman of the NHS Management Board should ensure that:-

• a property function is developed so as to give a major commercial reorientation to the handling of the NHS estate.

Patients and the community

The Management Board and Chairman should ensure that it is central to the approach of management in planning and delivering services for the population as a whole, to:-

• ascertain how well the service is being delivered at local level by obtaining the experience and perceptions of patients and the community: these can be derived from CHCs [Community Health Councils, set up in 1974] and by other methods, including market research and from the experience of general practice and the community health services.

• promote realistic public and professional perceptions of what the

NHS can and should provide as the best possible service within the resources available.

General observations

The clear similarities between NHS management and business management are much more important. In many organisations in the private sector, profit does not immediately impinge on large numbers of managers below Board level. They are concerned with levels of service, quality of product, meeting budgets, cost improvement, productivity, motivating and rewarding staff, research and development, and the long term viability of the undertaking. All things that Parliament is urging on the NHS.

The NHS does not have a profit motive, but it is of course, enormously concerned with control of expenditure. Surprisingly, however, it still lacks any real continuous evaluation of its performance against criteria such as those set out above. Rarely are precise management objectives set; there is little measurement of health output; clinical evaluation of particular practices is by no means common and economic evaluation of practices extremely rare. Nor can the NHS display a ready assessment of the effectiveness with which it is meeting the needs and expectations of the people it serves.

A general management process would be enormously important in:

(i) providing the necessary leadership to capitalise on the existing high levels of dedication and expertise among NHS staff of all disciplines, and to stimulate initiative, urgency and vitality.

(ii) securing proper motivation of staff. Those charged with general management responsibility would regard it as vital to review incentives, rewards and sanctions.'

How did all this work out?...

The Management Inquiry report was well received by the government, but less well received by the professions. I am given to understatement. The nurses saw it as a challenge to a carefully established career structure. The medical profession saw the report correctly as questioning whether their clinical autonomy extended to immunity from being questioned as to how resources were being used. All the professions saw the report as the introduction of economics into the care of patients, believing that this was inimical to good care. There was a deep-seated feeling that what distinguished the Health Service from the private sector or business or commerce was the very immunity of the Health Service from the supposedly corrupting influence of profit making and that this very immunity itself guaranteed high quality. This denies the fact that the hallmark of the truly great organisations in the private sector is that they have placed quality and customer satisfaction first and profit for a long time simply emerged as a by-product of effective service....

The report was never meant to be confrontational with the professions....

What the report did achieve was something more subtle. It forced the professions themselves to rethink their position....

The report was implemented.... So by the end of 1987, three years after implementation of the report ... authorities had in many cases reorganised to make their services more responsive and to take responsibility for quality assurance....

Just as general management was finding its effective feet the levels of decibels both in the Health Service and on the political front scaled new heights and Margaret Thatcher in early 1988 decided to establish her own Review and in the result to present new challenges for the recently established general management.... It was an astonishing episode in many ways.... It started out by seeking to examine new methods of funding the NHS and after careful consideration moved abruptly from this theme. It then switched to building on the existing management reforms and seeking to inject more competition and choice onto the service. It chose to do this by means which would have made strenuous demands on a well established management, let alone the still fledgling management process.

Sir Roy Griffiths, deputy chairman of the NHS Policy Board, *7 Years of Progress: General Management in the NHS*, London, 1991, pp. 2–5, 11–12, 14.

3.3.3 The 1988 Thatcher review

In her biography, Mrs Thatcher expounded retrospectively on the mix of objectives which underlay the improvised review, referred to by Griffiths. Some were reminiscent of views expressed earlier, above all by Powell, and the final paragraph contains a succinct summary of 'Thatcherism' as it affected welfare policy. This passage minimises the extent of the split in Cabinet over the future of the NHS (see 3.4.3).

I believed that the NHS was a service of which we could genuinely be proud. It delivered a high quality of care – especially when it came to acute illnesses – and at a reasonably modest unit cost, at least compared with some insurance-based systems. Yet there were large and ... unjustifiable differences between performance in one area and another. Consequently I was ... reluctant to envisage *fundamental* changes.... Although I wanted to see a flourishing private sector of health alongside the National Health Service, I always regarded the NHS and its basic principles as a fixed point in our policies....

There was bound to be a potentially limitless demand for health care ... for as long as it was provided free at the point of delivery....

In significant ways, the NHS lacked the right economic signals to respond to these pressures....

If one were to recreate the National Health Service, starting from fundamentals, one would have allowed for a bigger private sector – both at the level of general practitioners (GPs) and in the provision of hospitals: and one would have given much closer consideration to additional sources of finance for health, apart from general taxation....

The objective of reform ... was that we should work towards a new way of allocating money within the NHS, so that hospitals treating more patients received more income. There also needed to be a closer, clearer connection between the demand for health, its cost and the method of paying for it....

The pressure to provide more money for the Health Service was proving all but irresistible.... It seemed that the NHS had become a bottomless financial pit. If more money had to be provided, I was determined that there must at least be strings attached – and the best ways those strings could be woven together was in the form of a full scale NHS review....

I set out four principles which should inform its work. First, there must be a high standard of medical care available to all, regardless of income. Second, the arrangements agreed must be such as to give the users of health services, whether in the private or the public sector, the greatest possible choice. Third, any changes must be made in such a way that they led to genuine improvements in health care, not just higher incomes for those working in the Health Service. Fourth, responsibility, whether for medical decisions or for budgets, should be exercised at the lowest appropriate level closest to the patient....

M. Thatcher, *The Downing Street Years*, London, 1993, pp. 606–9.

3.3.4 The introduction of internal markets

The white paper *Working for Patients*, later given the force of
law by the 1990 National Health Service and Community Care
Act, finally identified the radical structural change that could
apply the 'Thatcherite' revolution to the NHS.

Key changes
1.9 The government is proposing seven key measures ...

First: to make the health service more responsive to the needs of
patients, as much power and responsibility as possible will be
delegated to local level....

Second: to stimulate a better service to the patient, hospitals will be
able to apply for a new self-governing status as NHS Hospital Trusts.
This means that while remaining within the NHS, they will take fuller
responsibility for their own affairs, harnessing the skills and dedication of their staff. NHS Trusts will earn revenue from the services they
provide. They will therefore have an incentive to attract patients, so
they will make sure that the service they offer is what their patients
want. And in turn they will stimulate other NHS hospitals to respond
to what people want locally....

Third: the money required to treat patients will be able to cross
administrative boundaries. All NHS hospitals, whether run by health
authorities or self-governing, will be free to offer their services to
different health authorities and to the private sector....

Fourth: to reduce waiting times and improve the quality of service
... 100 new consultant posts will be created over the next three
years....

Fifth: to help the family doctor improve his service to patients,
large GP practices will be able to apply for their own budgets to
obtain a defined range of services direct from hospitals.... GPs will be
encouraged to compete for patients by offering better services. And it
will be easier for patients to choose (and change) their own GP as they
wish.

Sixth: to improve the effectiveness of NHS management, regional,
district and family practitioner management bodies will be reduced in
size and reformed on business lines, with executive and non-executive
directors. The Government believes ... the era in which a £26 billion
NHS is run by authorities which are neither truly representative nor
fully management bodies must be ended. The confusion of roles will

be replaced by a clear remit and accountability.

Seventh: to ensure that all concerned with delivering services to the patient make the best use of the resources available to them, quality of service and value for money will be more rigorously audited. Arrangements for what doctors call 'medical audit' will be extended throughout the Health Service....

The best use of resources

1.15 If the NHS is to provide the best service it can for its patients, it must make the best use of the resources available to it. The quest for value for money must be an essential element in its work....

Public and private sector working together

1.18 The NHS and the independent health sector should be able to learn from each other, to support each other and to provide services for each other.... People who choose to buy health care outside the Health Service benefit the community by taking pressure off the Service and add to the diversity of provision and choice. The Government expects to see further increases in the number of people wishing to make provision for health care, but at the moment many people who do so during their working life find the cost of higher premiums difficult to meet in retirement. The Government therefore proposes to make it easier for people in retirement by allowing income tax relief on their private medical insurance premiums, whether paid by them or, for example, by their families on their behalf.

Working for Patients, Cm 555, 1989, pp. 4–5, 8–9.

3.3.5 New Labour and the NHS

New Labour quickly published a stinging critique of the Conservative reforms, whilst simultaneously disowning those of the 1970s. It applied its 'third way' philosophy to the NHS in a renewed attempt to marry the virtues of centralisation (common national standards and practices) with those of decentralisation (the encouragement of professional initiative and local responsiveness). However, two instincts which it shared with the Conservatives, suspicion of the professional 'suppliers' of welfare (para. 2.1) and an insistence on securing value for money (para. 2.24), favoured increased central regulation and thus led to the ultimate consolidation of many of the ear-lier reforms.

2. A new start
what counts is what works
Key themes
- the third way
- keeping what works
- discarding what has failed

The third way
2.1 In paving the way for the new NHS the Government is committed to building on what has worked, but discarding what has failed. There will be no return to the old centralised command and control systems of the 1970s. That approach stifled innovation and put the needs of institutions ahead of the needs of patients. But nor will there be a continuation of the divisive internal market system of the 1990s. That approach which was intended to make the NHS more efficient ended up fragmenting decision-making and distorting incentives to such an extent that unfairness and bureaucracy became its defining features.

2.2. Instead there will be a 'third way' of running the NHS – a system based on partnership and driven by performance....

Six key principles
2.4
- first, to renew the NHS as a genuinely *national* service. Patients will get fair access to consistently high quality, prompt and accessible services right across the country
- but second, to make the delivery of healthcare against these new national standards a matter of *local* responsibility. Local doctors and nurses who are in the best position to know what patients need will be in the driving seat in shaping services.
- third, to get the NHS to work in *partnership*. By breaking down organisational barriers and forging stronger links with Local Authorities, the needs of the patient will be put at the centre of the care process
- but fourth, to drive *efficiency* through a more rigorous approach to performance and by cutting bureaucracy, so that every pound in the NHS is spent to maximise the care for patients
- fifth, to shift the focus onto quality of care so that *excellence* is

guaranteed to all patients, and quality becomes the driving force for decision-making at every level of the service

• and sixth, to rebuild *public confidence* in the NHS as a public service, accountable to patients, open to the public and shaped by their views....

Keeping what works

2.6 The Government will retain the separation between the planning of hospital care and its provision....

2.7 The Government will also build on the increasingly important role of primary care in the NHS.... Family doctors who have been involved in commissioning services ... have welcomed the chance to influence the use of resources to improve patient care. The Government wishes to build on these approaches, ensuring that all patients, rather than just some, are able to benefit....

2.8 Finally, the Government recognises the intrinsic strength of *decentralising responsibility for operational management.* By giving NHS Trusts control over key decisions they can improve local services for patients.

Discarding what has failed

2.9 The internal market was a misconceived attempt to tackle the pressures facing the NHS. It has been an obstacle to the necessary modernisation of the health service. It created more problems than it solved. That is why the Government is abolishing it.

Ending fragmentation

2.10 The internal market split responsibility for planning, funding and delivering healthcare between 100 Health Authorities, around 3,500 GP fundholders (representing half of GP practices) and over 400 NHS Trusts. There was little strategic coordination. A fragmented NHS has been poorly placed to tackle the crucial issue of better integration across health and social care. People with multiple needs have found themselves passed from pillar to post inside a system in which individual organisations were forced to work to their own agendas rather than the needs of individual patients.

2.11 To overcome this fragmentation, in the new NHS all those charged with planning and providing health and social care services for patients will work to a jointly agreed local Health Improvement Programme. This will govern the actions of all parts of the local NHS to ensure consistency and coordination....

Ending unfairness

2.12 The internal market created competition for patients. In the process it created unfairness for patients. Some family doctors were able to get a better deal for their patients, for financial rather than clinical reasons. Staff morale has been eroded by an emphasis on competitive values, at odds with the ethos of fairness that is intrinsic to the NHS and its professions. Hospital clinicians have felt disempowered as they have deliberately been pitted against each other and against primary care. The family doctor community has been divided in two, almost equally split between GP fundholders and non-fundholders....

Ending inefficiency

2.16 ... [T]he internal market ... distorted priorities and – to the universal frustration of NHS staff – institutionalised perverse incentives which got in the way of providing efficient, effective, high quality services....

Ending instability

2.20 The internal market forced NHS Trusts to compete for contracts that at best lasted a year and at worst were agreed on a day-to-day basis. Such short-term instability placed a constant focus on shoring up the status quo rather than creating the space to plan and implement major improvement.

2.21 ... The new NHS will work on the basis of longer-term ... funding agreements that will allow clinicians and managers to focus on ways of improving care....

Ending secrecy

2.23 In the new NHS, all NHS Trusts will be required to open up their board meetings to the public....

2.24 These developments will place the traditional values of the NHS into a modern setting. They will be backed by the Government's commitment to extra investment in the NHS, year on year. But that extra money has to produce major gains in quality and efficiency.

The New NHS modern . dependable, Cm 3807, 1997, http://www.official-documents.co.uk/doh/newnhs/newnhs.htm, pp. 1–5.

3.4 CONTROVERSIES

3.4.1 Bevan's resignation

The first major political crisis provoked by the welfare state was over the introduction of charges into the 'free' NHS, which led to the resignation of Aneurin Bevan from the Cabinet in 1951 and a split in the Labour Party over the next decade. The allocation of scarce resources was at the root of the crisis. How should government allocate its limited resources between welfare and other policies (such as defence), and within the welfare budget, how much should be allocated to the NHS? The outbreak of the Korean War, and the consequent rise in defence expenditure, brought the issue to a head; but the NHS had also been overspending its budget since 1948 (by almost 100 per cent in 1948/49) and thus reduced the money available to other welfare services. This had led to considerable resentment and explains the willingness – as illustrated in this cabinet minute – of Bevan's successor as minister of health, Marquand, as well as a majority of cabinet ministers, to accept the need for charges. Charges, it was thought, would help to resolve the problem by raising extra income whilst reducing demand and thereby expenditure. Bevan was right to argue health expenditure was not out of control (see 3.2.2) and that more money had been allocated to defence than could be spent within a year. He was less justified in ignoring the need to agree clearer priorities within public, welfare and health expenditure.

One of the assumptions on which the Chancellor had constructed his Budget was that, in pursuance of the Cabinet's decision of 22nd March, expenditure on the National Health Service would be subject for the time being to an upper limit of £400 million. Before that decision was taken expenditure on the Health Service in the financial year 1951–52 had been estimated at £423 million; and, in order to keep it within the upper limit approved by the Cabinet, the Health Ministers had agreed to effect economies in hospital administration totalling £10 million and to introduce charges for dentures and spectacles which, in the coming year, would produce £13 million....

The Minister of Labour [Bevan] said that he had always been opposed to the introduction of charges for dentures and spectacles. In his view it would be undesirable in principle and politically dangerous, for the Labour Party thus to abandon the conception of a free Health Service. Now that he was aware of the details of the budgetary position he was able to add a further argument that this step was not financially necessary. In a Budget of over £4,000 million it should not be difficult to find so small a sum as £13 million in some way or another which would not breach the principle of a free Health Service. He was specially disturbed at the prospect that this inroad on the Health Service would be justified by the argument that the money to be saved was needed for the increased defence programme.... The Minister reminded the Cabinet that such charges could not be imposed without fresh legislation. Believing, as he did, that such charges would involve a serious breach of socialist principles, and having on numerous occasions proclaimed in public speeches his opposition to such a course, he did not see how he could be expected to vote in favour of such a Bill. If the Cabinet reaffirmed their decision that these charges should be imposed, he would be obliged to resign from the Government. A long discussion ensued.... The preponderant view in the Cabinet was that the Government, if they remained united on this issue, would have no substantial difficulty in persuading the Parliamentary Labour Party to support legislation authorizing charges.

Conclusions of a Meeting of the Cabinet, 9 April 1951, Public Record Office, CAB 128/19, p. 204.

3.4.2 Pay beds

The other major issue Bevan had had to face in setting up the NHS was that of professional power; and he had felt it necessary, to win hospital consultants' support, to permit them to continue treating private patients in either private hospitals or NHS ones ('pay beds'). To consultants this was a vital symbol of their independence. To others, including Bevan, it was a regrettable breach of the ideal of a free and equal service. Paying patients enjoyed faster treatment and better care, frequently subsidised surreptitiously from NHS resources. Barbara Castle, the secretary of state for health and social security between 1974 and 1976, had been one of Bevan's followers in the 1950s and was determined to capitalise on the radicalism of the time to fulfil Bevan's (Nye's) dream. In June

1974 members of the National Union of Public Employees (NUPE, a militant new organisation which had recruited many lower-paid hospital workers) refused to service private wards in the new Charing Cross Hospital and this provided the opportunity to publish plans to phase out the 4,500 pay beds and strictly license private hospitals. The resulting furore, which even led to consultants 'working to rule', illustrates the depth of mutual hostility within the NHS and the difficulty of implementing welfare reform through vested professional interests.

13 November 1975

The deputation from the BMA [British Medical Association] was led by Walpole Lewin and Rodney Smith. The only basis on which they had agreed to come was that there should be no 'preconditions' and, in welcoming them, I repeated this and invited them to give me their uninhibited view on the consultative document. A united hostile chorus then assailed me. Lewin declared that the phasing out of pay beds was not in the interests of the NHS and was a breach of the understanding the profession had had with successive governments. The licensing proposals threatened their independence. In certain areas it would be impossible to put in private specialised equipment. Private practice kept consultants working in ordinary District General Hospitals. 'We still hope you will reappraise your document,' he concluded. Sir Rodney, in that unctuous way of his, said that the Royal Colleges 'should not take part in detailed negotiations'. They were only concerned with standards of patient care, which they believed would suffer if pay beds went. Bolt, another surgeon, put his case more reasonably than most of them. He was concerned with the nitty gritty of the consultants' interests. If pay beds went, many consultants would not be able to do any private practice at all and would simply emigrate. All this was echoed by Simmons of the HCSA [Hospital Consultants and Specialists Association], Allen of the dentists, Gilmore of the juniors and Damerell of the Independent Hospitals Group. It was unanimous and I realised what a united front I was up against.

In reply, I nailed the canard that phasing out was in breach of the understanding on which they agreed to co-operate with Nye's NHS. I reminded them gently that the profession had continued to oppose Nye long after this concession had been made by him and that they had only been won over to accepting Nye's plans (and then only

105

grudgingly) by his legislative undertaking that doctors would be able to combine private practice with work for the NHS. That I was prepared to reaffirm in my Bill. I also told them that my proposals on licensing had been intended to safeguard the right to private practice by ensuring that private facilities would have an even geographical spread. They were merely put forward as a basis for discussion. If they preferred it, I would be prepared to consider a free-for-all, with total separation of all private facilities from the NHS and no licensing of the private sector. Stevenson [the Secretary of the BMA] bridled at this and said they were not prepared to discuss licensing at all, because they were opposed to the whole principle of phasing out. Was I in effect saying this was not negotiable? In fact, of course I was, but I merely said that I could not anticipate the Queen's speech. I would report to my colleagues what they had said.... An epoch of total non-cooperation lies ahead.

B. Castle, *Castle Diaries,* London, 1980, pp. 549–50.

3.4.3 Privatisation and the 1988 review

Nigel Lawson was chancellor of the exchequer from 1983 to 1989 and a leading advocate of privatisation. He was heavily involved in health care reforms under Mrs Thatcher and was a member of the 1988 review which introduced 'internal markets' (3.3.3–4). In his autobiography, he reviewed the familiar dilemmas faced by the NHS and identified the reasons why the 1988 review (contrary to received opinion) agreed privatisation was inappropriate for the NHS. There was less agreement, however, over the extent to which public expenditure should be used to subsidise private medicine as a competitor to, and thus a spur to efficiency in, the NHS – with Mrs Thatcher in the seemingly unfamiliar role of seeking greater expenditure. This extract provides an effective contrast between Conservative and Labour views on charges and private health care. Lawson's assurance over the success of 'internal market' reform should be compared to New Labour's actual reaction in the 1997 election (3.3.5) – and its later actions.

Health care: an intractable problem
There are in practice only two ways in which health care can be

106

financed. One is by the taxpayer, and the other through the individual taking out an insurance policy. The latter method, which is the basis of the US system, inevitably results in a massive further escalation in the cost of health care....

The UK system of taxpayer finance avoids these problems. But it cannot escape the fact that, when finite resources ... are faced with infinite demand, there will always be frustrated demand....

As if this were not sensitive enough, the political problem in the UK was compounded by two other factors. The first was the sheer size of the Health Service. It was the third biggest employer and bureaucracy in the world.... The second factor was even more delicate. The National Health Service is the closest thing the English have to a religion, with those who practice in it regarding themselves as a priesthood. This made it extraordinarily difficult to reform.... Faced with a dispute between their priests and Ministers, the public would have no hesitation in taking the part of the priesthood....

The Health Service Review
On 28 January 1988, Margaret set up a small ministerial group under her chairmanship....

My own idea had been that the review should be confined entirely to the hospital service. It was here that all the obvious problems were, from waiting times for operations to babies dying. Moreover the general practitioners came face to face with the public all the time, and the political cost of alienating them could be very high.... Margaret, however, having initially been too nervous to do anything at all ... characteristically decided to go the whole hog, and reform everything at once....

The Labour party subsequently alleged that what we were proposing amounted to the privatisation of the Health Service; and even those who do not subscribe to this foolish charge often suspect that that was what we wished to do. As both arch-promoter of privatisation and one of the only three members of the review group from its inception to its conclusion, I can state quite categorically that there is not a word of truth in it. Some, I realise, will say 'So much the worse' – to which I would have to reply that the provision of medical care is *sui generis*, and should not be assimilated to other activities where full-blooded privatisation is entirely appropriate. In this particular area the ground on which to stand firm is support for the parallel availability of private medical treatment, against those who inveigh against a so-called 'two-tier' system and imply that the provision of private health care should be a criminal offence. This would not only be an intolerable restriction of individual freedom but almost certainly contrary to both the UN [United Nations] Declaration of Human Rights and its European counterpart, and thus itself illegal.

Of course, the maintenance of a largely tax-financed Health Service in no way rules out the use of specific charges for particular items and facilities. Indeed, it is highly desirable that people should be reminded that nothing is free: it is simply a matter of how it is paid for. During the course of the review discussions I argued for a considerable extension of charging, pointing out how absurd it was that the proportion of total NHS spending financed by charges was lower in the 1980s than it had been in the 1950s, despite the huge increase in real incomes in the meantime. Margaret was not prepared to touch it, fearing the political unpopularity.

A private diversion
In the early months ... I came under heavy pressure from Margaret ... to introduce tax relief for private health care....

In the end the pressure was such that, mistakenly, I offered Margaret a compromise. There would be no change in the tax treatment of the benefit of company health insurance schemes. Nor would there be a general tax relief for contributions to private health insurance schemes; but what I was prepared to offer ... was tax relief for contributions to private health insurance schemes by or on behalf of the over sixties.... Margaret clearly snapped up my compromise.

How the reforms emerged
There was much criticism when the White Paper was published that the government was being characteristically doctrinaire and arrogant in imposing its reforms.... I found this very puzzling. No hospital was obliged to become an NHS Trust Hospital.... Similarly, no doctors were obliged to become fund-holders....

The mistake ... was to use the phrase 'trust hospitals'. Margaret always had a weakness for the word 'trust', which certainly went down well in financial circles. But in the NHS context it encouraged absurd talk of such hospitals opting out of the Health Service....

Teething troubles are inevitable, but the balance of judgement so far is that [the reforms] have made a substantial improvement.

The old argument that nothing whatever needed to be done except inject more taxpayers' money is no longer heard.... The opposition from the BMA, once so strident and vituperative, is now little more than a whimper. Perhaps most striking has been the experience of GP fundholders, who are convinced that they are performing a far better service for their patients.... I very much doubt if, at the next election, the Labour Party will again be foolish enough to pledge itself to undo all the Thatcher Government's health reforms.

Nigel Lawson, *The View From No. 11: Memoirs of a Tory Radical,* London, 1992, pp. 612–19.

3.5 HEALTH OUTCOMES

3.5.1 The 1980 Black Report

The Labour government between 1974 and 1979 committed itself to reducing inequality both within and outside the NHS. The chief scientist at the Department of Health and Social Security, Sir Douglas Black, was commissioned in 1977 to investigate health inequality, and his report's identification of its socio-economic causes, outside the formal health care system, transformed international analysis – much to the embarrassment of governments seeking to reduce public expenditure in a depression. The Thatcher government, to which the report was submitted, was one such government and it sought to suppress the report. The Major government's adoption of health targets in 1991 was, however, belated recognition of the report's call for more wide-ranging preventive measures. In this extract Black, with his fellow authors Jerry Morris, Cyril Smith and Peter Townsend, retrospectively summarises the report's findings and reception.

In 1977 a Working Group was set up to review evidence about differences in health status among social classes, identify possible causes of those differences and draw implications for policy as well as for further research. At that stage the health of the British population was not improving on some indicators quite as fast as that of a number of other industrial societies. Despite strong support for the National Health Service, and especially for the principle of equal access to health care irrespective of income ... inequalities in health between classes remained disturbingly high.

Early in 1980 the Working Group submitted its report to the incoming Secretary of State of a new Government, Patrick Jenkin. He published it later that year under a short preface which described the cost of meeting the recommendations in the report as 'quite unrealistic in present or foreseeable economic circumstances, quite apart from any judgement that may be formed of the effectiveness of such expenditure in dealing with the problems identified'. Copies of the report were scarce, because few were printed by the DHSS. Nonetheless the report attracted, and continues to attract, interest.

There seem to be at least two reasons for this interest. One is that an obligation to review patterns of health in a population encourages the objectives and priorities of health care policies to be specified in greater detail and perhaps more plausibly; for example, the standards achieved by some social groups can be properly regarded as attainable by others. A second reason for the interest in the type of review embodied in the Black report is that an obligation to provide a scientific explanation for inequalities in health is bound to lead to a better definition of responsibilities for a nation's health – especially the balance of responsibilities as between health care services and other social institutions – like housing, education, industry, agriculture and environmental health. Social and not just individual health has to be defined, measured and explained....

Despite the provisional or general nature of the evidence the Working Group found that material deprivation played a major role in explaining the very unfavourable health record of the poorer sections of the population (especially of the partly skilled and unskilled manual groups making up more than a quarter of the entire population), with biological, cultural and personal lifestyle factors playing a contributory role. This conclusion carried a powerful implication for the construction of policy. The elimination or reduction of material deprivation and not just the organisation of more efficient health care services had to become a national objective for action. Policies external to the National Health Service were therefore of crucial importance if inequalities were to be reduced.... The report also called attention to the fact that insufficient attention was being paid to the need to promote healthier life-styles more equally among the population. There were financial, educational and other restrictions on the opportunities of some groups to achieve better life-styles. This tended to sharpen health inequalities in Britain....

M. Whitehead, *The Health Divide: Inequalities in Health in the 1980s*, London, 1987, pp. i–iii.

3.5.2 Health inequalities

The key statistical findings of the Black Report are summarised in this extract. Some critics have questioned the causal relationship between, for example, ill-health and class. Does poverty lead to poor health or poor health to poverty?

The pattern of present health inequalities
On the basis of figures drawn from the early 1970s ... men and women in occupational class V had a two-and-a-half times greater chance of dying before reaching retirement age than their professional counterparts in occupational class I....

Table 1: *Death rates by sex and social (occupational) class (15–64 years) (rates per 1,000 population, England and Wales, 1971)*

Social (occupational) class	Males	Females*	Ratio M/F
I (Professional)	3.98	2.15	1.85
II (Intermediate)	5.54	2.85	1.94
III (Skilled non-manual)	5.80	2.76	1.96
IIIM (Skilled manual)	6.08	3.41	1.78
IV (Partly skilled)	7.96	4.27	1.87
V (Unskilled)	9.88	5.31	1.86
Ratio V/I	2.5	2.5	

* In this table women with husbands have been classified by their husband's occupation, women of other marital statuses are attributed to their *own* occupational class.

Race, ethnicity and health
Another important dimension of inequality in contemporary Britain is race. Immigrants to this country from the so-called New Commonwealth ... are known to experience greater difficulty in finding work and adequate housing.... Given these disabilities it is to be expected that they might also record rather higher than average rates of mortality and morbidity....

[But] The age standardised mortality ratios of immigrant males compares favourably with their British-born equivalents in occupational classes IV and V.... This rather favourable comparison ... may

... reflect the underlying tendency for migrants to select themselves on the grounds of health and fitness. Men and women prepared to cross oceans and continents in order to seek new occupational opportunities or a new way of life do not represent a random cross-section of humanity. A better comparison for exploring health inequality would ideally involve second- or third-generation immigrants, but these are the very groups that are difficult to trace for statistical purposes....

Table 3: *Mortality by country of birth and occupational class (SMR) (males 15–64)*

Country of Birth	I	II	III	IIIM	IV	V	All
India and Pakistan	122	127	114	105	93	73	98
West Indies	267	163	135	87	71	75	84
Europe (including UK and Eire)	121	109	98	83	81	82	89
UK and Eire (including England and Wales)	118	112	111	118	115	110	114
England and Wales	98	99	99	99	99	100	100
All birth places	100	100	100	100	100	100	100

Source: *Occupational Mortality, 1970–72*, pp. 186–7.

Housing tenure and mortality
... When the population is divided into housing tenure groups ... class gradients vary considerably.

Table 4: *Mortality by tenure and class (SMR) (males 15–64)*

Class	Tenure		
	Owner-occupied	Privately rented	Local-authority tenancy
I	79	93	99
II	74	104	99
IIIN	79	112	121
IIIM	83	99	104
IV	83	100	106
V	98	126	123

Source: Unpublished data, Medical Statistics Division, OPCS, preliminary results of the LS 1970–75.

P. Townsend and N. Davidson (eds), *Inequalities in Health: The Black Report*, Harmondsworth, 1990, pp. 43, 49, 50–2.

4

Education

The Appointed Day in 1948 brought together legislation covering four of the five core welfare services. The exception was education. This did not mean, however, that education was relatively unimportant. On the contrary, its importance was such that it had already been the subject of the one major piece of reconstruction legislation during the war: the 1944 'Butler' Education Act. Thereafter it remained central to both the expansion and contraction of the welfare state, as epitomised by the definition of New Labour's priorities in the 1997 election as being 'education, education, education'.

There was a simple reason for its importance. Education was seen to be the key to the attainment of the two major welfare goals of individual freedom and economic efficiency. The 1944 Act attracted immense public and political support, for example, because it promised greater equality of opportunity. Whatever their background, all children would have a chance to develop their talents to the full – both for their own individual satisfaction and to the economic advantage of society. Given the breaking down of barriers to individual fulfilment, the country would become more genuinely democratic; and given the fuller development of talent it would be the better able to compete in the international economy. Social justice would thus be allied to and reinforce national efficiency. This dual objective was never a source of political dispute. What eventually did arouse controversy – and quite bitter controversy – was the compatibility of its constituent parts (the issue of 'equality' versus 'quality') and the means by which they should be delivered.

The 1944 Act ushered in a period of expansion in which education expenditure doubled (to 12.5 per cent of public expenditure by 1975) and overtook the NHS as the second most expensive welfare service. The Act's principal impact was at the secondary level. Before 1939, the school leaving age had been fourteen and only 20 per cent of children over eleven had been taught outside 'all age' elementary schools, of whom half had had to pay. After 1944 all children were guaranteed four years of free, specialist secondary education between the ages of eleven and fifteen. This represented a major increase in equality in terms of class (because poorer families had been unable to afford secondary fees), gender (because parents had been less willing to pay fees for girls) and region (because all-age schools – in which children had remained for all their schooling from five to fourteen – predominated in rural areas).

The way in which children were selected for different forms of secondary education, however, soon aroused criticism. Educational psychologists at the time conventionally divided children between the 'academic', the 'mechanical' and the 'practical'; and in most European countries three types of education were provided to cater for these different aptitudes. In Britain, an examination at the age of eleven (the 'eleven plus' with its notorious IQ test) duly distinguished between children and assigned them to grammar, technical or secondary modern schools. In the 1950s this process was exposed as flawed in a variety of ways. Most importantly, research by educational sociologists suggested that the eleven plus was not an objective test of innate ability: children with supportive parents or from better-off backgrounds had typically developed their potential more fully by eleven and so were favoured by the examination. The broad result was that middle-class children were disproportionately assigned to grammar schools. In contrast, the majority of poorer children were branded as having 'failed' the examination and consigned to secondary moderns which, until the late 1950s, did not enjoy the promised 'parity of esteem' in terms of resources and staffing. Transfers between schools for children who were 'late developers' were rare. In short, social inequality was being reinforced rather than reduced.

The remedy, advanced by the Labour Party after 1953, was comprehensive schooling. All children in a given neighbourhood should attend the same school, thereby breaking down class distinctions and ending any sense of 'failure'. To develop individual aptitudes fully, education in these schools could remain divided between three academic streams – with the advantage of ease of transfer for late developers. Alternatively, and more controversially, to engineer greater equality the teaching could be unstreamed ('mixed ability').

The consequent introduction of comprehensive education in the 1960s ignited the battle between quality and equality. Its focus, particularly at a popular level, was the closure of grammar schools. These schools were seen, not least by many traditional Labour voters, as centres of educational excellence and proven vehicles for working-class upward mobility. Comprehensives, by contrast, were seen to threaten pastoral care (because of their size) and academic standards (particularly when they were unstreamed). The low standards of high schools in the USA, it was argued, provided a dire warning (4.2.2).

The controversy over secondary education has tended to dominate other educational issues, and it should be placed in perspective. Central government until the 1980s, it should be remembered, delegated decision-making to local government and teachers. Here there was a groundswell of support for comprehensive education which ensured continuity of policy whatever the ideology of the party in power. By the time the Conservatives left office in 1964, for example, over half of local authorities had plans to go comprehensive; and the greatest concentration of grammar school closures was between 1970 and 1974. The minister of education then was Mrs Thatcher. Secondly, the 1960s – as in all western countries – saw radical reform and expansion at *all* levels of education. Amongst the boldest endorsements of this expansion was the white paper *Education: A Framework for Expansion* (Cmnd 5174), which promised to increase expenditure by 50 per cent over the following ten years. It was published as late as 1972 and the author was again Mrs Thatcher.

Even before this white paper, however, fundamental doubts started to be expressed about the wisdom of expansion. Student unrest in 1968 sowed the first doubts; the Black Papers, published after 1969, provided an academic critique of 'progressive' teaching methods (4.2.2); and the 'anarchy' at the William Tyndale school and the Polytechnic of North London (4.3.1) appeared to confirm the worst fears. Consequently the Labour government launched a 'great debate' in 1976 designed to enhance the teaching of 'core skills' and to address long-standing concerns about the bias against vocational education (4.3.2).

These objectives were endorsed by the Conservatives after 1979. The first led in 1988 to the introduction of a national curriculum (4.3.4–6). The second led not only to attempts to alter the culture of teaching at all levels but also to the entrusting of vocational training to a range of bodies (ultimately Training and Enterprise Councils) run by industry rather than educationalists. The declared intention was to improve overall standards by empowering parents, above all, in relation to local authorities and the teaching profession, which were deemed to have abused the earlier trust placed upon them (4.2.5). Hence, for example, the publication of league tables for schools and universities to enable informed choice, and increased powers for parents as school governors.

The degree of empowerment achieved is debatable. What undoubtedly was achieved – as in the NHS – was an unprecedented centralisation of power. After 1994, for example, the Funding Agency for Schools rather than local authorities determined the financing of schools, whilst the national curriculum supported by inspectors from Ofsted (the Office for Standards in Education), rather than individual teachers, determined what was to be taught and how. Similarly local autonomy over the funding of post-school education was lost in 1991 and 1993 respectively with the appointment of the Further Education and the Higher Education Funding Councils. New Labour welcomed and reinforced this centralisation.

Education has traditionally been the welfare policy most open to expert advice and academic research. Extensive extracts from the relevant reports and legislation for most of the period have been published in S. Maclure, *Educational Documents* (4th edition, 1979) and H. Silver, *Equal Opportunity in Education* (1973). The purpose of this chapter is not to reproduce them yet again. Rather it is to provide an insight into the early vision for the principal areas of education, two of the main controversies (comprehensive education and the national curriculum) and the new consensus of the 1990s. The extracts refer essentially to England and Wales not to Northern Ireland and Scotland, which have their own distinctive educational systems – the one ironically favouring selective and the other comprehensive education.

4.1 THE VISION

4.1.1 Wartime ideals

On the outbreak of war, civil servants immediately started to plan the radical reshaping of the education system. This resulted in the *Educational Reconstruction* white paper, upon which the 1944 Act was based. It contained, as this extract shows, a bold vision of equal opportunity and specialist secondary education, whilst trying to forestall future problems such as competitive examinations at eleven and the bias against vocational skills. For all its apparent boldness, it has been subsequently attacked as an attempt to head off a more radical agenda which would have included the abolition of independent schools, the secularisation of education (as in France and the USA) and the imposition of comprehensive schools (rather than their half-hearted endorsement, as in para. 31).

1. The Government's purpose in putting forward the reforms described in this Paper is to secure for children a happier childhood and a better start in life: to ensure a fuller measure of education and opportunity for young people and to provide means for all of developing the various talents with which they are endowed and so enriching the inheritance of the country whose citizens they are. The new educational opportunities must not, therefore, be of a single pattern. It is just as important to achieve diversity as it is to ensure equality of opportunity. But, such diversity must not impair the social unity within the educational system which will open the way to a more closely knit society and give us the strength to face the tasks ahead....

2. With these ends in view the Government propose to recast the national education service. The new layout is based on the recognition of the principle that education is a continuous process conducted in successive stages. For children below the compulsory school age of 5 there must be sufficient supply of nursery schools. The period of compulsory attendance will be extended to 15 without exemptions and with provision for its subsequent extension to 16 as soon as circumstances permit. The period from 5 to the leaving age will be divided into two stages, the first, to be known as primary, covering the years up to about 11. After 11 secondary education, of diversified types but of equal standing, will be provided for all children.... The provision of school meals and milk will be made obligatory.

3. When the period of full-time compulsory schooling ends the young person will continue under educational influences up to 18 years of age either by remaining in full-time attendance at a secondary school, or by part-time day attendance at a young people's college....

15. The first stage in the process of compulsory schooling is the infant stage which lasts from 5–7 or 8.... Many of the infants' schools are among the most successful of the publicly provided schools. The junior schools for children between 7–11 have, however, tended to be

the 'Cinderellas' of the public system of education.... Little new and up-to-date accommodation has in recent years been provided for junior children.

16. Another feature common to both infants' and junior schools ... is that their classes are in many cases far too large. No teacher, however competent, can see to the development of an individual child's innate potentialities, or foster in it a healthy development of mind, body and character, if she has to deal single-handed with a class of 50 small children. This is not education but mass production.

17. More serious still is the effect on junior schools and on their pupils of the arrangements for transition from junior schools to the various types of post-primary education.... There is nothing to be said in favour of a system which subjects children at the age of 11 to the strain of a competitive examination on which, not only their future schooling, but their future careers may depend. Apart from the effect on the children, there is the effect on the curriculum of the schools themselves. Instead of the junior schools performing their proper and highly important function of fostering the potentialities of children at an age when their minds are nimble and receptive, their curiosity strong, their imagination fertile and the spirits high, the curriculum is too often cramped and distorted by over-emphasis on examination subjects and on the ways and means of defeating the examiners. The blame for this rests not with the teachers but with the system....

27. At the age of 11 comes the change from junior to the more senior stage.... In the future children at the age of 11 should be classified, not on the results of a competitive test, but on an assessment of their individual aptitudes largely by such means as school records, supplemented, if necessary, by intelligence tests, due regard being had to their parents' wishes and the careers they have in mind. Even so the choice of one type of secondary education rather than another for a particular pupil will not finally be determined at the age of 11, but will be subject to review as the child's special gifts and capacities develop. At the age of 13, or even later, there will be facilities for transfer....

28. If this choice is to be a real one, it is manifest that conditions in the different types of secondary school must be broadly equivalent. Under the present system the secondary school enjoys a prestige in the eyes of parents and the general public which completely overshadows all other types of school for children over 11. Inheriting as it does a distinguished tradition from the old English Grammar School it offers

the advantages of superior premises and staffing and a longer school life for its pupils.... But ... an academic training is ill-suited for many of the pupils.... Further, too many of the nation's abler children are attracted to the type of education which prepares primarily for the university and for the administrative and clerical professions; too few find their way into schools from which the design and craftsmanship sides of industry are recruited. If education is to serve the interests of both the child and of the nation, some means must be found of correcting this bias....

29. Compared to the grammar schools the senior schools have a recent history.... Their future is their own to make.... They offer a general education for life, closely related to the interests and environment of the pupils and of a wide range embracing the literary as well as the practical....

30. Junior Technical Schools ... hold out great opportunities for pupils with a practical bent.

31. Such then will be the three types of secondary schools. It would be wrong to suppose that they will necessarily remain separate and apart. Different types may be combined in one building or on one site as considerations of convenience and efficiency may suggest. In any case the free interchange of pupils from one type of education to another must be facilitated.

Educational Reconstruction, Cmnd 6458, 1943, Chapter 1, pp. 3, 5–6, 9–11.

4.1.2 Scientific manpower

Educational Reconstruction had identified a bias against science and technology and this was addressed, with similar boldness, by the 1945 Percy and the 1946 Barlow Committees. The former recommended a hierarchy of technical colleges, peaking with institutions of university status (the future colleges of advanced technology, such as Aston and Heriot-Watt, which actually became universities in 1965). The latter, as shown here, called for a doubling of science graduates not at the expense of arts but through capitalising on the equality of opportunity promised by the 1944 Act. Equally remarkable, given the chairman (Sir Alan Barlow) was a Treasury official, was the call for the proper funding and independence of universities.

2. ... If we are to maintain our position in the world and restore and improve our standard of living, we have no alternative but to strive for that scientific achievement without which our trade will wither, our Colonial Empire will remain undeveloped and our lives and freedom will be at the mercy of a potential aggressor....

The longer term problem
(1) Supply and demand
15. It is only to the Universities that we can look for any substantial recruitment to the ranks of qualified scientists. The proportion that has come from other sources in the past is very small indeed and we do not favour any attempt to add a responsibility for producing a substantial number of pure scientists to the existing and prospective burdens of the Technical Colleges.... The Technical Colleges will be hard put to it to produce the number of technologists that are required to support and apply the work of the scientists....

23. ... It is too early to attempt to estimate exactly what the output should be once the nation has settled down to peace-time conditions *but we are satisfied that the immediate aim should be to double the present output, giving us roughly 5,000 newly qualified scientists per annum....*

(2) Doubling the output of scientists
(i) The talent available
25. We need to form an estimate of the proportion of the population that is inherently fitted to benefit from a university education....

26. We have surveyed the results obtained in recent years on the distribution of intelligence, as measured by 'intelligence tests', among the whole population and among samples of the members of certain Universities....

At present rather less than 2 per cent of the population reach the Universities. About 5 per cent of the whole population show, on test, an intelligence as great as the upper half of the students.... We conclude, therefore, that only about one in five of the boys and girls who have intelligence equal to that of the best half of the University students, actually reach the Universities.... There is clearly an ample reserve of intelligence in the country to allow a doubling of the University numbers and at the same time a raising of standards.

27. There is also evidence that the great majority of the intelligent persons who do not reach the Universities are ex-pupils of the elementary schools. If university education were open to all on the basis of

measured intelligence alone, about 80 per cent would be expected to come from those children who started their education in the public elementary school and only 20 per cent from those whose education had been in independent schools.... These figures ... do make clear that a high proportion of the reserve of potentially able students comes from families that are unable to afford the cost of higher education. If, therefore, it is not to be lost to the Universities, greatly increased financial assistance both at the secondary school and at the university level is essential....

(iii) The relation between science and other faculties
(a) Engineering and technology
30. In the figures that we have quoted we have made no estimates for the vitally important studies in engineering and related technologies....

31. The Percy Committee, reporting in July 1945, drew a distinction between the functions of Universities and Technical Colleges. Industry, they said, must look mainly to the Universities for the training of scientists and mainly to the Technical Colleges for technical assistants and craftsmen. Both Universities and Colleges must share the responsibilities for educating the future senior administrators and technically qualified managers of industry. We are more concerned here with the need for those whom the Percy committee call engineer-scientists and development engineers. There must be a large increase in the number of these highly trained technologists capable of appreciating the latest progress in the research laboratories and applying the results to practical engineering or processes in industry. The solution offered by the Percy report is the development of full-time technological courses of university degree standard at a selected and limited number of Technical Colleges.

32. We cordially support this recommendation....

(b) The humanities
36. ... We would deprecate any attempt to meet the increased demand for scientists and technologists at the expense of students of other subjects....

(5) The implementation of our proposals
64. ...

(a) Each University and University College ... must be invited to consider its position and form an assessment of the way it can best contribute to the expansion demanded....

(c) It is probably not possible to assess statistically the demand for graduates in the humanities and other branches of learning. But the expansion of these faculties cannot be left entirely to trial and error if there is to be no danger of a growing 'lack of balance' in the Universities....

(f) Arrangements need to be made to ensure an adequate supply of the best students from the schools.... If the best available talent is to reach the Universities, then financial assistance must be made available to the great majority of university students....

(h) The parallel needs of the special Technical Colleges must be met and a regional and national system developed for knitting together the Schools, and the Technical Colleges, the Higher Technical Institutes, the Universities and Industry.

(i) Finally, this heavy programme will have to be financed very largely at the expense of the Exchequer....

65. We must here record that we are unanimously opposed to any infringement of the cherished independence of the Universities, even if it could be justified on the ground that it would facilitate the execution of the expansion programme....

Scientific Man-Power: Report of a Committee Appointed by the Lord President of the Council, The Barlow Report, Cmd 6824, 1946, pp. 3–11, 20–1.

4.1.3 The Conservative ambitions

The postwar priorities for welfare expenditure were initially the NHS and housing, but by the mid-1950s the Conservative minister of education, David (later Lord) Eccles, initiated an unparalleled period of expansion to fulfil belatedly the Butler vision and exceed it. The peculiar mix of political, social and economic motives for the expansion is here summarised in a letter to the prime minister.

We must consider it a stroke of fortune to find ourselves the first administration which can, if it so chooses, identify itself with bringing the Butler Act to life. There are very good reasons why this chance should be taken with both hands.

(a) A half-educated electorate is fodder for the class war and a menace to free institutions. Problems such as forestalling inflation, preventing and settling strikes and abandoning restrictive practices will, in the end, only be solved by better education....

(b) The rate at which new industries can be developed and the old ones modernised must depend largely on the supply of scientists and technicians. Indeed the corollary of your strong lead in this field is a sharp expansion in technical education and, equally important, an improvement in the standard of primary and secondary schools designed to make boys and girls anxious to continue their studies.

(c) The Conservative Party needs to be able to claim some outstanding sector of the Welfare State as its own. Pensions and other social benefits are the work of all parties. Bevan fathered the Health Service. The credit for housing ... must be shared with the local authorities. But education can be ours. It is very Conservative in spirit; it began with the Church; its purpose is to fit man to take opportunities and to lead balanced lives; this purpose is achieved by home and school and the Church working together; the Act of 1944 was introduced by the present Chancellor of the Exchequer; if we now carry out its provisions with vigour modern education, i.e. education adequate for conditions of universal suffrage and full employment, will be seen to be Conservative alike in origin and administration....

Better education is the wisest investment the country can now make, having regard to the demands of the scientific revolution and the need to develop a sense of responsibility towards the problems and pitfalls of full employment. I would also argue that a political party, aiming to poll more than half the votes at future general elections, must be clearly identified with one sector of the sprouting Welfare State, and that education is a service marked out as peculiarly Conservative in purpose....

Letter from David Eccles to Anthony Eden, 6 June 1955, Public Record Office, PREM 11/1785.

4.1.4 Higher education

The 1963 Robbins Report was the major catalyst for the expansion of student numbers in higher education from the 2 per cent of the population, noted by Barlow, to over 30 per cent by 1997. Commissioned by Eccles and chaired by the economist Lord Robbins, it called for the doubling of student numbers by 1980/81. Its short-term target was an increase of 59 per cent by 1970/71, which was immediately accepted by the Conservative government. In the event, an increase of 104 per cent was achieved. The justifications for expansion included the provision of places to all who were qualified, bringing Britain up to international norms and the need for competitive efficiency: two-thirds of the new students were to be in science and technology (although this aim was not met). This extract, based on the research which had discredited the eleven plus exam and selective secondary schooling, typified contemporary determination to counteract the social pressures which were restricting the full development of genetic ability.

Guiding principles

133. In principle, the problem of estimating the number of places required can be approached in two ways: by considering what supply of different kinds of highly educated persons will be required ... or by considering what the demand for places in higher education is likely to be. We have decided that the second approach presents the sounder basis for estimates....

The so-called pool of ability

137. It is sometimes argued that growth in the number of those able to benefit from higher education is something that is likely to be limited in the foreseeable future by biological factors. But we believe that it is highly misleading to suppose that one can determine an upper limit to the number of people who could benefit from higher education, given favourable circumstances. It is, of course, unquestionable that human beings vary considerably in native capacity for all sorts of tasks.... But while it would be wrong to deny fundamental differences of nature, it is equally wrong to deny that performance in examinations or tests – or indeed any measurable ability – is affected by nurture in the widest sense of the word. Moreover, the belief that there exists some easy method of ascertaining an intelligence factor unaffected by education or background is outmoded....

138. Considerations of this sort are important at all stages of education, but especially at the higher stages. For by then the effects of earlier education and environment in moulding and modifying fundamental biological equipment have produced a cumulative effect. It is

no doubt true that there are born a number of potential 'firsts' whose qualities are such that they win through whatever their environmental disadvantages, and another, considerably larger, number who, if trained by the most famous teachers in history, would still fail their examinations. But in between there is a vast mass whose performance, both at entry to higher education and beyond, depends greatly on how they have lived and been taught beforehand....

139. The Crowther Report ['15–18'] had already indicated the close association between a father's level of occupation and the educational achievement of his children at school.... [O]ur survey confirmed that the association with parental occupation is ... still closer where higher education is concerned.... The underlying reasons for this are complex, but differences of income and that of parents' educational level and attitudes are certainly among them....

140. ... [J]ust as since the war more children have stayed on at school for a full secondary education, so in turn more of their children will come to demand higher education during the 1970s....

141. This in itself is ... no guarantee that the quality of students will be maintained if there is an increased entry. There is, however, impressive evidence that large numbers of able young people do not at present reach higher education....

142. While the reserves of untapped ability may be greatest in the poorer sections of the community, this may not be the whole of the story. It is sometimes imagined that the great increase in recent years in the numbers achieving good school-leaving qualifications has occurred almost entirely among the children of manual workers. This is not so. The increase has been almost as great among the children of professional parents, where the pool of ability might have been thought more nearly exhausted.... The desire for education, leading to better performance at school, appears to be affecting the children of all classes and all abilities alike, and it is reasonable to suppose that this trend will continue....

145. Finally, it should be observed that fears that expansion would lead to a lowering of the average ability of students in higher education have proved unfounded. Recent increases in numbers have not been accompanied by an increase in wastage and the measured ability of students appears to be as high as it ever was.

Higher Education, The Robbins Report, Cmnd 2154, 1963, Chapter VI, pp. 48–53.

4.1.5 Primary education

Educational Reconstruction had identified primary education in 1943 as a 'Cinderella' service (para. 15). It remained so until the Conservatives commissioned the Plowden Report in 1963. Its report to a Labour government in 1967, as this extract shows, promoted the progressive 'child-centred' learning which was to lead to the backlash after 1976 – and ultimately the reintroduction of testing which it vigorously opposed. It, like the Robbins Report, epitomised the determination in the 1960s to remove social constraints on the development of natural ability; and, in line with USA thinking, it concluded that equality of opportunity could only be fully achieved by positive discrimination. Accordingly it recommended the establishment of Educational Priority Areas to channel extra resources to children in deprived areas.

519. Research into the ways in which children learn had produced ... two interpretations of the learning process. One ... is concerned with simple and complex operant conditioning, the place of reinforcement in learning, habit formation and the measurement of various kinds of stimulus-response behaviour....

521. ... A second school of research, which is dominant in Great Britain ... is associated with the names of Baldwin, Isaacs, Luria, Bruner and in particular Jean Piaget.... One of its most important conclusions is that the great majority of primary school children can only learn efficiently from concrete situations, as lived or described. From these situations children acquire concepts in every area of the curriculum.... Learning takes place through a continuous process of interaction between the learner and his environment, which results in the building up of consistent and stable patterns of behaviour, physical and mental. Each new experience reorganises ... the structure of the mind and contributes to the child's world picture.

522. ... Piaget's explanations appear to most educationalists in this country to fit the observed facts of children's learning more satisfactorily than any other....

Aspects of children's learning
523. Play is the central activity in all nursery schools and in many infant schools.... We know now that play – in the sense of 'messing about' either with material objects or with other children, and of

creating fantasies – is vital to children's learning and therefore vital in school.... In play, children gradually develop concepts of causal relationships, the power to discriminate, to make judgements, to analyse and synthesise, to imagine and to formulate. Children become absorbed in their play and the satisfactory conclusion fixes habits of concentration which can be transferred to other learning....

529. The child is the agent in his own learning.... Activity and experience, both physical and mental, are often the best means of gaining knowledge and acquiring facts.... We certainly would not wish to undervalue knowledge and facts, but facts are best retained when they are used and understood, when right attitudes to learning are created, when children learn to learn....

530. The intense interest shown by young children in the world about them ... is apparent to both teachers and parents. Skills of reading and writing ... can best be taught when the need for them is evident to children.... There is, therefore, good reason for allowing young children to choose within a carefully prepared environment....

533. Learning is a continuous process from birth. The teacher's task is to provide an environment and opportunities which are sufficiently challenging for children and yet not so difficult as to be outside their reach....

Some practical implications
The time table
536. These beliefs about how children learn have practical implications for the time table and the curriculum. One idea now widespread is embodied in the expression 'free day' and another, associated with it, is the 'integrated curriculum'.... If teachers encourage overlap between what is done in periods of self chosen activity and in the times allocated ... to reading and writing, a good learning situation will probably result.... Some infant schools are now confident enough in the value of self chosen activity to give the whole day to it.... The tendency is spreading to junior schools. Children may plan when to do work assigned to them, and also to have time in which to follow personal or group interests of their own choice....

537. These changes represent a revolution....

Flexibility in the curriculum
540. The idea of flexibility has found expression in a number of practices, all of them designed to make good use of the interest and curiosity of children, to minimise the notion of subject matter being rigidly

compartmental, and to allow the teacher to adopt a consultative, guiding, stimulating role rather than a purely didactic one....

Evaluation of children's progress

551. ... It is not possible to describe a standard of attainment that should be reached by all or most children. Any set standard would seriously limit the bright child and be impossibly high for the dull. What could be achieved in one school might be impossible in another.... With the ending of selection examinations, teachers – and parents – will need some yardstick of the progress of their children in relation to what is achieved elsewhere.... We therefore envisage that some use will continue to be made of objective tests within schools. Such tests can be helpful – and their norms can serve as a basis of comparison – as long as they are used with insight and discrimination, and teachers do not assume that only what is measurable is valuable....

Department of Education and Science, *Children and Their Primary Schools*, The Plowden Report, vol. 1, London, 1967, pp. 192–202.

4.1.6 Nursery education

Nursery education had been identified by the Plowden Committee as an ideal vehicle for positive discrimination to offset social disadvantage, and its recommendations were endorsed by Mrs Thatcher in the last comprehensive plan for postwar educational expansion, published in 1972. Discrimination was endorsed but, mindful of Eccles's vision, the object could be portrayed as a desire to control ('socialise') rather than encourage individual development. Concern over the balance between state and voluntary provision (also examined by the 1968 Seebohm Report, see 6.1.1 and 6.2.2) anticipated debates in the 1980s. It was made particularly pertinent by the phenomenal success since the 1960s of the voluntary Pre-School Playgroups Association.

13. ... This will be the first systematic step since 1870, when education was made compulsory at the age of five, to offer an earlier start in education....

16. There is now considerable evidence pointing to the importance

of the years before five in a child's education – and to the most effective ways of providing for the needs, and potential which children display at this age.... The Plowden Committee estimated that provision for 90% of four year-olds and 50% of three year-olds would be adequate to meet demand.

17. The action the Government now propose will give effect to these recommendations....

Objectives
19. The value of nursery education in promoting the social development of young children has long been acknowledged. In addition we now know that, given sympathetic and skilled supervision, children may also make great educational progress before the age of five....

20. The opportunities which the new policy offers for families living in deprived areas – both urban and rural – in bringing up their young children will be particularly important. There, as elsewhere, the Government believe that provision for the under fives should build on, not supplant, parents' own efforts.

21. The expansion of nursery education will also provide an opportunity for the earlier identification of children with special difficulties....

Nature of expansion
22. Planning the provision required to meet the aims of the new policy is complicated in two ways. First, the Government are not laying down a uniform detailed pattern; they hope that local plans will reflect local needs and resources, particularly the contribution of playgroups. Secondly, demographic factors apart, the extent of demand and its future growth are uncertain....

23. ... The government ... welcome diversity in provision so long as it is efficient and there is no sacrifice of standards in the education and care of children....

Disadvantaged children
28. All children can gain from nursery education but it is particularly valuable for children whose home and life are restricted, for whatever reason. While the Government's aim is that nursery education should be widely available within ten years for children of three and four, priority will be given in the early stages of the programme to areas of disadvantage....

The rôle of parents

29. Local Education authorities will also wish to adapt and apply to nursery education lessons which can be learnt from the experience of playgroups. The most successful of these have derived much strength from the support of parents, which the playgroup can generate by providing a focus of interest in education in the community. Some mothers have been able to give practical help in running playgroups ... many more may wish to have some training.... Their maturity and experience with children are important assets. In addition, nursery education probably offers the best opportunities for enlisting parents' understanding and support for what schools are trying to achieve, which is of key importance to successful education at subsequent stages.

Education: A Framework for Expansion, Cmnd 5174, 1972, Chapter 3, pp. 4–7.

4.1.7 Special needs

The concept of equality of opportunity was extended in the 1970s to handicapped children in relation to education as well as care (see Chapter 6). The Warnock Committee, chaired by an Oxford philosopher who had been a headmistress, favoured integration in ordinary schools rather than specialist institutions. Commissioned by a Conservative government in 1973, it reported to a Labour one in 1978 and had its recommendations enacted by the Conservatives in 1981 – thereby demonstrating the continuance, in some educational areas, of an informed educational consensus after the mid-1970s.

The criteria by which to judge the quality of educational provision is the extent to which it leads a pupil ... towards understanding, awareness of moral values and enjoyment and towards the possibility of independence. It is progress towards these goals which alone can justify a particular course of education for anyone, whatever his abilities or disabilities....

There is in our society a vast range of differently disabled children, many of whom would not have survived infancy in other periods of history. In the case of the most profoundly disabled one is bound to face the questions: Why educate such children at all? Are they not ineducable? How can one justify such effort and such expense for so small a result? Such questions have to be faced, and must be answered. Our answer is that education, as we conceive it, is a good, and a specifically human good, to which all human beings are entitled. There exists, therefore, a clear obligation to educate the most severely disabled for no other reason than that they are human. No civilized society can be content just to look after these children; it must all the time seek ways of helping them, however slowly, towards the educational goals we have identified....

If we fail to do this, we are actually increasing and compounding their disadvantages.

Moreover there are some children with disabilities who, through education along the common lines we advocate, may be able to lead a life very little poorer in quality than that of the non-handicapped child, whereas without this kind of education they may face a life of dependence or even institutionalisation....

Our concept of special education is thus broader than the traditional one of education by special methods appropriate for particular categories of children.... It extends beyond the idea of education provided in special schools, special classes or units for children with particular types of disability, and embraces the notion of any form of additional help wherever it is provided and whenever it is provided, from birth to maturity, to overcome educational difficulties. It also embodies the idea that, although the difficulties which some children encounter may dictate WHAT they have to be taught and the disabilities of some HOW they have to be taught, the point of their education is the same.

Report of the Committee of Enquiry into the Education of Handicapped Children and Young People, Cmnd 7212, 1978, Chapter 1, pp. 5–7.

4.1.8 Multicultural education

One of the last areas of inequality to be addressed was racial inequality. Since the 1960s there had been concern at the underperformance of West Indian students, and multicultural programmes had been introduced, particularly since 1972, in an attempt to combat this by encouraging minority groups to take pride in their culture. These programmes were attacked on the right for discouraging assimilation and on the left for leaving the white majority untouched. Mounting racial tension, especially in the early 1980s, demanded an answer. The Swann Report in 1985 (drafted under the chairmanship of the vice-chancellor of Edinburgh University) recommended how education, by itself and with other agencies, could help to remedy the situation. It was rejected by Keith Joseph as minister of education.

Main conclusions and recommendations

1.1 This report is concerned primarily to change behaviour and attitudes. They need to change throughout Britain, and, while the education system must not be expected to carry the whole burden of that change, schools in particular are uniquely well placed to take a lead role. Britain has evolved, over many centuries, institutions and traditions which, whatever their shortcomings, have been taken as models by many nations, and were indeed an important part of the attraction of this country to the ethnic minorities who are an essential concern of our report. It is because we believe that everyone in Britain has a direct interest in ensuring that those institutions, and attitudes which inform them, change to take full account of the pluralism which is now a marked feature of British life, that we make our recommendations....

2.3 School performance has long been known to show a close correlation with socio-economic status and social class, in the case of all children. The ethnic minorities, however, are particularly disadvantaged in social and economic terms, and there can no longer be any doubt that this extra deprivation is the result of racial prejudice and discrimination, especially in the areas of employment and housing. The resulting deprivation, over and above that of disadvantaged Whites, leads in many instances to an extra element of underachievement....

2.4 Not all underachievement, where it occurs, is to be accounted for in these terms, and the rest, we believe, is due in large measure to prejudice and discrimination bearing *directly* on children, within the educational system, as well as outside it. We have received much oral and written evidence ... referring in particular to stereotyped attitudes amongst teachers, as well as other factors....

2.6 It will be evident that society is faced with a dual problem:

eradicating the discriminatory attitudes of the white majority on the one hand, and on the other, evolving an educational system which ensures that *all* pupils achieve their full potential.

2.7 In the short term, the first of these problems is a matter for the Law, the Government, Housing Authorities, Employers, Unions, the Commission for Racial Equality, and many others. But in the long run we believe that it is a matter for schools to bring about this much-needed change in attitudes amongst coming generations.

2.8 The second problem is specifically one for the educational system....

2.9 The dual approach to one of Britain's most serious social concerns, leads us to the concept that we have called 'Education for All' – an attempt simultaneously to change attitudes amongst the White Majority, and to develop a pattern of education that enables *all* pupils to give of their best.

3.1 The essential steps on the argument for our concept of 'Education for all' are as follows:

(a) The fundamental change that is necessary is the recognition that the problem facing the educational system is not how to educate children of ethnic minorities but how to educate *all* children.

(b) Britain is a multi-racial and multi-cultural society and all pupils must be enabled to understand what this means.

(c) This challenge cannot be left to the separate and independent initiatives of LEAs and schools: only those with experience of substantial numbers of ethnic minority pupils have attempted to tackle it, though the issue affects all schools and all pupils.

(d) Education has to be something more than the reinforcement of beliefs, values and identity which each child brings to school.

(e) It is necessary to combat racism, to attack inherited myths and stereotypes, and the ways in which they are embodied in institutional practices.

(f) Multi-cultural understanding has also to permeate all aspects of a school's work. It is not a separate topic that can be welded on to existing practices.

(g) Only in this way can schools begin to offer anything approaching the *equality of opportunity* for all pupils which it must be the aspiration of the education system to provide.

Education for All, The Swann Report, Cmnd 9453, 1985, pp. 768–9.

4.2 CONTROVERSY: COMPREHENSIVE EDUCATION

4.2.1 The case for the defence

Educational sociologists undermined faith in the tripartite system during the 1950s and opened the door for the introduction of comprehensive secondary schools in the 1960s. Here Robin Pedley, the director of education at Exeter University, in a famous Penguin book expresses the moral fervour with which the educational and social advantages of comprehensives were advocated.

'Nothing,' said Victor Hugo, 'is so powerful as an idea whose time has come.'

The arguments against our divided system of education mount higher day by day. Parents are no longer content to accept the verdict of mental tests at eleven as authoritative....

In examination, comprehensive schools are already turning the tables on those who raised the alarm about the threat to academic standards. Despite the serious handicaps imposed upon them, these schools are beginning to suggest that it is the segregated system whose performance may be inferior.... Their continued success ... will produce a growing flood of young people eager to continue their studies beyond the secondary stage....

Large changes in the framework of our educational system are required, but ... what matters most of all is what goes on inside our schools. It is very important that our comprehensive schools shall not content themselves with merely achieving equal opportunity for the competitive success of individual pupils. In the year ahead, now that the folly of eleven-plus segregation is everywhere being recognised, they will be tempted of the devil. They will be shown and offered all the scholastic kingdoms, including Oxford and Cambridge.... Tempting though such prizes are, they must not be allowed to divert the new schools from their larger purpose: the forging of a communal culture by the pursuit of quality with equality, by the education of their pupils in and for democracy, and by the creation of happy, vigorous, local communities in which the school is the focus for social and educational life.

R. Pedley, *The Comprehensive School*, Harmondsworth, 1963, pp. 197–200.

4.2.2 The case for the prosecution

In 1965 Anthony Crosland as the new Labour minister of
education issued the famous Circular 10/65 declaring the government's objective 'to end selection at eleven plus and to
eliminate separatism in secondary education'. Its gradual
implementation by most local authorities prompted a backlash
which was spearheaded by a series of Black Papers, edited by
two university academics. In the second, detailed objections
were summarised in the form of a letter addressed to Labour
MPs, from which this extract is taken.

A major irony is that the Labour Party 'reforms' particularly harm the
intelligent working class child.... Both editors of the Black Papers
were born in working class areas, and they feel bitter and angry that
the fine opportunities given to them in Grammar Schools in the 1940s
are from now on to be denied to children with similar backgrounds....

[The] usual method now is to allow only certain neighbourhoods
to send children to a specific comprehensive school – a plan which
removes parental choice, limits the size and intake of a school in a
manner often fatal to real comprehensiveness, and produces other
adverse results.... It is also, of course, grossly non-egalitarian, since
the parents who want their children well-educated in the state system
might now have to move to another district where the comprehensive
achieves a high standard, and how many working-class parents will
have the money, the opportunity or the inclination to do this? Some
areas are bound to fall into decline, and it is here that clever working
class boys [sic] will be victimised.... This pattern has produced well-
known adverse effects in America and Russia, from whose mistakes
we seem unable to learn....

Possibly the most serious defect of the comprehensive is the failure
of their sixth forms.... In a neighbourhood of mixed and unselected
ability, you need a far larger number of students than such schools are
likely to have to run a fully viable academic sixth form. As a result we
are now seeing the development in many areas of 'tertiary education'
– a system whereby pupils leave comprehensive school at around 16
and proceed to a Sixth Form College or a Technical College.... For the
comprehensive school the result can only be disastrous. It will lose its
best teachers, who will surely choose to teach in a Sixth Form College
if they can.... It will lose all its senior pupils – all those who most help

to develop the traditions of a school, and define its identity. Decapitated in this way, it can only become an uneasy transit camp between the primary school ... and the tertiary school.... It is not unrealistic to fear that in a few years time standards will very dramatically decline. There will be many children who spend their junior years in a 'progressive' primary school, and who then pass to an unstreamed, unexamined comprehensive with no sixth form. At sixteen, many will be semi-literate, at a stage when such basic defects are almost impossible to correct. The possibility of this situation was amply demonstrated in the 1950s in America. But why are we risking it in Britain? Why are we undermining a primary system which has proved its ability to produce numeracy and literacy? Why are we destroying the finest secondary schools in the world?

C.B. Cox and A.E. Dyson, *The Crisis in Education*, Black Paper Two, London, 1969, pp. 5–8.

4.2.3 Reinstating choice

On their return to power in 1970, the Conservatives issued Circular 10/70 restoring to local authorities the freedom they had enjoyed since 1944 to decide which structure of secondary education to adopt. This freedom is here justified in Parliament by the minister of education. Surprisingly, given the emphasis on pragmatism and 'rejecting compulsion on democratically elected authorities', the minister was Mrs Thatcher.

The cardinal issue of secondary reorganisation was whether the existing rights of local education authorities to decide what is best for their area should be upheld....

The powers under the [1944] Act ... which places the duty on local education authorities to secure the provision of schools sufficient in number, character and equipment to afford for all pupils ... opportunities for education appropriate to their ages, aptitudes and abilities. Wisely that provision did not lay down the type of institution in which that duty should be discharged. Had it at that time adopted such a rigid policy and stipulated the best school system then known, and none other, the comprehensive system could never have developed as it has from the early 1950s.

A rigid system is the enemy of advance. Almost every practical educationist advises one to have policies which are flexible so that one can stand ready to take advantage of new methods and new research....

The Government accept the view that the age of 11 is too early to make final decisions about a child's future.... In some ways the debate about the type of schools has perhaps distracted attention away from what is every bit as important; namely, what happens inside schools. At present there is a mixed system of schools and, because the cost of comprehensivisation would be so great there will be a mixed system for some time to come....

I believe it is possible to have a mixed system of both comprehensive and grammar schools.... This is not a contradiction.... Certainly, with a small rural area, I do not believe it would be possible to have a comprehensive school and a grammar school, but in some very large urban areas it is possible, because the grammar school and direct grant school have quite different catchment areas from the comprehensive school....

The second paragraph of the circular points out that authorities will now be freer ... to determine the shape of secondary provision in their areas. I believe the best educational schemes have come when authorities have not been coerced....

The main purpose of this circular is to honour an election pledge to reject compulsion on democratically elected authorities.

Parliamentary Debates, vol. 803, 8 July 1970, cols 667–88.

4.2.4 Reinforcing compulsion

On its return to power in 1974, the Labour government issued Circular 4/74 and reinforced it with the 1976 Education Act which instructed local authorities that secondary education could not be 'based (wholly or partly) on selection by reference to ability or aptitude'. The decision was retrospectively justified in a green paper.

1.11. ... The comprehensive school reflects the need to educate our people for a different sort of society, in which the talents and abilities of our people in all spheres need to be developed and respected; the education appropriate to our Imperial past cannot meet the requirements of modern Britain....

Secondary schools

2.6 Four fifths of our boys and girls now attend comprehensive schools. The comprehensive school is at the centre of the Government's policy on secondary education. The objective of the comprehensive system is to offer to every boy or girl educational opportunities appropriate to his or her ability, aptitudes and personal motivation. It recognises the importance of educating together young people from different backgrounds, as an essential preparation for a united and understanding society....

2.8 The curriculum is not the school's sole means of realising the purposes of comprehensive education. The creation of a lively and caring community, where pupils have the opportunities to exercise initiative and responsibility; the sensitive organisation of groups for learning and other activities; the establishment of an unobtrusive system of effective guidance and support for the adolescent are crucial to success. But all these serve the cause of pupils' learning.... The comprehensive school's curriculum must reflect the diversity of its pupils' individual needs. In educational terms, the comprehensive school aspires to educate all our children to the highest standards of which they are capable....

2.9 The curriculum now offers a greater spectrum of learning and a broader range of choices than did the traditional selective system. A much higher portion of pupils now take public examinations.... New content and new styles of learning in the sciences and mathematics have helped to make these subjects more interesting and more accessible to many pupils. The opportunity to learn a modern language has been given to a much wider range of pupils of different abilities than in the past.

Education in Schools: A Consultative Document, Cmnd 6869, 1977, pp. 4, 10.

4.2.5 The Thatcherite response

After 1979 the Conservatives revoked Circular 4/74, but rather than embarking on a frontal attack, they decided to erode comprehensive schools by initiatives such as the assisted places scheme (financing selected pupils in independent schools) and city technology colleges. Finally, in order to create a 'market' in which the teaching profession would have to respond more sensitively to parents and pupils alike, the 1988 Education Act permitted schools to opt out of local government control and be financed directly from Whitehall. This led directly to New Labour's promotion of 'specialist' schools to replace traditional comprehensives which Tony Blair's press secretary was notoriously to condemn as 'bog standard' in 2000. The Act is defended here in Parliament by the then minister of education, Kenneth Baker.

Chapter IV [of the Bill] deals with the establishment of grant-maintained schools. Our proposal will allow all secondary schools and primary schools with more than 300 pupils, to opt out of local authority control and to apply for direct funding. This will widen choice for many parents in the state-maintained sector for whom all too often the only choice is to take it or leave it. The wider choice will help improve standards in all our schools, not just those who opt-out. The local education authorities will want to hold onto their schools and will therefore have a far greater incentive to respond to the wishes of parents. For the first time in eighty years they will face competition in the provision of free education so standards will rise in all schools as we introduce a competitive spirit into the provision of education – and at no extra cost to the consumer.

Meanwhile let me stress and make clear that these schools will offer free education. They will be funded at the same level as they would have been had they remained under the local authority. There will continue to be an equality of public resourcing.

When it opts out a grant-maintained school will retain the character that it had and will continue to admit pupils on the same basis.... Grant-maintained schools will have to agree their admissions arrangements with the Secretary of State and these arrangements will be published annually so the parents will know how places will be allocated in the event of over subscription.... Opting out will be an open, democratic process.

Parliamentary Debates, vol. 123, 1 December 1987, col. 778.

4.3 CONTROVERSY: THE NATIONAL CURRICULUM

4.3.1 William Tyndale

Britain was exceptional in not having a national curriculum, and although one had been contemplated in the early 1960s, it took events in the mid-1970s such as the 'scandal' at William Tyndale, a North London primary school, to make it a political possibility. There teachers put into practice an extreme form of 'child-centred' learning advocated by the Plowden Committee, which led to falling pupil numbers, a critical inspection and a teachers' strike in 1975. Following a public inquiry, the teachers were dismissed and the school reorganised. This account by two journalists on the *Times Educational Supplement* illustrates the new willingness to accept increased centralisation to defend the interests of consumers of education (parents) against overbearing and incompetent producers (local government and teachers) – three themes which were to dominate the 1980s.

The main ingredients of William Tyndale could be found all over the country: a staff with strong radical convictions, a weak headteacher, a dithering inspectorate, worried parents and a local education authority that did not know what it wanted from its primary schools.... The mixture was common enough, but previously it had not been thought of as dangerously explosive. The zeitgeist, however, had changed. Gone were the heady spendthrift days of the 1960s when education and all social services boomed, and books like Anthony Crosland's *The Future of Socialism* could paint a rosy picture of a future full of beautiful people all happily caring for one another. In their place was the pessimism of the seventies, with their rapidly deteriorating cities and their visions of permanent economic decline.... Combined with the fact that people's expectations of the Welfare State had outrun their willingness to pay the consequent taxes, this meant in education a decline in the power of the teacher (the labour market was no longer running in his favour) and a concern for minimum standards for all children....

Attainment
Mr Ellis, Mr Haddow and Mr Austin [the head and teachers at Tyndale], if not all their followers, had a fairly clear idea of what they expected schools to do. Schools for them had a profound effect on

children: the point was how to use that effect. Rather like social workers their main preoccupation was with the (largely false) dilemma of
whether they and schools were agents of change or agents of social
control. They wanted change and that was a perfectly respectable
position. That sort of thinking had not only inspired much of the
Plowden Report on primary education, it had been responsible for the
millions of pounds invested in Western type education in the newly
independent countries of the third world....

Another view was that schools existed not to change society but to
prepare for change.... The world of tomorrow was bound to be a
world of group activity and co-operative projects and it was important that children be prepared for a world of continuous adaptation.
All questions of social reform apart, co-operative informal teaching
methods would be more suitable for this purpose than formal, traditional ones.

What was left then, as an aim of primary education? Once the
eleven plus had gone, there was no measure of achievement at all,
however unsatisfactory. Children moved on up into secondary school
when they were eleven or twelve whether or not they had learnt to
read and write; there was no question of keeping anyone back. The
notion, popular among parents, that children should be taught the
'basics' while at primary school was the only hint of a minimum
standard. Even that, though, if it were to be formalised would require
some form of attainment testing and since the abolition of the eleven
plus it had become impossible for educationists to reach agreement
among themselves on a value-free objective test – or even on the
merits of testing at all.

Assessment

It is difficult to talk of assessing the performance of teachers when
there is no agreement on what teachers are supposed to be doing....
There was no basis on which one school could be compared with
another – except the subjective impressions of the inspectors, a group
of men and women whose sole qualification for the job was that they
had once been good teachers. Moreover, the touchiness of many
teachers and their unions, concerned with their status as qualified professionals ... contributed to the general unwillingness of the inspectors
to force their opinions down anybody's throat....

But if inspectors abandoned their role as assessors, who was to
make judgements about how well or how badly teachers might be

doing their job?...

Accountability

All of these issues we have mentioned – the powers and responsibilities of the local authorities, the control of the curriculum, the criteria for assessing a school's efficiency, the aims of primary education, the need for testing, the role of the inspectorate, the function of managers and the professionalisation and accountability of teachers – are proper subjects for consideration by the Secretary of State for Education. Only he can ... take an overview of the issue which underlies every other: the proper balance to be struck between politicians and the community on the one hand, and teachers and the other professionals on the other. After William Tyndale, the Secretary of State can no longer pretend, as he and his predecessors have so often tended to do, that all is happening somewhere else.

John Gretton and Mark Jackson, *William Tyndale: The Collapse of a School – or a System*, London, 1976, pp. 121–5.

4.3.2 Launching the 'great debate'

> The Labour prime minister, James Callaghan, responded to the perceived crisis in a speech at Ruskin College, Oxford in October 1976. Designed to stimulate a 'great debate' on education, it was a skilful blend of traditional and progressive concerns. The need for basic skills and an end to anti-industrial bias was stressed, but Black Paper prejudices were rejected and the need for individual fulfilment defended.

I am concerned on my journeys to find complaints from industry that new recruits from the schools sometimes do not have the basic tools to do the job that is required.

   I have been concerned to find that many of our best trained students who have completed the higher levels of education at university or polytechnic have no desire to join industry. Their preferences are to stay in academic life or to find their way into the Civil Service. There seems to be a need for a more technological bias in science teaching that will lead towards practical applications in industry rather than towards academic studies. Or to take other examples why is it that such a high proportion of girls abandon sciences before leaving school? Then there is the concern about the standards of numeracy of school-leavers. Is there not a case for a professional review of the mathematics needed by industry at different levels? To what extent are these deficiencies the result of insufficient co-ordination between schools and industry? Indeed how much of the criticism about basic skills and attitudes is due to industry's own shortcomings rather than to the educational system? Why is it that 30,000 vacancies for students in science and engineering in our universities and polytechnics were not taken up last year when the humanities courses were full?

On another aspect there is unease felt by parents and others about the new informal methods of teaching which seem to produce excellent results when they are in well-qualified hands but are more dubious when they are not.... There is little wrong with the range and diversity of our courses. But is there sufficient thoroughness and depth in those required in after life to make a living?

These are proper subjects for discussion and debate. And it should be a national debate based on the facts. My remarks are not a clarion call to Black Paper prejudices. We all know those who claim to defend standards but who in reality are simply seeking to defend old privileges and inequalities.

It is not my intention to become enmeshed in such problems as whether there should be a basic curriculum with universal standards – although I am inclined to think there should be – nor about ... the position and role of the inspectorate.... What I am saying is that where there is legitimate public concern it will be to the advantage of all involved in the education field if these concerns are aired and shortcomings righted or fears put at rest....

For many years the accent was simply on fitting the so-called inferior group of children with just enough learning to earn their living in the factory. Labour has attacked that attitude consistently.... There is now a widespread recognition of the need to cater for a child's personality, to let it flower in the fullest possible way.

The balance was wrong in the past. We have a responsibility now to see that we do not get it wrong in the other direction. There is no virtue in producing well-adjusted members of society who are unemployed because they do not have the skills. Nor at the other extreme must they be technically efficient robots. Both the basic purposes of education require the same essential tools. These are basic literacy, basic numeracy, the understanding of how to live and work together, respect for others, respect for the individual. This means acquiring certain basic knowledge and skills and reasoning ability. It means developing lively inquiring minds and an appetite for further knowledge that will last a lifetime. It means mitigating as far as possible the disadvantages that may be suffered through poor home conditions or physical or mental handicap....

Let me repeat some of the fields that need study because they cause concern. There are the methods and aims of informal instruction; the strong case for the so-called 'core curriculum' of basic knowledge; next what is the proper way of monitoring the use of resources in order to maintain a proper national standard of performance; then there is the role of the inspectorate in relation to national standards; and there is the need to improve relations between industry and education.

J. Callaghan, 'Towards a national debate', *Education*, 17:148, October 1976, pp. 332–3.

4.3.3 Old Labour and a 'core' curriculum

> Shirley Williams, as minister of education, responded to Callaghan's allusion to a core curriculum and inspection in a consultative document. Its hesitancy reflected not just the minister's personality but also a lack of certainty within education as a whole following the ending of expansion. League tables of schools and standard assessments tests were, however, firmly ruled out.

2.14 ... Unease about the curriculum is expressed in many forms but the principal points of concern appear to be:

(i) the curriculum has become overcrowded; the timetable is overloaded and the essentials are at risk;

(ii) variations in the approach to the curriculum in different schools can penalise a child simply because he has moved from one area to another;

(iii) even if the child does not move, variations from school to school may give rise to inequality of opportunities;

(iv) the curriculum in many schools is not sufficiently matched to life in a modern industrial society.

2.15 Not all these comments may be equally valid, but it is clear that the time has come to try to establish generally accepted principles for the composition of the secondary curriculum for all pupils. This does not presuppose uniform answers.... But there is a need to investigate the part which might be played by a 'protected' or 'core' element.... Properly worked out, it can offer reassurances to employers, parents and the teachers themselves, as well as a very real equality of opportunity for the pupils....

And on standards:

3.1 ... the conviction has been expressed that deterioration has occurred....

3.2 Within the general broadening of the curriculum there has been an extension of the range of skills and ideas that have been looked for in children. This may cut both ways. It has been alleged that, in primary schools, improved fluency in writing has been achieved at the expense of accuracy in spelling and punctuation; and that efforts to introduce modern aspects of mathematics and to reduce apprehension in pupils have been accompanied by diminished accuracy in traditional arithmetic.... Some of these problems are essentially transitional; they will disappear as teachers gain more experience in their new schools and with the new methods. Others can be overcome by preparation, in-service training and so on. But what must be recognised is that it is not sufficient just to maintain present standards; like the nation as a whole the schools have to meet the growing and changing demands of the future.

Assessment
3.3 Growing recognition of the need for schools to demonstrate their accountability to the society which they serve requires a coherent and soundly based means of assessment....

(i) The national level
3.4 The traditional and long established means for assessing the performance of the educational system as a whole rest with HM Inspectorate....

3.5 Inspection seeks in the first place to answer the question: is the work upon which the pupils are engaged suited to the circumstances in which they are growing up, and is it pitched at a level and conducted in a way that will enable them to make the progress they should? It then seeks to analyse and interpret the findings of the inspection process in order to arrive at wider educational conclusions.... The conclusions reached by HM Inspectorate must be capable of being related nationally to the education system....

(ii) The schools

3.7 Local education authorities need to be able to assess the relative performance of their schools.... In particular, it is an essential facet of their accountability for educational standards that they must be able to identify schools which consistently perform poorly, so that appropriate remedial action can be taken.... There is scope here for the authorities to try to achieve a greater degree of uniformity in their approach to the assessment of schools. But 'league tables' of school performance based on examination or standardised test results in isolation can be seriously misleading because they fail to take account of other important factors such as the wide differences between school catchment areas.

(iii) The pupils as individuals

...

3.11 It has been suggested that individual pupils should at certain ages take external 'tests of basic literacy and numeracy', the implication being that those tests should be of national character and universally applied. The Secretaries of State reject this view. Because of differing abilities and rates of development of children of school age, tests pitched at a certain level could be irrelevant for some and beyond the reach of others. Moreover the temptation for schools to coach for such tests would risk distorting the curriculum and possibly lowering rather than raising average standards.

Education in Schools: A Consultative Document, Cmnd 6869, 1977, pp. 10–18.

4.3.4 Mrs Thatcher's response

Mrs Thatcher's memoir admitted few doubts in the endorsement of a core curriculum and assessment tests.

The starting point for the education reforms outlined in our general election manifesto was a deep dissatisfaction with Britain's standard of education. There had been improvement in the pupil–teacher ratio and real increases in education spending per child. But increases in public spending had not by and large led to higher standards.... Precisely what conditions and qualities made for good schools was a matter for vigorous debate. I had always been an advocate of relatively small schools as against the giant, characterless comprehensives. I also believed that too many teachers were less competent and more ideological than their predecessors. I distrusted the new 'child-centred' teaching techniques, the emphasis on imaginative engagement rather than learning facts, and the modern tendency to blur the lines of discrete subjects and incorporate them in wider, less definable entities like 'humanities'. And I knew from parents, employers and pupils themselves that too many people left school without a basic knowledge of reading, writing and arithmetic....

One option would in theory have been to advance much further along the path of centralisation. In fact, I did come to the conclusion that there had to be some consistency in the curriculum, at least in the core subjects. The state could not just ignore what children learned: they were, after all, its future citizens and we had a duty to them.... Alongside the national curriculum should be a nationally recognised and reliably monitored system of testing at various stages of the child's school career, which would allow parents, teachers, local authorities and central government to know what was going right and wrong and take remedial action if necessary.

M. Thatcher, *The Downing Street Years*, London, 1993, pp. 590–1.

4.3.5 Attacking the national curriculum

Kenneth Baker's call for a debate provoked an angry response from many educationalists. The chief education officer for Oxfordshire, Tim Brighouse, wrote an article in the *Times Educational Supplement* (24 April 1988) entitled 'A dangerous dash to totalitarianism' in which he likened the initiative to those introduced by Napoleon and Hitler. The educational journal *Forum* organised a well-attended conference in March 1988, at which Michael Armstrong (representing primary schools) delivered this broadside.

The national curriculum which this government now seeks to impose on maintained schools depends upon three great fallacies. The first of these is the fallacy of the SUBJECT....

The Government's list, as it stands, is more or less arbitrary. Why, for example, should science be closer to the heart of the primary school curriculum than art – except on the most crassly utilitarian grounds? Why should the moral sciences – ethics, civics, philosophy – be less fundamental than the physical sciences – unless it be that the latter might appear to be less politically sensitive? Why should history and geography be preferred to Social Studies – other than for reasons of political prejudice? Or art and music to drama and dance? Why is there no mention of craft – or is it simply subsumed under technology? The Government may like to argue that there cannot be time for everything and that choices have to be made, but it refrains from defending the particular choices which it HAS made.

But in any case the entire argument about which subjects to make compulsory and which to leave optional misrepresents the way in which individual subjects permeate a curriculum and subserve it.... Most of the really fruitful classroom inquiries, whether on the part of an individual child, a small group of children or an entire class, have a way of moving in and out of subjects, conflating traditions, confusing boundaries, eliminating distinctions and creating new ones. So a study of the life of a frog becomes an exercise in philosophical speculation, scientific observation, literary fantasy and artistic method....

In learning, from nursery to university, the significant insights tend to come to those, teachers and pupils alike, who refuse to be bounded by subjects, who are prepared to move freely between traditions and beyond traditions – from science to philosophy to art to some new field of inquiry – without embarrassment....

The second great fallacy that bedevils the national curriculum is the fallacy of the TEST.

... For the tests ... measure no more than a SHADOW of achievement. Their role is peripheral to assessment. They help us to diagnose particular weaknesses, to locate gaps in knowledge, to detect unevenness in development, or to estimate proficiency at accomplishing a limited number of set tasks. But when the shadow is mistaken for the substance – when nationally prescribed tests are placed at the CENTRE of a school's assessment of its pupils and become the chief criterion of comparison between children, teachers and schools – then children's individual accomplishments will at best be caricatured and at worst altogether denied....

In the end individual achievement is incommensurable. The act of measurement is inevitably an act of reduction and rejection – an act which deprives many children of the value of their own accomplishments, confining knowledge to the interests and purposes of the privileged and the selected.

And this brings me to the third and greatest fallacy of the national curriculum, the fallacy of DELIVERY.

Throughout the consultation document, throughout the Bill itself, knowledge is portrayed as a commodity, delivered by teachers, grocery boys, as it were, of the curriculum, to children. The metaphor of delivery diminishes the status both of teachers and of children at the same time as it lends a spurious authority to the concept of knowledge.... It is to suppose that knowledge is altogether independent of the circumstances of human experience and the social order: independent of social conditions, relationships of power, of the interest and purposes of those by whom or to whom it is to be delivered. It places knowledge above reproach. It makes it mysterious and impenetrable, something to be taken on trust at the valuation of those who are placed in authority....

Whatever slender plausibility this naïve understanding of knowledge may possess depends upon the twin assumptions that neither teachers nor children are capable, or to be trusted with, a critical engagement in subject matter....

Yet critical enterprise is inseparable from learning.... The central responsibility – and the unfulfilled but attainable goal – of popular education is to provoke and sustain the critical enterprise of every child in every school. The present Government has chosen to ignore, to evade, and in the last resort to deny this responsibility. I find it hard to imagine that the children of this country have ever been more grossly betrayed.

Michael Armstrong (Harwell County Primary School), 'Popular education and the national curriculum', *Forum* 30:3, 1988, pp. 74–6.

4.4 THE CONSENSUS OF THE 1990S

4.4.1 The Thatcherite revolution

In 1992 the Conservatives reviewed the impact of a turbulent decade of educational change and identified the national curriculum, stricter inspection and the greater responsiveness of teachers to outside demands as its key achievements.

1.12 ...The National Curriculum provides clear objectives and a basic framework of standards.... Debate is no longer about the principle of a national curriculum but about the detail....

1.13 The Government is firmly wedded to quality ... measured by the school assessment and examination process and – very importantly – judged by a powerful inspectorate.

1.14 Previous local authority inspection arrangements in some areas were shameful – irregular and unsystematic visits followed by unpublished reports with little or no evaluation.... Inspectors in some areas were reported to be spending as little as 3% of their time in the classrooms; too often there was no clear distinction between inspection and advice, so that sometimes inspectors told schools what to do and then checked up to see if they were doing it – rather than the proper task of evaluating whether or not it worked.... From next year, all schools will be subject to regular and rigorous inspection under the watchful eye of the new and powerful Chief Inspector of Schools....

Greater accountability

1.19 The corollary of increased autonomy for schools is greater accountability by them to parents, employers and the wider community. This finds its roots in the Education Act 1980, which took the first step towards requiring the publication of performance data in school prospectuses. That requirement was strengthened in 1986; again in 1988; and was completed in the Education (Schools) Act 1992 which, in line with the Citizen's Charter, made provision for the publication of data about performance and school attendance, as well as four-yearly inspection reports. Annual meetings with parents to consider a report from the governing body and the publication of financial data under the local management of schools are part of the same process. Scrutiny by parents, employers and the local community at large will be intense, interested and increasingly informed, to the benefit of our children.

Choice and Diversity: A New Framework for Our Schools, Cm 2021, 1992, pp. 3–5.

4.4.2 New Labour, same policies

New Labour made education its top welfare priority, but its first major policy statement – with references to basic skills, a national curriculum and strict inspection – largely endorsed the Thatcherite revolution rather than promoting, as claimed, a 'new approach'. A relatively minor switch of resources from assisted places to reduction in class sizes reflected a residual commitment to engineering greater equality of opportunity. A less confrontational approach was promised, although a suspicion of the teaching profession was hardly disguised.

1. ... Our goal is a society in which everyone is well educated and able to learn throughout life. Britain's economic prosperity and social cohesion depend on achieving that goal.

2. Good teachers, using the most effective methods, are the key to higher standards. The Government values teachers and intends to build on the knowledge and skills they have developed over the years....

3. The first task of the education service is to ensure that every child is taught to read, write and add up. But mastery of the basics is only a foundation. Literacy and numeracy matter so much because they open the door to success across all the other school subjects and beyond....

5. There are wider goals of education which are also important. Schools, along with families, have a responsibility to ensure that children and young people learn respect for others and for themselves. They need to appreciate and understand the moral code on which civilised society is based and to appreciate the culture and background of others....

Tackling the problems we face
12. The demands for equality and increased opportunity in the 1950s and 1960s led to the introduction of comprehensive schools. All-in secondary schooling rightly became the normal pattern, but the search for equality of opportunity in some cases became a tendency to uniformity. The idea that all children had the same rights to develop their

abilities led too easily to the doctrine that all had the same ability. The pursuit of excellence was too often equated with elitism.

13. It was right in the 1980s to introduce the National Curriculum – albeit that it was 20 or 30 years too late. It was right to set up more effective management systems; to develop a more effective inspection system; and to provide more systematic information to parents. These changes were necessary and useful. We will keep and develop them. But they were not and are not enough in themselves. We face new challenges at home and from international competitors, such as the Pacific Rim countries. They do not rely on market forces alone in education and neither should we....

Our policy principles

14. We have consistently made clear that there will be unrelenting pressure on schools and teachers for improvement....

15. Our first principle is to ensure that education must be at the heart of government.... A clear sign of this is our pledge that over the lifetime of the Government we will increase the proportion of national income spent on education....

16. Our second principle is that, in deciding our priorities, we shall put in place policies that benefit the many, not just the few. Hence ... the shift of resources as a matter of urgency from the Assisted Places Scheme to the reduction of classes for all 5, 6 and 7 year olds. Our policies will be designed to achieve early success rather than later attempts to recover from failure.

17. ... We know what it takes to make a good school: a good head who understands the importance of clear leadership, committed staff and parents, high expectations of every child and above all good teaching. These characteristics cannot be put in place by altering the school structure or by legislation and financial pressure alone. Effective change ... requires millions of people to change their behaviour. That will require consistent advocacy and persuasion to create a climate in which schools are constantly challenged to compare themselves to other similar schools and adopt proven ways of raising their performance....

19. ... Hence our commitment to zero tolerance of underperformance.... Our policy will be driven by our recognition that children only get one chance. We intend to create an education service in which every school is either excellent, improving or both.

20. Government will lead the drive to raise standards and create

the right framework, but it cannot succeed alone. It must work in partnership with all those who have a part to play[:] ... parents, teachers and governors, local authorities, churches and business. Parents are a child's primary educator and our partnership approach will involve them fully. We want to put the years of division, conflict and short-term thinking behind us.

Excellence in Schools, Cm 3681, 1997, pp. 9–12.

5

Housing

Housing is the 'core' social service least readily associated with the welfare state. It is also the most complex and politically contentious. The three characteristics are closely related. For instance, housing appears to many to be an essentially private matter because most post-war stock has been built by private companies and an increasing proportion has been owned by the occupier – with the assistance of other private agencies, such as banks and building societies. The Conservative Party, in particular, promoted this creation of a 'property-owning democracy' in the belief that it would safeguard individual freedom against an over-powerful state. However, the 'right' to decent housing was the pre-eminent desire of ordinary people as expressed in opinion polls in 1945; and the Labour Party, in its turn, was aware of how private landowners and landlords had in the past often denied this right by exploiting their ownership of scarce building land and rented accommodation. Hence its particular promotion of publicly owned 'council' housing. Such a mix of conflicting political motives and housing tenures inevitably resulted in a complex system of controls and public subsidies.

This complexity is best simplified by distinguishing between four key policy objectives:

• *Numbers*. The initial priority was to end the crude housing short-age inherited from the war. This was achieved in England by the 1960s, in Scotland by 1970 and in Northern Ireland by 1979. New construction was needed thereafter to replace slums and to meet additional needs generated by a mobile population and demographic change (increasing numbers and different family structures). Changing incentives resulted in a revolution in housing tenure. Between 1945 and the mid-1990s, privately rented accommodation fell from 54 to 7 per cent of housing stock, while owner-occupancy rose from 26 to 66 per cent. Council housing rose from 12 per cent in 1945 to

154

32 per cent at its peak in the early 1980s.

- *Quality*. Other than the replacement of slums, the priority here was renovation of older properties (by ensuring 'basic amenities' such as a fixed bath and an indoor lavatory) and improvements to meet rising public expectations.

- *Price*. A key political challenge – as in all European countries – was to ensure that everyone paid a proper ('economic') price for their home, whilst relieving those on low incomes who clearly could not. After the mid-1950s, there was a consequent reduction in universal measures, such as subsidies (to all council housing) and wartime rent controls (affecting over five million properties in the privately rented sector). They were replaced by more targeted assistance such as rent and rates rebates and, increasingly after 1972, benefits from the social security budget. Owner-occupants received a variety of tax breaks – although, perversely, they benefited most those with the more expensive properties.

- *Planning*. This was the most politically contentious policy area. There was broad agreement that, to protect the environment, all building development should be subject to planning permission. Who, however, should benefit from such development? Should it be the private property owner via the free market (as favoured by the Conservatives) or the general public through the nationalisation of development land or a 'betterment' tax on windfall profits (as advocated by Labour)? Less controversial issues, after enabling legislation in the 1940s, were the development of new towns and national parks.

Each of these objectives, as indicated, aroused intense ideological differences; but, once in office, both the Conservative and Labour Parties tended to adopt practical consensual policies (see also pp. 10–11). The forging of consensus between 1945 and 1976, however, did not follow the conventional pattern of welfare expansion.

Until 1955 the emphasis was on construction and, despite Bevan's initial hostility (5.1.2), a mix of public and private housing was accepted. The greatest concentration of council house building occurred, for instance, between 1952 and 1955 under the Conservatives. Once the shortage was deemed to be over, however, the Conservatives immediately sought a return to the market. In 1955 they ended general subsidies for council house building, which meant that fewer such houses were built and those that were had to be let at an 'economic' rent. In 1957 they then passed the Rent Act which started the progressive deregulation of the private rented market, with the declared objective of restoring profitability and thus landlords' ability to maintain high standards (5.2.1–3, 5.4.1). This policy was completed by the 1972 Housing Finance Act, which switched subsidies from property to people to ensure equal treatment for each sector of the housing market (5.2.6–7). In relation to planning, the 1959 Town and Country Planning Act similarly restored a free market in land sales.

Labour vigorously opposed each of these developments but eventually accepted them. Despite its traditional commitment to council housing, it announced in 1965 that any further expansion was 'to meet exceptional needs. The expansion of buildings for owner occupancy on the other hand is normal; it reflects a long-term social advance which should gradually pervade every region' (*The Housing Programme, 1965–1970*, Cmnd 2838, p. 8). In the same document it also accepted the need for economic rents, although after the 1972 Housing Finance Act this led to severe political embarrassment (see 5.4.4). Acceptance was at least tempered by the provision, under the 1965 Rent Act, of greater security of tenure for tenants and safeguards against excessive rent rises (5.2.4). In relation to planning, legislation in 1967 and in 1975 (the Community Land Act) sought to reassert the control over land sales attempted in the 1948 Town and Country Planning Act, but once again it was not vigorously implemented and was thus ineffective.

After 1976, housing policy conformed more closely to the general pattern of welfare reform as public provision was rapidly reduced. Most famously, greater inducements were given to tenants to buy their council houses (5.3.1). By the mid-1990s 1.5 million had exercised their right and thereby reduced council-owned property by one-sixth. Simultaneously, responsibility for the building of new 'social' housing was largely taken from local government and entrusted to non-profit-making housing associations – on the European model. Finally the purchaser–provider divide was enshrined in the 1988 Housing Act, which permitted private landlords and housing associations (after a vote by tenants) to take over the management of any council-run estate. Independent housing action trusts could also renovate run-down estates and then pass them on to any landlord – so long as it was not a local authority. By such means, the power of local government in the postwar housing market was broken, although central government was still left with high, and often unnecessarily high, costs (5.3.2–3). These reforms were accepted by New Labour (5.3.4–5).

156

The following extracts are designed to illustrate these three policy phases, with the battle over rented accommodation being selected as the most telling symbol of the return to market forces in the second phase. It links directly to the final section, illustrating the exceptional social and political tensions generated by housing policy.

5.1 ENDING THE SHORTAGE, 1945–1955

5.1.1 Wartime plans

Housing, because it aroused such political controversy, was the last of the core services to be covered by a reconstruction white paper. The target of 300,000 houses and plans for a public–private mix were significant for the future.

2. In the years 1934–39, the total output of houses exceeded 300,000 a year. In 1939 the number of houses was approximately equal to the number of separate families, and a campaign for slum clearance and the abatement of gross overcrowding was in full swing.... By 1939, the proportion of people still living in unfit or overcrowded houses had been reduced to some 6 per cent; and over 30 per cent of the population were living in new houses which had been built since 1919.

3. This progress was cut short by the war. The number of houses built between 1939 and 1945 has not exceeded 200,000. Meantime about 200,000 houses have been entirely destroyed, and a further 250,000 made uninhabitable by enemy action. In addition, a very much larger number of houses have been damaged but are still occupied in varying degrees of repair. Current repair – the first line of defence in the maintenance of health and comfort in housing – has perforce been neglected and the condition of large numbers of houses has therefore progressively deteriorated.

Objectives
4. The Government's first objective is to afford a separate dwelling for every family which desires to have one. For this purpose it is estimated that some three-quarters of a million dwellings are needed.

5. The second objective is to provide for the rapid completion of the slum clearance and overcrowding programmes which were already in course of execution before the war. To remove houses

already condemned as unfit and to abate overcrowding condemned since 1935, a further half-million houses are needed.

6. The long-term objective of the Government is to secure a progressive improvement in the conditions of housing in respect both of standards of accommodation and of equipment, and to attain this objective by a continuous programme of new building. This continuous programme must include provision year by year for any increase in the number of separate families, the needs which arise out of redistribution of the population, and the replacement of obsolescent houses.

Programme

7. The Government propose to treat the first two years after the end of hostilities in Europe as a period of national emergency when exceptional measures must be taken to meet the housing shortage.... The primary aim of the Government is to produce the largest practicable number of separate dwellings in this emergency period....

14. ... [T]he Government have already announced that the maximum target which they can properly adopt is one of 300,000 permanent houses built or building by the second year after the end of hostilities in Europe.... If more houses can be built they will be built, but the programme will be based on evidence of the building resources likely to be available....

39. The execution of this programme depends on collaboration between private industry and public authority.

Housing, Cmd 6609, 1945, pp. 2–3, 7.

5.1.2 Bevan's vision

As minister of health between 1945 and 1950, Bevan was responsible for housing; and although better housing is arguably the optimum means of preventing ill health, it was relatively overlooked during the creation of the NHS. Bevan's commitment to engineer a more equal society through welfare policy, however, is evident from his determination to extend public control over both building and land purchase. He also wished to 'municipalise' all private rented accommodation.

I want to explain ... the broad outlines of the Government's housing policy. Before the war the housing problems of the middle classes were, roughly speaking, solved. The higher income groups had their houses: the lower income groups had not.... We propose to start to solve, first, the housing difficulties of the lower income groups. In other words we propose to lay the main emphasis of our programme upon building houses to let. That means that we shall ask local authorities to be the main instruments for the housing programme.... It is ... a principle of the first importance that the local authorities must be looked to as the organisation and source for the building of the main bulk of the housing programme....

Each year before the war about 260,000 houses were built for private enterprise alone, for sale, while the local authorities were confined largely to slum clearance schemes. They built about 50,000 houses a year under those schemes.... I would like to ask the House to consider the grave civic damage caused by allowing local authorities to build houses for only the lower income groups living in their colonies. This segregation of the different income groups is a wholly evil thing, from a civilised point of view.... It is a monstrous affliction upon the essential psychological and biological one-ness of the community....

One of the consequences of this segregation was to create an insistence on uniformity.... I am going to encourage the housing authorities in their lay-outs to make provision for building some houses also for the higher income groups at higher rents....

I hope that all age-groups will be found hospitality in their schemes, and that they will not be segregated. I hope that old people will not be asked to live in colonies of their own – after all they do not want to look out of their windows on an endless processions [*sic*] of the funerals of their friends; they also want to look at processions of perambulators....

The main emphasis, in the housing programme, will be on the local authorities. I am fully aware there are certain forms of building organisations that may not be available for the public building programme. The local authorities are, therefore, allowed to license private buildings for sale up to a limit of £1,200 in the provinces, and £1,300 in London.... These licences are for the purpose of supplementing the main housing programme, and not for diverting building labour and materials that would otherwise flow into the public housing programmes....

I should like ... to warn hon. Members against one aspect of this matter. There is a great deal of money available in this country for investing in house-building.... I do not propose ... to let this vast mass of accumulated money on a scarcity market, and to encourage people to acquire mortgages that will be gravestones around their necks....

It is not that we ourselves are against people owning their own houses.... There is no desire on our part to prevent people owning their own houses....

The Leader of the Opposition when he was Prime Minister ... said that this business of housing was going to be treated as a military operation. I entirely agree with him. If you wanted land for an airfield during the war, you did not have protracted negotiations with the landlord. We are going to have no protracted negotiations with the landlord for getting houses.... We are going to ask the House to approve a Bill by which land for all public purposes, including housing, will be acquired by all those agencies which have powers of compulsory purchase.... If it is agreed, as it is by the House, that land is needed for public purposes, there is no logic in those purposes being frustrated or held up because protracted negotiations have to go on with the owners of the land....

We, on this side of the House, have committed ourselves to no figures.... The fact is that if at this moment we attempted to say that, by a certain date, we will be building a certain number of houses that statement would rest upon no firm basis of veracity....

When the materials and labour have been provided to the local authorities, we will provide the local authorities with housing targets....

In conclusion I would say this: I believe that this housing shortage can be solved.

Parliamentary Debates, vol. 414, 17 October 1945, cols 1223–34.

5.1.3 The Conservative vision

A group of Conservative backbenchers (led by future 'One Nation' ministers such as Iain Macleod) attacked Bevan's record and also matched his vision of the 'one-ness of the community'. This extract illustrates the determination of the younger generation of MPs to reconcile the Conservative Party to the welfare state.

We do not condone the bad quality and deplorable appearance of some of the speculative building between the wars, nor the lack of physical planning and the wasteful development of land.... But Mr. Bevan's ranting polemics on the subject would perhaps sound better in the mouth of a Minister of Health who was getting enough houses built....

Although there is no survey which would give the extent of over-crowding and involuntary sharing, the evidence of the local authority waiting lists and of everyone's personal experience shows it to be very great.

These conditions touch on many aspects of our national life: health threatened by overcrowded and insanitary homes; education retarded when children have no room in which to do homework, or arrive tired at school after sleeping in a room with several others; marriages broken up through the strain of sharing a home or making do in cramped and uncomfortable quarters; Borstal institutions, remand homes and approved schools filled by the products of an unhappy home life. A home of the right size and in the right place and at the right rent is everybody's first need. Less would need to be spent on the other social services if housing conditions were drastically improved.

One Nation: A Tory Approach to Social Problems, London, 1950, pp. 29–31.

5.1.4 Macmillan's achievement

In the 1950 and 1951 elections, the Conservatives targeted Labour's 'failed' housing policy and promised to realise the wartime building target of 300,000 houses per year. Macmillan achieved this as early as 1953 and thereby consolidated both his Party's commitment to the welfare state and his own career. His success was a result of putting into practice Bevan's rhetoric about the need for a military operation. 'This is a war job. It must be tackled in the spirit of 1940', he insisted, when extracting extra resources from the Treasury.

The Conservative Party had certainly given hostages to fortune. Whatever the refinements about targets, the country expected 300,000 houses a year. Since the figures were published at monthly intervals, here was a score-board on which the eyes of all critics, friendly and hostile, would be continually riveted. There would be no evasion by indefinite excuses about the economic climate or the difficulties of labour and materials. The relentless figures would tell their own tale.... [B]y the time the election came we were drifting before another economic storm.

This would be the first obstacle; for if the classical methods were to be applied, the Treasury would certainly demand the cutting of imports, a rise in the Bank Rate and a reduction of the so-called 'capital investment programme'.... As a result I was destined during the first months, even years to wage a continual battle with the Treasury for my fair share....

If the financial hurdle could be overcome, or evaded, my next problem lay with the administrative instrument available for the jobs to be done. The Ministry ... was staffed in the main by officials who had dealt with local government affairs, and was, therefore, a department concerned with guidance, advice, supervision. Sometimes even warning and reproof, but never with positive action.... Moreover ... it had no direct powers.... 1,500 or more local housing authorities in England and Wales were responsible for licensing 'private enterprise' housing and for ordering and programming 'council' houses. But there was no urgency or drive; no production organisation, central or local; no progress officers; no machinery for identifying and breaking 'bottlenecks'. The Ministry was in no sense a 'Production Department' – yet somehow or other ... it had to be turned into an active and vibrant machine. I had given it a new name – the Ministry of Housing; I must breathe into it a new spirit.

Next came the vital questions of policy. During the years of the Labour Government, building for sale by private enterprise had been greatly reduced.... The building industry which had been under rigid control during six years of war and six years of socialism, had lost all elasticity.... There was also the need to prevent the old houses from falling into disrepair and ruin. If this question was to be dealt with we must make at least some impact on the question of rents, millions of which were still controlled, some at pre-1914 levels. Closely connected was the scandalous condition of the slums....

It is difficult now to realise the atmosphere of stringency and even defeatism in which we still lived six years after the war. Nor was it possible ... to sweep away at one blow all the hampering regulations.... No house of any kind could be built without license issued by a local authority. No local authority could build council houses or allow private houses to be built, whether for rent or sale, except within the allocation made to it yearly for the minister. The size and cost of such houses were rigidly controlled. At the same time local authorities had been instructed not to issue more than one licence in every ten for private building. This rule had been modified to one in five.... On 19 November 1951 I put forward a plan to raise this to one in two, making at the same time administrative arrangements to continue to control the maximum size and conditions of resale to ensure that the house went to people genuinely in need of a home. Secondly, I proposed to allow the sale of municipal houses subject to appropriate safeguards....

During all these months I had been considering the most intricate and politically dangerous of the problems connected with housing ... the system of rent control. I argued that rent restriction and new housing were closely interlocked. The former could only be dealt with, at any rate politically, in the climate of success of the latter. There were nine million houses occupied at artificially low rents of between 6s and 8s a week as against the economic rent of 30s a week.... This large pool of houses at frozen rents was a deterrent to unsubsidised building and to house-owning.... Rents could equitably be raised on the understanding that no increase should be payable unless the houses were put into a good condition by their owners.

H. Macmillan, *Tides of Fortune,* London, 1969, pp. 374–7, 403–4, 444–5.

5.2 RESTORING THE MARKET, 1955–1978

5.2.1 The 1957 Rent Act

The most controversial initiative to restore the market, once Macmillan was deemed to have ended the housing shortage, was the 1957 Rent Act. In order to achieve more 'economic' rents, it removed rent controls from half a million expensive properties and permitted rent increases elsewhere so long as the proceeds were used on repairs. Here it is defended on the grounds that the majority would benefit whilst only a minority would be immediately 'decontrolled'.

Now the government has had the courage to tackle the injustices of the Rent Acts. It is wrong that many house rents are lower than the rents of weekly instalments on TV sets, and that landlords should be forced to subsidise tenants indiscriminately. It is wrong that old houses should be allowed to decay for want of money to keep them repaired. It is wrong that many dwellings should be half used or empty because of unfair rents. The right policy now that acute housing shortage has been relieved is progressively to remove houses from the Rent Acts as the housing situation improves.

The Rent Bill, therefore, will decontrol the higher valued dwellings ... subject to real and fruitful safeguards to tenants in the transition period. Decontrol will mean less waste and underoccupation and therefore more accommodation for all. Six out of seven tenants will, however, remain controlled, with new rent limits which reflect present day repair costs.

Conservative and Unionist Central Office, *Background Material for Election Addresses*, London, 1957.

5.2.2 Attacking the Conservative record

In its 1959 manifesto the Labour Party expressed its opposition to the Conservatives' market philosophy, playing on fears that lower value flats would be progressively decontrolled (which, because of the resulting denials, did not happen). Nevertheless, continuation of Bevan's commitment to 'municipalise' privately rented accommodation was significantly linked with the right of tenants to buy their refurbished homes and support for owner-occupation.

Labour's policy has two main aims: to help people buy their own homes and to ensure an adequate supply of decent housing to let at a fair rent.

As a first step we shall repeal the Rent Act, restore security of tenure to decontrolled houses, stop further decontrol, and ensure fair rents by giving a right to appeal to rent tribunals.

The return of a Tory Government would mean further rent increases and the decontrol of many more houses. We say this despite the official Tory assurance that there will be no decontrol during the life of the next Parliament – for we remember what happened last time.

During the 1955 Election Mr. Bevan prophesied that rents of controlled houses would be increased if the Conservatives came back into power. Two days later the Conservative Central Office ... said there was no truth in the allegation. In 1957 the Conservative Government introduced the Rent Act....

Council building of rented houses has been slashed under the Tories.... We shall reverse their policy by restoring the subsidy and providing cheaper money for housing purposes. We shall encourage councils to press on with slum clearance.

At the last count there were seven million households in Britain with no bath, and over three million sharing or entirely without a w.c. The Tories have tried to induce private landlords to improve their property by means of public grants, with very small success. Labour's plan is that, with reasonable exceptions, local councils shall take over houses which were rent-controlled before 1 January, 1956, and are still tenanted. They will repair and modernise these houses and let them at fair rents.... Every tenant, however, will have the chance to buy from the Council the house he lives in.

F.W.S. Craig (ed.), *British General Election Manifestos, 1959–1987*, Aldershot, 1990, p. 13.

5.2.3 The Milner Holland Report

The implementation of the 1957 Act eventually resulted in the Rachman scandal (see 5.4.1). The resulting inquiry found that exploitation by private landlords, despite claims by Labour in the 1964 election, was not widespread. It did identify, however, serious policy deficiencies which resulted in part from a lack of constructive political consensus.

We now set out the principal points of importance to which we draw special attention:

1. There is an acute shortage of rented housing in London and many difficulties and hardships arise from it. The number of households whose housing conditions cause hardships is substantial.... The people most affected are those with low incomes who have neither a controlled nor a council tenancy – families with several children, newcomers to London, and a smaller but growing number of elderly

people.

2. This acute shortage and these difficulties and hardships are the product of social and economic trends which will continue for the foreseeable future; and they cannot be eliminated without a radical appraisal of the present policies and procedures.

3. The supply of privately rented accommodation in Greater London has diminished…. This trend will not be halted, still less reversed, unless investors can be assured that, provided their properties are properly maintained and managed, they will be free from the hazards of political uncertainty and able to obtain an economic return.

4. This stability cannot be assured unless tenants have a corresponding assurance that they will be protected from abuses, their houses will be properly maintained and managed and they will … enjoy security of tenure. Any measure which confers this security must carry with it a proper and well-considered measure of rent regulation; rents must be open to periodical review….

5. Nearly 50 years of rent control … have masked the true cost of housing and the cost of maintaining it. Neither a policy of rigid rent restriction, without any mitigation of its adverse effects on the provision and maintenance of rented housing, nor a policy of piecemeal and haphazard decontrol unaccompanied by any provision for security of tenure, have led to any real relief of the stresses of London housing….

7. Whatever arrangements may be made to assist the great majority of landlords who behave responsibly, and at the same time control the activities of the minority of irresponsible landlords, there will remain many thousands of families who are unable to pay an economic rent … or obtain a council tenancy. To meet their needs, a very great addition to the stock of assisted housing will be required; and for this purpose all possible agencies for the provision of rented housing must be used to the full….

8. We have examined the extent of abuses by landlords of their tenants. Although they affect only a small proportion of tenants, we are satisfied that they are general in incidence and too numerous to be dismissed as isolated instances or in any way insignificant. Where they do occur, their nature is such as to constitute a serious evil which should be stamped out….

14. Finally, we think that what … is needed for the remedy of London's ills is a common frame of mind. Housing has for too long been the sport of political prejudice. The need now is for a common

approach to the problem and for a fully considered development of
policy based on an understanding of the whole housing situation and
purged of irrelevant prejudice against landlords, tenants or any other
groups of the population.

Report of the Committee on Housing in Greater London, The Milner
Holland Report, Cmd 2605, 1965, pp. 226–9.

5.2.4 Establishing 'fair' rents

> On return to office, the Labour Party passed the 1965 Rent
> Act, which established a semi-legal framework in which a 'fair'
> compromise could be reached between controlled and fully
> 'economic' rents. This Conservative response to this delay in
> restoring market conditions demonstrated that, despite Milner
> Holland, adversarial politics still flourished.

Conservatives recognise that there were serious localised problems in
areas of acute housing shortage, and this is why, amongst other measures, they set up the Milner Holland Committee.... The Labour Party's
answer to the ... Report is the biased, doctrinaire and largely irrelevant Rent Act, to which the Conservative Opposition put forward
three main objections –

The Act's Coverage. Conservatives pointed out the stupidity of the
Act applying rent regulations to the country as a whole, irrespective of
whether any specific area has a housing shortage or not....

Rateable Value Limits Too High ... bringing under regulation and
control virtually all rented property in the country....

The Definition of 'Fair' Rents. The criteria in the Act for regulating
rents through rent officers and rent assessment are completely unsatisfactory. By largely excluding any consideration of supply and demand
the Act removes the one possible objective economic criterion....

Labour Prejudice and Housing Sense. Above all the Act takes no
account of one of the most important conclusions of the Milner Holland Report, namely, that the private landlord must be encouraged to
play his full part if housing shortages are to be overcome.... In most
European countries, including Sweden, this point is fully recognised as
the Report showed.

Yet *Mr Crossman* admitted in the debate on the ... Report that he had a 'natural prejudice against landlords' and made it clear that he did not intend to give them any support that the Report so clearly thought to be vital.... As *The Times* concluded its leader on the original Bill: – 'Instead of using the Report as a stimulus to more open-minded and more ambitious policies, the Minister picked out from amongst its arguments and conclusions those which suited the accumulated prejudices of his own party, learning little from its impartial analysis or from its highly relevant study of the experiences of other countries'.

Conservative and Unionist Central Office, *The Campaign Guide 1966*, London, 1966, pp. 205–7.

5.2.5 The shift to renovation

> More consensual was the policy shift from building new houses to renovating old ones, as announced in this Labour government white paper. This was motivated, amongst other things, by growing public disquiet at the destruction of historical city centres and the collapse of a new tower block in London (see 5.4.2). Shortage of money, owing to Britain's economic difficulties, was also important. The principal role of local government was significantly identified as facilitating private initiative.

Since the war the first aims of housing policy have been to provide enough houses to overcome the shortage, to keep up with the growing number of households and, since 1955, to replace the worst of the older houses. At the same time house owners and local authorities have been encouraged by subsidies and other means to carry out improvements. But for the most part improvement has been left to individual initiative, and the results have been patchy. Now, as a result of the very large increase in housebuilding in the last few years, it is possible to plan for a shift in emphasis of the housing effort.... The Government intend that within a total public investment in housing at about the level it has now reached, a greater share should go to the improvement of older houses.

III The general policy
6. Bad housing, disrepair, lack of basic necessities like hot water and

baths, are not limited to any one part of the country, or to the big cities or towns, or to houses of particular tenure. True, conditions are worse in the North than elsewhere: and worse in privately let houses than in owner-occupied houses or local authority houses. But in all parts of the country and in all kinds of accommodation there are far too many people living in bad conditions and without the comfort and convenience they ought to have in their homes. The policy behind the legislative changes now put forward is simply that much more should be done year by year to improve and repair houses....

IV Improvement and repair
Powers and procedures
11. The government want local authorities to direct their main efforts in future to the development of whole areas, not just individual houses....

12. Local authorities should have the power to declare General Improvement Areas. The aim in these areas would be to help and persuade owners to improve their houses, and to help them also by improving the environment. Authorities would be able to buy land and buildings and carry out work for this purpose. They would also have power to buy houses for improvement and conversion and to buy any houses which were unfit and which stood in the way of the improvement of the whole area....

15. In suitable cases where an owner needs a loan as well as a grant, but could not afford to repay the principal for a period, or during his occupancy, the Government propose that the local authority should be able to charge interest only, the principal being secured on the property and recovered later on....

29. All these provisions together are intended to give local authorities working with housing associations and with householders, a new opportunity to bring basically sound old houses up to modern standards, and to make many run-down neighbourhoods into pleasant and comfortable places to live in....

Old Houses Into New Homes, Cmd 3602, 1968, pp. 1–7.

5.2.6 The 1972 Housing Finance Act

The 1972 Act revolutionised policy and was believed by the Conservatives finally to realise their postwar economic and social objectives. All tenants had to pay 'economic rents'. This provided local councils with sufficient income (together with central government grants) to repair their housing stock, clear slums and grant rent rebates to *all* those on low income. The Act was justified in the Conservatives' February 1974 manifesto. Its claims for 'fairness' should be qualified by the fact that even 'bigger subsidies' were paid to owner-occupiers through tax relief, which were not withdrawn until the 1990s.

Our Housing Finance Act has, for the first time, brought fairness between one tenant and another by concentrating help with the rent on those areas and those families who most need it. Today, by law, and for the first time, everyone in a rented home – whether council or private, unfurnished or furnished – can get such help if they need it.

This help has to be paid for. This has meant rent increases for the better off tenants who had hitherto often been enjoying bigger subsidies than many poorer families. But with nearly two million tenants already receiving rent rebates and allowances, a large number of families are now paying less rent than before the Act was passed.

F.W.S. Craig (ed.), *British General Election Manifestos, 1959–1987*, Aldershot, 1990, p. 174.

5.2.7 Attacking the 1972 Act

During the Act's passage through Parliament, Anthony Crosland delivered a stinging attack which forecast the administrative chaos and the authoritarian consequences that were characteristic of attempts to 'roll back the state', both in the 1970s and 1980s. He also foresaw the dangers of confrontation, which were realised in Clay Cross (see 5.4.4) and with which he had himself had to deal as secretary of state for the environment after Labour's 1974 electoral victories.

I can state our view of the Bill quite simply: it is the most reactionary and socially divisive measure....

The crux of the Bill lies in Parts V and VI which impose so-called fair rents on 5.5 million local authority dwellings. We have ... in the past ... made our basic objections to this principle – to the drastic effect which it will have on the cost of living, to the spread of means testing to millions more tenants, to the reversion which it implies to one-class welfare housing, and also to the sharp consequent increase in inequality....

Today, I want to discuss the practical implications of this new method of rent fixing for council tenants, and show that they will be both totally muddled ... and highly authoritarian....

It is a muddle because ... local authorities are not and cannot be in a market situation. They have certain social responsibilities which the private landlord does not have. They have to rehouse people from clearance areas and from the waiting lists. One cannot transfer a market concept to a non-market situation....

[Moreover] we find only 200,000 fair rents have been registered in the private sector.... It is on this tiny and incomparable base that we are to build a new rent structure for 5.5 million council house tenants.... The result will be a total muddle. The ensuing rents will be haphazard and capricious and every housing manager and treasurer in the country knows it.

That muddle might be just tolerable if the tenants had any democratic rights in the matter, rights of appeal or of argument, either through their elected representatives or by the proper processes of law. But they have no such rights: the whole process ... is arbitrary and authoritarian....

What is to happen ...? The elected councillors will lose all their traditional powers over rent policy. It is true that they make the provisional assessment of fair rents in conjunction with the rent officers. But then this goes to the rent scrutiny committee, which has the absolute power to alter it in any way it chooses. It is the committee which takes the final decision and neither the councillors nor tenants have any say whatsoever.

The elected local authorities lose to an appointed body their traditional freedom and autonomy, within the limits of national policy, to set rents for their areas and to exercise their local judgement on local needs. Instead we are to have rents by Whitehall direction....

If the councillors should object, as well they might, to being policed in this way and try to do the job for which they are elected, the job of protecting their tenants and mitigating hardship, they find themselves policed in an even more disagreeable way. I very much hope hon. Members have read Clauses 93 to 95. They give unprecedented default powers to the Government, power to discontinue subsidies, to fine councillors and officials up to £400 and eventually to send in a housing commissar ... from Whitehall, to take over the housing functions of the local authority....

I turn to ... certain Clauses ... dealing with rebates and allowances. The need for such an elaborate apparatus stems from the simple fact that we are abandoning one principle – of providing homes at rents that most people can afford to pay – and substituting for it another principle – of setting rents at a level which most people will not be able to afford to pay. In other words, rents will be set at a level where we have to give a proportion of them back to most of our tenants and employ an army of bureaucrats to do so. This is the most stupid imaginable principle on which to operate.

Parliamentary Debates, vol. 826, 15 November 1971, cols 48–53.

5.3 ERODING PUBLIC PROVISION, 1979–1998

5.3.1 The sale of council houses

Within thirteen days of Mrs Thatcher's 1979 electoral victory, new inducements were announced to make effective old commitments to enable council tenants to buy their houses. In this parliamentary exchange Michael Heseltine, as secretary of state for the environment, detailed the political, economic and social advantages to be gained (whilst omitting the obvious political point that owner-occupiers tended to vote Conservative). Peter Shore's reply, for Labour, repeated many of Crosland's objections in 1972 (5.2.7).

[Michael Heseltine]
We intend to provide as far as possible the housing policies that the British people want.... We propose to create a climate in which those who can prosper, choose their own priorities and seek the rewards and satisfactions that relate to themselves, their families and their communities. We shall concentrate the resources of the community increasingly on the members of the community who are not able to help themselves....

I want to talk about tenants in the public sector.... First, I believe that, in a way and on a scale that was quite unpredictable, ownership of property has brought financial gain of immense value to millions of our citizens.... It is my purpose to argue that this dramatic change in property values has opened up a division in the nation between those who own their own homes and those who do not.

The further prices advanced, the further the tenant fell behind, and no tenant fell further behind than the public authority tenant....

My second general point is that this policy also carries great economic advantage. We are a society where one of our greatest natural resources, our working people, is rendered immobile – unable to move from one part of the country to another as a consequence of the rigidity of the bureaucratic control over 5 million homes.

The owner can sell and move. The local authority tenant faces virtually impossible obstacles to movement. Trapped as he is by waiting lists, he is also subjected to a range of restrictions as to improvements, pets, lodgers, decoration and a range of pettifogging details that no freeholder would ever be expected to tolerate. Often maintenance is inadequate and the environment neglected.

We have the distressing phenomenon of millions of our citizens living in an environment from which they would like to escape but cannot, and administered by well-meaning officials who would ... never dream of living on the estates that are their responsibility.

Too many of our people are forced to accept the restrictions of tenancy. We are determined to give them the freedom and opportunities of freeholders. There will be two stages: first, a more liberal consent under which authorities which wish to sell will have greater discretion to do so; secondly, we shall introduce a Bill giving local authority and new town tenants the right to buy their own homes.

[Peter Shore]
This must be the first Gracious Speech at the opening of a Parliament in which a newly elected Government have not seen fit to refer to the primary task of meeting housing need....

Britain can now rightly claim to be among the best housed nations in Europe ... [but] there are still about 2 million families living in seriously unsatisfactory conditions. That problem should and could be eliminated in the next decade.... If this prospect is not to be chucked away, there has to be a substantial programme of house building and house improvement.... Since it is the poorer people who have to bear the brunt of bad housing, provision must include a substantial programme of housing for rent.

All we have in the Gracious Speech is the proposal to give local authority and new town tenants the right to buy the house they occupy....

The argument is not about encouraging owner-occupation but about the Government's proposal for the compulsory selling of local authority rented property....

The Secretary of State must face some basic problems. How does he reconcile the freedom of democratically elected local authorities to determine their housing policies, including housing sales policies, with the compulsory right to buy?...

How can the Government reconcile with the right to purchase the obligation placed on local authorities since the Housing Act 1957 to consider ... the needs of the districts with respect to the provision of further housing accommodation? Where demand and supply for rented accommodation are in balance, the right hon. Gentleman can say that there is no insuperable problem, but how can he argue the case for the right to buy in areas of housing need, particularly the big cities and great conurbations?

In London, 70 per cent of local authority tenants live in flats. The government know that only a handful of flats will be sold, but a considerable number of the houses with gardens will certainly go. Has the Secretary of State never heard of families living in high-rise flats or on older estates whose main hope for the future lies in seeking a transfer to a local authority house with a garden? What prospect will they have now?

Does the Secretary of State not know that 41 per cent of local authority tenants are receiving either rent rebates or supplementary benefits, or that more than 50 per cent of council tenants have as the head of their household someone who is unemployed? Is the right hon. Gentleman seriously suggesting that the right to buy has any meaning at all for those public sector tenants?

Parliamentary Debates, vol. 967, 17 May 1979, cols 408–9, 418–20.

5.3.2 The fiasco of housing benefit

The 'muddle' predicted by Crosland in 1972 arrived with a vengeance with the introduction of a 'simplified' housing benefit in 1984. Here *The Times* analyses the political and administrative factors behind the fiasco.

Anatomy of a bureaucratic bungle

Today dozens of council housing offices across the country will close their doors early, some leaving long queues out in the cold. Housing managers will order phones taken off the hook in an effort to ration staff time for the sake of the desperate cases....

The cause is what the Social Security Advisory Committee in its restrained way called the 'remarkably troubled birth' of a new social benefit which since last April, has been gradually revealed as the biggest administrative fiasco in the history of the welfare state....

The queues are of claimants, poor, not so poor, in work, unemployed, deserving or undeserving, who qualify for state assistance towards housing costs. Some have been left for weeks, a number for months, without money for rent and rates. Some have been evicted as a result. Others have paid rent out of money intended for food, gas or electricity. Many have run up hundreds of pounds of rent arrears despite never having been in debt before.

All are victims of a would-be reform, Housing Benefit. Here was a bid by the Thatcher Government to make the system fairer, easier for beneficiaries to understand, and an end to what the Government's own advisers labelled 'fragmentation of responsibilities between the Department of Health and Social Security [DHSS], the Department of the Environment [DOE] and local authorities'.

Councils are victims, too. They were sold the reform on the grounds it would cut their rent arrears, but they have seen them rocket.... Some housing associations, although favoured by the Government, are in deep trouble. Private landlords' income is in disarray....

The sorry tale of Housing Benefit's introduction is not a poverty lobby sob story. It is one of a government desperate to cut Civil Service manpower; a battle between two departments, Social Services and Environment, with the umpire, the Treasury, uninterested in details as long as the bottom line showed only zeroes....

Housing Benefit is a case study in the sheer scale of modern social assistance, paid to 60 per cent of Glasgow's council tenants and to 30,000 people even in affluent Croydon. The story also illuminates political courage. Ministers were warned, in 1978–81, that a streamlined working scheme would cost money; they were prepared neither to find the extra money nor take the political opprobrium of imposing appreciable benefit loss on some people in order to make the scheme simpler.

Housing benefit was a bright idea in the mid-1970s. The spark came from Professor David Donnison, appointed by Barbara Castle in 1975 to chair the Supplementary Benefits Commission. Donnison was unusual in the world of social administration: he knew about housing. Reform of the overlapping and confused housing assistance scheme was high on his list and, despite the reluctance of the Callaghan government to think radically about anything, survived until 1979. It was seized on by the incoming Conservative government.

Housing assistance was a mess because two schemes ran side by side. The first was from the DHSS which paid money for rent and rates to its clients on Supplementary Benefit, which they in turn paid to their landlords, whether private or council. The second ... consisting of a completely separate system of rent-and-rates subsidy under the aegis of the DOE, run by councils. It had been introduced in the 1972 Housing Finance Act to protect pensioners and others on low incomes when council rents were pushed up and private sector rents made 'fair'.

The dual schemes got in each other's way. Families in exactly the same circumstances could end up getting quite different amounts of housing aid....

Donnison ... had envisaged a unification of all state assistance for housing, including DHSS payments to poor people who were owner occupiers. He thought some of the money spent on tax relief for mortgages could be channelled into aligning all benefits. No government, certainly [not] Mrs Thatcher's or Mr Callaghan's, has dared tackle tax relief on mortgages, and that idea was dropped.

What was left was called Unified Housing Benefit. All payments should be the responsibility of a single office, which Donnison and the DHSS thought should be the town hall.... A key attraction, when the Conservatives took office in May 1979, was that the scheme shed civil service jobs....

Donnison had consistently warned that the scheme 'could not be introduced in a politically acceptable way without some increase in public expenditure'. His reason was that Supplementary Benefit and rent rebates were calculated on different tests of income and means: aligning them meant someone would lose. To have avoided some of the complexities that were produced would have cost an extra £50 million to £100 million on top of the £3.2 billion that housing benefit was expected to cost in its first year.

From its earliest days the planning of the scheme was bedevilled by rivalry between the DHSS and the DOE....

A result of the confusion was that the DOE's acknowledged expertise in rent and rate rebates remained locked up in the department....

The gaps showed. Led by minister Hugh Rossi, DHSS planners chose the easy legislative course: an 'enabling bill', the details to be filled in later by a myriad regulations. Between August 1982 and April 1983 no fewer than nine sets of regulations were issued....

Despite protests from councils, now realizing the enormity of their inheritance, the scheme started life in November, 1982....

The problems under an impossibly tight timetable began....

Payments to claimants started to be missed: housing offices were besieged and in more than one case police had to be called to quell disturbances....

It has become clear that what was meant to be a 'unified' Housing Benefit is no such thing. The two old schemes are still effectively running in parallel with their two sets of means test....

To try to align the old rent rebates with the DHSS scale, the reformers had changed the tapering scale at which assistance was provided at various levels of income. In principle, the Government said, more would gain than lose. In practice the losers included many pensioners, notably with works or occupational pensions, presenting the spectacle of a Conservative government penalizing people for a lifetime of prudence and thrift....

The Times, 21 January 1984.

5.3.3 The 1988 Housing Act

The 1988 Act instituted the purchaser–provider divide in housing policy. In her memoirs, Mrs Thatcher placed the reform in its historical context.

By the mid-1980s everything in housing pointed to the need to roll back the existing activities of government. Although the country's housing stock needed refurbishment and adaptation, there was no pressing need now – as arguably there had been after the war – for massive new house building by the state. Furthermore, rising incomes and capital ownership were placing more and more people in a position to buy their homes with a mortgage.

State intervention to control rents and give tenants security of tenure in the private rented sector had been disastrous in reducing the supply of rented properties. The state in the form of local authorities had frequently proved an insensitive, incompetent and corrupt landlord.... Moreover, new forms of housing had emerged. Housing Associations and the Housing Corporation which financed them ... offered alternative ways of providing 'social housing' without the state as landlord. Similarly, tenant involvement in the form of co-operatives and the different kinds of trust being pioneered in the United States offered new ways of pulling the state out of housing management. I believed that the state must continue to provide mortgage tax relief in order to encourage home ownership, which was socially desirable. (Far better and cheaper to help people to help themselves than to provide housing for them.) The state also had to provide assistance for poorer people with housing costs through housing benefit. But as regards the traditional post-war role of government in housing – that is building, ownership, management and regulation – the state should be withdrawn from these areas just as far and as fast as possible.

This was the philosophical starting point for the housing reforms on which Nick Ridley was working from the autumn of 1986.... The beauty of the package which Nick devised was that it combined a judicious mix of central government intervention, local authority financial discipline, deregulation and wider choice for tenants....

Central government would play a role through Housing Action Trusts (HATs) in redeveloping badly run down council estates and passing them on to other forms of ownership and management – including home ownership, ownership by housing associations and transfer to a private landlord – with no loss of tenant rights. Second, the new 'ring-fenced' framework for local authority housing accounts would force councils to raise rents to levels which provided money for repairs. It would also increase the pressure on councils for the disposal of part or all of their housing stock to housing associations, other landlords or indeed home ownership. Third, deregulation of new lets

– through development of shorthold and assured tenancies – should at least arrest the decline of the private rented sector.... Finally, opening up the possibility of council tenants changing their landlords, or groups of tenants running their estates through co-operatives under our 'tenants' choice' proposals, could reduce the role of local authority landlords still further.

The most difficult part of the package seemed likely to be the higher council rents, which would also mean higher state spending on housing benefit. More people on housing benefit means more welfare dependency; on the other hand, it seemed better to provide help with housing costs through benefit than through subsidising the rents of local authority tenants indiscriminately. Moreover, the higher rents paid by those not on benefit would provide an added incentive for them to buy their homes and escape from the net altogether.

M. Thatcher, *The Downing Street Years*, London, 1993, pp. 599–601.

5.3.4 New Labour, same principles

It took New Labour thirteen months to announce its housing policy. Then in June 1998 the minister of housing, Hilary Armstrong, sought to stress the novelty of policy whilst actually endorsing key Thatcherite principles such as reliance on the market and empowerment of tenants. The creation of a Housing Inspectorate, which could recommend the take-over of 'failing' councils, was simultaneously announced. This would have concerned the Clay Cross councillors (see 5.4.4) as much as abstention from ideological commitment would have concerned Bevan.

Let no-one say we've changed nothing. Let no-one say we're carrying on where the Tories left off. Yes, we have had policy reviews and spending reviews to get things right but we've spent a year beginning to change what the Tories got most wrong....

If the housing market worked perfectly there would be no need or rationale for government intervention but the free market cannot accommodate the needs and aspirations of all. Governments must intervene – but that intervention must be limited and strategic, empowering and enabling, not centralising and controlling.... [New

Labour] will exercise no preference between public or private sectors.... I have no ideological objection to, or ideological obsession
with, the transfer of local authority housing. If it works, and it is what
tenants want, transfer may be an appropriate option. What matters is
what works....

Restore choice and power, self-reliance and personal responsibility
to the social housing tenant. We will give tenants in council and housing association properties a direct say, a direct stake, in the running of
their homes.

M. Powell (ed.), *New Labour, New Welfare State?*, Bristol, 1999, pp. 134–8.

5.3.5 Implementing the purchaser–provider divide

> Scotland's housing stock, for political and social reasons, had
> always been radically different from England's: at its peak 56
> per cent was publicly owned and in some areas of Glasgow the
> figure was 99 per cent. The efficiency with which it was man-
> aged did not justify Bevan's faith in the municipalisation and
> by the 1990s its condition was deplorable, as this extract
> reveals. Two years after the advent of New Labour, Thatcherite
> reforms were duly contemplated. This was not the first time
> that Scotland, even before devolution, set precedents in welfare
> policy which England later followed.

Her flat is damp. It has no central heating. Pipes are 'constantly' leak-
ing. Now her one-year-old son has asthma. Charlotte can rattle off a
long list of other complaints about high-rise living on the edge of
Glasgow city centre. But like many tenants battered by bureaucracy's
apparent inability to tackle basic repairs, she has given up hope....
'Everything is bad, really bad.... I hope to get out soon – to England'.

Across what passes for a square in the St. George's Cross district,
littered with rubble and broken glass ... Gordon Dodd is walking his
six-year-old son home in the late evening. While his low-rise flat
nearby is in slightly better repair – 'although heating would be nice' –
he is under no illusion about the scale of the problem facing Britain's
biggest council landlord. 'To be honest, half the houses in Glasgow
need to be bulldozed and rebuilt....'

A mile away ... the man charged with sorting out a housing crisis would not disagree. 'The stock is in a hellish condition and everyone realises it is not fit for the 21st century, for the dignity of people who want to stay in their own homes,' admits Bob Allan, chief executive of the embryonic Glasgow Housing Association....

After years of defensiveness, no one in authority disputes that the city's 94,000 council flats and houses are amongst the worst in Britain. Only a quarter reach acceptable standards, while a further quarter are seen as 'saveable'....

Saddled with debts approaching £1bn and facing a repairs backlog of £1.2bn for stock deteriorating by the day, Glasgow city council has thrown ideology to the wind. Memories of that old political cliché, Red Clydeside, may linger in old hearts ... but now the Labour pragmatists running the city chambers have decided to get rid of that monument to municipal socialism – council housing. In a move certain to set the pace for big English cities – notably Birmingham – it is preparing to hand over its entire stock to Allan's housing association next year, provided tenants vote 'yes' in a city wide ballot.

The move has become a *cause célèbre* for the Scottish executive and the young minister for communities, Wendy Alexander.... 'We have the opportunity to create a new, positive spirit in many communities,' Alexander has said.... 'There is a genuine desire for constructive change. Tenants will lead the way throughout the entire process ... this will be for the people of Glasgow, by the people of Glasgow.'

Peter Hetherington, 'Out of stock', *Guardian*, 6 September 2000.

5.4 CAUSES CÉLÈBRES

5.4.1 The Rachman scandal

Perec Rachman was a Polish immigrant who owned some 150 properties in London by the late 1950s and exploited a clause in the 1957 Rent Act which allowed rented properties to be decontrolled once the sitting tenants left. He devised means of encouraging them to leave, such as the removal of roofs and the transformation of basements into all-night clubs. After his death in 1962 his name became associated with the Profumo sex scandal, and poor housing conditions were effectively linked to political corruption by Labour in the 1964 election. The Milner Holland Report (5.2.3) concluded that Rachman was atypical but the poor condition of rented property in London is graphically described in this contemporary newspaper extract.

Terrified tenants live among the rats
Landlords listed for ministry

The Ministry of Housing has been sent the names of 15 persons who, it is claimed, have been making large sums of money out of the misery and helplessness of the homeless. These names include landlords of large blocks of decaying flats and houses, mainly in the East End of London, at least one estate agent and two notorious brothel owners who operate closely with some of the landlords.

Following in the footsteps of the late Peter Rachman, these men have been growing rich at the expense of those least able to help themselves, mainly working class families with small children....

Girl near tears

A tour this week of some of these premises in Stepney showed clearly the squalor and misery out of which a few men are growing rich. A young girl, near to tears, showed the pitifully small room in which she and her husband had to live. There was no water, except for a cold tap in the backyard, down three flights of dark rickety stairs. The one lavatory, for the 11 people living in this building, was too filthy to use. Cooking facilities had to be shared.

The house was rat-infested and the walls so ridden with bugs and beetles that the girl was afraid to replace the ancient wallpaper which helped, to some extent, to keep them from crawling into the room.

Suicide attempt

A few broken bits of furniture were provided by the landlord. For this he charged £3 a week. The rates on this building were £46 15s 4d a year and the landlord was receiving £19 a week in rent from the tenants, who also paid for their gas and electricity. It was obvious that nothing had been spent on decorations for many years.

Her husband had tried to commit suicide, the girl said. They would have liked children but in these surroundings 'they would only turn into pimps or prostitutes'.

Her marriage had already broken up once and, in a pitiful attempt to save it, she had bought a tank of tropical fish for which the landlord made her pay another 5s a week....

There are stories like this all over Stepney. Another family of six, living in a dingy basement flat of three rooms, the father and mother sharing their bed with two of their children, pay £3 10s a week. A few years ago they had the courage to appeal to a rent tribunal, which judged the flat to be worth 14s a week. At this they were given notice by their landlord and only after intercessions by their local councillor was it agreed that they could stay – under a new agreement by which they paid the original high rent.

Again there was no hot water, garbage from all the flats above rotted outside their window and there were continual floods after heavy rains....

One family said they felt as though they were completely without any rights. They had to conform completely to the landlord's wishes, they could ask for nothing, they did not dare complain. They lived in a state of terror because they could be kicked into the street at any time. One man who had fallen behind with his rent had been thrown out and his belongings sold by the landlord.

Coal shed homes

Many of the landlords are of Maltese, Indian or Pakistani extraction. They are no more charitable to their own people than to white families and in one seven-roomed house there were – until the health authority recently stepped in – 40 Indians, sleeping in shifts and paying £1 a week rent. The name of one landlord is always coupled with a curse almost anywhere in Stepney. In one of the squares largely owned or leased by this man ... even the coal sheds in the back yards have been turned into temporary living accommodation....

Throughout this area there are three classes of rent, for the controlled, the decontrolled and the coloured. It is hoped that new legislation may be introduced to enable these situations to be brought to light by someone other than the tenant so avoiding the possibility of victimization.

The Times, 28 August 1963.

5.4.2 Ronan Point

Between 1955 and 1968 the efficient 'modern' way to eradicate slums was to replace them with tower blocks. They transformed the skyline of all major British cities. The policy abruptly ended in part because of an explosion in a recently completed block in London and its partial collapse. This extract describes not only the tragedy but also the conspiracy of political, commercial and professional interests which led to the building, to low standards, of a type of flat tenants least appreciated. Slum clearance schemes at this time provided one of the few instances of systematic corruption within the British welfare state.

Terrified families, many barefoot and in their night clothes, poured out of their homes in the block of flats in Butchers Road, Custom House E, after the dawn explosion shook out an entire corner of the building. In addition to the three dead and one missing, 11 of the residents were injured.

At the scene, in the heart of London's dockland, it was said that the signs pointed to a gas explosion. It had occurred on the eighteenth floor, punched out the walls, ripped through the four flats above, and sent floors below crashing to the ground.

The whole corner section, containing mainly living rooms, fell just before 6 a.m. Dressing tables, electric fires, chairs and sofas were left perched on the remains of some of the floors. The bodies of two men and a woman were brought out during the morning from the rubble.

The block, Ronan Point, was one of four in a £2,100,000 slum clearance contract awarded by Newnham Council to Taylor Woodrow-Anglian. It had been occupied for less than two months. Eighty families had so far moved into the 110 flats....

The building is similar to those in the Maurice Walk area for which Taylor Woodrow won for the G.L.C. a Civic Trust award....

From her hospital bed where she is recovering from burns to face and arms, Miss Ivy Hodge ... spoke last night about the explosion which is thought to have originated in her flat on the eighteenth floor.

She said she had got up and remembered filling a kettle to make tea. 'Then I found myself on the floor'. She did not recollect turning on the gas or trying to light it....

Dearer and fewer flats the best safeguard

Britain's industrialised building manufacturers ... reacted yesterday with shock and incomprehension....

Industrialised buildings are seen by many as the solution to Britain's housing problem. We must build up, and we must build cheaply, successive governments have told planners. Mass production makes system-building cheap, and the standardisation possible in a tall, symmetrical structure makes it readily applicable to these....

In a competitive business, builders build what they are asked to; it is not for them to double and strengthen the already stringent safety factors insisted upon by their clients, who are likely to be local authorities where industrialised building is concerned. If the builder does make extra sure he pays for the privilege himself or else risks losing the contract....

Mr. Sydney Lenssen, editor of *Construction News,* said the general reaction in the industry had been that it would be unrealistic to abandon the present method of system building....

Mr. Lenssen described the damaged building as a series of boxes one on top of another. 'When one goes, they all go. It was a domino collapse.' But the same thing would happen in a traditional building, he added. The only way to overcome it would be to have lateral supports taking the weight for every, or every other, floor. Then if one flat exploded you would lose that, but nothing below, 'but the cost would be tremendous'.

It would also take much longer, and speed of construction is becoming a commercial and political must. The damaged flats were built at the rate of about one floor a week, the whole building taking no more than 18 months to construct.

Mr. Patrick Davies, Newnham housing manager, pointed out that the borough had 8,000 on its housing waiting list and another 1,000 a year to be rehoused from slums. Because of this, speedy erection was essential, and with this in mind the use of industrialised blocks was a 'first-class scheme' which provided excellent accommodation quickly....

Londoners who could remember the war recalled that when the bombs fell one of the safest places was the Dorchester Hotel, reputed to have a steel frame and thus be safer in a blast. Amid the rubble and rescue workers yesterday, the gaunt tower looked exactly like a block hit by a high explosive bomb. The same cascading wave effect was visible, with huge concrete slabs torn from their mountings and tossed around like leaves.

Architects confirmed yesterday that in a bombing raid steel frame buildings were safer than other types of building, but they insisted that they were not designing buildings for a third world war, but for a peaceful and highly competitive London....

The Times, 17 May 1968.

5.4.3 The founding of Shelter

Two years earlier in 1966 there was a more propitious event, the founding of Shelter, the pressure group for the homeless. Here its first director describes the various events, planned and unplanned, attending its launch and thereby illustrates the 'spirit of the 1960s' which saw an unexpected revival in voluntarism upon which the Seebohm Report and later governments sought to capitalise (6.1.1 and 6.2.1–4). Shelter's definition of the homeless, again reflecting the idealism of the time, was any family 'nagged by insecurity, or overcrowded so that it lives with constant strain and tension ... or cheated of the essential facilities that others take for granted'.

My report suggested a number of themes for the campaign:

(1) We should convince people that the housing situation was out of control and only an all-out effort from everyone could save hundreds of thousands of families from disaster. We decided to emphasise that Shelter was a 'rescue operation' in a national emergency. 'This is a national emergency, and in an emergency we all unite', our literature said.

(2) We should emphasise the statistics of the housing problem to show that people were not homeless because of their own inadequacy but because of the scarcity of housing....

(3) We should emphasise the Shelter definition of a homeless family, and constantly refer to 'the hidden homeless'.

(4) Recognising that the particular spirit of the Sixties was a desire by people to become involved, we should emphasise involvement in all our publicity. 'Shelter involves you' became a campaign theme, and the slogan on T-shirts and badges....

The name Shelter was chosen. This did not emerge overnight. Lists of possible names were circulated.... The word SHELTER speared on a number [of them].... Some reacted unfavourably, saying that it would be confused with air-raid shelters or tramps (one person helped to collect £26 in the north of England in the belief he was raising money for a new bus shelter) but, once the campaign was launched, everyone seemed to think the word Shelter was a 'natural'.

There were to be three main elements to the launch:

• National newspaper advertising;
• Editorial coverage;

• Direct mail to churches and other bodies most likely to be supportive....

There was, however, one unexpected factor. Every campaign needs a bit of luck.... With Shelter, it was the screening on television a few nights before the launch of Jeremy Sandford's now famous documentary-drama about a homeless family, 'Cathy Come Home'. It is often presumed that the launch of Shelter resulted from Cathy, or was planned to follow the screening of Cathy. This was not so. We had no idea the play was planned. In fact, I did not see it. I was busy in my office that night putting the finishing touches to the print material for the campaign....

In the days after Cathy was screened there was uproar about its revelations about the nature of the housing problem and the way the homeless were dealt with. It had created the ideal atmosphere for the launching of Shelter, for when our press conference took place on December 1 everyone knew exactly what we were talking about. The impact was immediate. The months of pressure and persuasion had worked and the media coverage was enormous.

Des Wilson, *Pressure*, London, 1984, pp. 140–2.

5.4.4 Clay Cross

Just as Shelter symbolised the voluntarism of the 1960s, so Clay Cross epitomised the political attempts in the 1970s to radicalise the welfare state which were to culminate with the 'winter of discontent'. Local councillors in this small Derbyshire mining village refused to introduce 'economic' rents under the 1972 Housing Finance Act, with the dire consequences predicted by Crosland (5.2.7). The key parts of their struggle are recounted here by one of the leading councillors. His anger was focused as much on the Labour Party as the Act because of its ambivalence over whether to support 'social justice' or the rule of law (which included a special party conference in 1974). Councillors were surcharged and debarred from public office but the 1974–79 Labour government retrospectively cancelled the surcharge and made good the losses sustained by the council.

[1] A stern warning from the Department of the Environment was sent to the Clay Cross council shortly before the day on which rents were due to be raised by £1 a week....

[2] An extraordinary audit of the council's books was ordered. The news was broken at a protest rally in Chesterfield, and it brought an angry response. The chairman of the Chesterfield Trades Council said that Clay Cross was the cradle of local socialism, and 'these lads' should not be left isolated.

The staff of Clay Cross council took care to see that they were not. On the day the deputy district auditor arrived for the extraordinary audit, the entire 100-strong work force of the public works department took over an hour to greet him with a rousing chorus of the Red Flag....

This spontaneous gesture by the council staff and residents of the town was followed by a week-long series of protest meetings, by pickets in the town and then by the first big Clay Cross demonstration. It was organised by tenants' associations elsewhere in the country.... An estimated crowd of about 3,000 turned up in this small mining town....

[Next] time it was the District Auditor himself ... who arrived in the town to continue the extraordinary audit.... A brave man Mr Lacey. He announced he would hold the audit in public, and found himself in a packed council chamber, which had been filled out with men, women, babies, prams, and banners long before he arrived. He also found himself, rather incongruously, sitting flanked on both sides by assistants, under the well known Clay Cross Will Not Implement The Act banner, held either side by council supporters....

[3] Mr Skillington's appointment was announced exactly a year after the Housing Finance Act had come into effect, and 18 months after Clay Cross had first served official notice on the Government that a Housing Commissioner should be sent to the town if the rent was to be collected....

He attempted on his first visit to the town to keep his cool, but he was eventually obliged to beat a tactical retreat. He had been advised ... to visit the town in secret. No, said Mr Skillington, he would go in the front door. He arrived in a chauffeur-driven car to find the council doors pasted with scarlet notices declaring: 'No Increases Here' and to be greeted as 'scab labour'....

Once inside he was told he would not be given a desk, or a chair by the council. Well then, he said, it looked as though he would have to stand. They would not give him a pencil either, but he had one of them with him and used it to write a letter to the councillors who had not responded to an invitation to meet him. 'I am sorry you have been unable to meet me today ...'

The Housing Commissioner's rent increase of £1 a week was due to be collected in the first weeks of the new year. The council redeployed its rent collectors to office duties. Mr Skillington recruited his own rent collectors. The council ordered its staff back on the streets, but instructed them only to collect the old rent.... Mr Skillington gave in.

D. Skinner and J. Langdon, *The Story of Clay Cross*, Nottingham, 1974, pp. 49–76.

5.4.5 The homeless

One major initiative by New Labour on taking office was the appointment of a Social Exclusion Unit to identify a coherent ('joined-up') strategy to tackle the complex mix of factors causing social inequality. It focused first on what was seen to be a principal example of the 'evils' of Thatcherism: not 'homeless' families as earlier defined by Shelter but literally homeless individuals frequently to be found begging on the streets. This report identified who was at risk, but a humane determination to resolve the problem was marred by a typically authoritarian commitment 'to deliver clean streets'.

Foreword by the Prime Minister

The sight of a rough sleeper bedding down for the night in a shop doorway or on a park bench is one of the most potent symbols of social exclusion in Britain today. It is a source of shame for all of us that there are still about 2,000 people out on the streets around England every night, and 10,000 sleep rough over the course of a year.

There are good reasons for aiming to end rough sleeping. It is bad for those who do it, as they are intensely vulnerable to crime, drugs and alcohol, and at high risk of serious illness, and premature death. And rough sleeping is bad for the rest of society. The presence of some rough sleepers on the streets will attract others – often young and vulnerable – to join them. Many people feel intimidated by rough sleepers, beggars and street drinkers, and rough sleeping can blight areas and damage business and tourism....

Chapter 1: Who sleeps rough?
...
1.6 The information we have tells us that:
- there are very few rough sleepers aged under 18;
- around 25 per cent are between 18 and 25;
- six per cent are over 60; and
- around 90 per cent are male....

1.9 The single most common reason given for the first episode of rough sleeping is relationship breakdown, either with parents or partner:
- research by Centrepoint with homeless young people across the country found that 86 per cent had been forced to leave home rather than choosing to....

1.10 Older homeless people also identify family crisis as key with the main factor being widowhood and marital breakdown, as well as eviction, redundancy and mental illness....

1.11 A disproportionate number of rough sleepers have experience of some kind of institutional life.

1.12 Between a quarter and a third of rough sleepers have been looked after by local authorities as children....

1.13 Unlike other young people leaving home, many care leavers lack any sort of on-going parental support which can act as a back up when a first attempt at independent living goes wrong....

1.14 Around half of rough sleepers have been in prison or a remand centre.... Those who have been in prison typically experience serious problems obtaining both housing and jobs, frequently exacerbated by the problems of relationship breakdown, drugs etc....

1.16 Repeated studies have found that between a quarter and one fifth of rough sleepers have been in the services....

1.17 Some 30–50 per cent of rough sleepers suffer from mental health problems. The great majority (88 per cent) of those with mental health problems became ill before they became homeless....

1.18 Research does not support the widespread belief that the closure of long-term psychiatric hospitals has resulted in former patients sleeping rough....

1.19 As many as 50 per cent of rough sleepers have a serious alcohol problem and some 20 per cent misuse drugs....

1.20 Rough sleepers are disproportionately likely to have missed school....

1.21 Generally, single people will only get assistance under the homelessness legislation if they are unintentionally homeless and in priority need....

1.22 Researchers ... agree that a number of changes in social security policy ... in the late 1980s were closely associated with a squeeze on the ability of single people on low incomes to gain access to suitable housing....

Rough Sleeping Report by the Social Exclusion Unit, Cm 4008, July 1998, pp. 1, 4–6, 16.

6

The personal social services

The 'personal social services' was a term coined in the 1960s to describe, and to create a common identity for, a wide range of services provided for an equally wide range of people whose exceptional needs were not fully met by other core services. Amongst those helped were neglected and abused children; the 'frail' elderly; the physically and mentally handicapped; the mentally ill; those on probation; and those described even by a sympathetic report as 'the flotsam and jetsam of society' (6.1.1) or, more disparagingly, 'problem families' and the 'underclass'. The term was the invention of the Seebohm Committee on Local Authority and Allied Personal Services, which reported in 1968 at the peak of the expansionary phase in state welfare. Indeed the Committee could be said to have epitomised the optimism and ambitions of that phase (6.1.1, 6.2.2). The full implementation of its recommendations, however, occurred after the economic crisis of the mid-1970s and the resulting 'sea change' in both government policy and public opinion. This meant that the services continued to lack adequate resources and public sympathy – a neglect until recently mirrored in academic analysis.

There were four main reasons for this continuing traditional neglect. First, those served by the personal social services had little in common – except a lack of political influence. Consequently there was little pressure on government to prioritise their needs.

Second, pressure could have been exerted by a powerful professional body. This was part of the political thinking behind the Seebohm Committee's recommendation for the unification of the service. However, the social work profession was historically split between jealously guarded specialisms; and attempts to provide 'generic' training and social workers (both to establish the profession's academic credibility and, in the field, to ensure those in need had to deal only with a single case worker) were criticised for failing to provide the necessary skills to identify and resolve problems. There was consequently continuing suspicion that resources targeted on the personal social services would be largely wasted.

Third, the ultimate objective of policy was never agreed. To what extent, for example, should cost limit attempts to ensure the handicapped enjoyed as normal a life as possible (their 'right' to 'full citizenship')? Should those who challenged or rejected society's norms be required, as a condition of help, to accept those norms? In other words, to what extent should taxation be raised to meet the needs of a disadvantaged minority; and should the ultimate objective of social work be individual empowerment or control? Both questions raised fundamental issues concerned with the redistribution of resources (see, for example, 6.2.4) and of power (see 6.3.9), which proved easier to evade than confront.

Finally, there was continuing controversy over how far government should become involved in such essentially private matters as the care of neglected children or 'frail' pensioners. If it intervened to support – or even supplant – traditional carers such as family, friends and voluntary agencies, would it not undermine, rather than strengthen, an active and caring society? Might not bureaucratic and inflexible services supplant adaptable – and cost-effective – ones? In the 1980s it was estimated that the personal social services provided by government had an annual value of £3,800 million, whilst those of organised charity were costed at £400 million and those of informal care at £24,000 million. This continuing mix of care (the 'mixed economy' of welfare) demonstrated the distinctly limited role of government.

Before 1968, the personal social services were largely neglected. To the extent that need was formally recognised, responsibility was left largely to family, friends or organised charities. National Assistance and other core services provided a basic means-tested income and care for many. However, charities remained responsible for meeting the exceptional needs of certain groups, such as the blind and deaf; and local government was forbidden by law to move into new areas such as the prevention of child neglect (which remained the domain of the National Society for the Prevention of Cruelty to Children until 1963) and the provision of services to the homes of the frail, such as meals on wheels (which was the exclusive responsibility of voluntary organisations such as Age Concern until 1962). Trained social workers, employed as much by charities as by government, remained largely convinced that those in poverty were the authors of their own fate ('problem families') and should be either educated or shocked into better ways. There was no need for further state intervention.

With increasing affluence, however, attitudes began to change. As noted in the Introduction, the 1948 Children Act had rejected Poor Law attitudes towards needy children and created specialist bodies in central and local government, which lobbied for increased resources (see also 6.3.3). 'Generic' training courses, pioneered in the 1950s, became increasingly common and the social work profession became more united. Rising public concern about juvenile delinquency led to recognition of the need for a more preventive and comprehensive 'family' service (6.3.4). This led to legislative change in England and more especially Scotland, where the 1968 Social Work Act – in line with progressive thinking in the USA and Sweden – set up children's hearings which replaced concepts of 'guilt' and 'punishment' with 'failure of upbringing' and 'education'. The 1960s also saw a flowering of self-help groups, such as the Disabled Income Group and Shelter, which both provided services for their members and lobbied for change (see 6.2.2–3).

The Seebohm Committee built upon all these positive trends to recommend 'generic' training for all social workers, the creation of a unified social service department in each local authority and, under these departments' direction, constructive co-operation between the statutory and voluntary sectors (6.1.1). These recommendations aroused little political controversy and having been submitted to a Labour government were enacted by the Conservatives in 1970. The percentage of public expenditure devoted to the personal social services quickly doubled (to 3.9 per cent by 1976). Services accordingly improved, with the needs of long-neglected groups being belatedly recognised. The 1970 Chronically Sick and Disabled Persons Act, for example, paved the way for the registration of those in need and the payment of their carers; and targets were set for the first time, in 1971 and 1975 respectively, for the treatment of the mentally handicapped and the mentally ill.

Political and public support for expansion, however, was shallow-rooted and did not survive the fiscal crisis of the mid-1970s. Scandals, starting with the murder of Maria Colwell in 1973, reinforced historic doubts about the effectiveness of social workers employed by the state (6.3.5). Resources from central government were cut in real terms by the Labour government after 1977; and later attempts by local authorities to maintain services led directly to their rate-capping by the Conservative government in 1985. Coincidentally many of those in poverty were blamed once again for their own misfortune ('the underclass') and the importance of the voluntary sector was re-emphasised. Most significantly, for example, the 1981 white paper *Growing Older* redefined community care as care in the community not *by* the community but by family or voluntary agencies (6.2.4). The natural corollary was the 1990 National Health Service and Community Care Act, which transformed social service departments from the direct providers of services to care managers: they were to identify the needs of individuals and open tenders, for which the private and voluntary sectors should compete. In 1993 it was made plain that no more than 15 per cent should be awarded to public sector agencies. Central government thereby retained the responsibility for the regulation and, to a varying extent, the financing of care, but provision was largely the province of family, friends and both voluntary and private agencies.

Throughout the postwar period, the need for the personal social services grew for medical, social and demographic reasons. Medical advance extended both the length and the potential quality of many people's lives. Increasing family breakdown put children at risk and complicated care for the elderly. Demographically the ageing of society and particularly the increase in the numbers of people over 75 raised major questions about care – and above all the fine distinction between health care (free under the NHS) and personal care (outside the NHS to release beds for the acutely ill). The depressing fact, as underlined by New Labour's analysis on entering office (6.1.4) and its later record, is that – despite the potential advances of the early 1970s – little concrete progress was apparently made. This is all the more damning because welfare systems are typically judged by how they treat the most vulnerable, and the personal social services raise in the starkest way questions concerning the respective rights and responsibilities of government and individuals.

The following extracts are divided between the organisation and role of both the statutory and the voluntary sector, and their consequences for one particularly vulnerable group, children. Space precludes the in-depth coverage of other groups.

6.1 THE STATUTORY SECTOR

6.1.1 The Seebohm Report

The Seebohm Committee was originally commissioned in 1965 as a response to mounting concern over juvenile delinquency and the perceived need for a new 'family service'. It mirrored the Beveridge Report by both evading its terms of reference and providing a vision of the future. Indeed it was the last bold affirmation of principle behind the postwar expansion of the welfare state. Its principal recommendation was the creation within each local authority of unified social service departments to care for everyone in need. This extract reflects the Committee's desire to break down barriers between specialisms and between the statutory and voluntary services so that the new departments could effectively serve the whole community.

Chapter VII A social service department
139. We are convinced that if local authorities are to provide an effective family service they must assume wider responsibilities than they have at present for the prevention, treatment and relief of social problems.... Much more ought to be done for example, for the very old and the under fives, for physically and mentally handicapped people in the community, for disturbed adolescents and for the neglected flotsam and jetsam of society.... Much more ought to be done in the fields of prevention, community involvement, the guidance of voluntary workers and in making fuller use of voluntary organisations. We believe that the best way of achieving these ends is by setting up a unified social service department which will include the present children's and welfare services together with some of the social service functions of health, education and housing departments....

The unified approach
141. ... There is a realisation that it is essential to look beyond the immediate symptoms of social distress to the underlying problems. These frequently prove to be complicated and the outcome of a variety of influences. In many cases people who need help cannot be treated effectively unless this is recognised. Their difficulties do not arise in a social vacuum.... The family and the community are seen as the contexts in which problems arise and in which most of them have to be resolved or contained....

142. The present structure of the personal social services ignores the nature of much social distress. Since social need is complex it can rarely be divided so that each part is satisfactorily dealt with by a separate service....

143. Because problems are complicated and interdependent, co-ordination in the work of social services of all kinds is crucial.

Chapter XVI The community

474. ... We see our proposals not simply in terms of organisation but as embodying a wider conception of social service, directed to the well-being of the whole of the community and not only of social casualties, and seeing the community it serves as the basis of its authority, resources and effectiveness. Such a conception spells ... the death-knell of the Poor Law legacy and the socially divisive attitudes and practices which stemmed from it....

Community development

480. There are many benefits to be gained for individuals and families from the sense of belonging to a community and of participating in its various common activities.... Community development ... is seen as a process whereby local groups are assisted to clarify and express their needs and objectives and to take collective action to meet them. It emphasises the involvement of the people themselves in determining and meeting their own needs....

483. A clear responsibility then should be placed upon the social service department for developing conditions favourable to community identity and activity....

The role of volunteers and voluntary organisations

495. Linked with the idea of the importance of the participation of consumers of the social services is the question of the role of the volunteer and of the voluntary organisation....

496. The social service department should play an important part in giving support, both financial and professional, to vigorous, outward-looking voluntary organisations which can demonstrate good standards of service, provide opportunities for appropriate training for their workers both professional and voluntary, and show a flair for innovation....

Chapter XVIII Training

528. If the country is to have effective personal social services, those who staff these services must have the knowledge, attitudes and skill

which will enable them to respond appropriately and sensitively to people in need.... The demands on the staff of the social service department will require a high standard of training for their professional and administrative practice; the increasing importance of teamwork ... emphasises the need for a good deal of interdisciplinary training....

532. At the present time, most social work courses claim to provide a training in those principles and skills that are common to casework.... In practice, however, nearly all students are recruited for some special service, usually child care, medical social work, probation or the local authority health and welfare services.... Separate recruitment, finance and the anticipation of specialised practice are all impediments to a genuinely common training and to the development of those common attitudes, interests and sympathies which will be essential in the new social service department.

New aspects of social work training
555. ... It is only within the last fourteen years that courses have been established in this country in which the principles and methods common to all case-work practice have been taught. This training is called 'generic' because the principles and methods taught belong to the whole 'genus' of social case-work, whether practised for instance in hospital, or with offenders, with mentally disordered people or with children and their families....

558. We consider that there is room for experiment with a wider concept of generic training which aims to equip students to work as appropriate with individuals, groups or communities. The justification for this approach is the belief that the divisions between different methods of social work are as artificial as the difference between various forms of casework and that in his daily work the social worker needs all these methods to enable him to respond appropriately to social problems which involve individual, family, group and community aspects. This newer concept of generic training has obvious attractions as a preparation for work in the social service departments.

Report of the Committee on Local Authority and Allied Personal Services, The Seebohm Report, Cmnd 3703, 1968, pp. 44–5, 147–9, 152–3, 164–6, 171–2.

6.1.2 The failure of community care

In 1982 the Conservative government established the independent Audit Commission to check the accounts, and thereby
the efficiency, of local authorities in England and Wales. In
1986 it turned its attention to the personal social services and
in particular to community care – the policy, inaugurated at the
time of the 1962 Hospital Plan, to discharge people from large
institutions and care for them either in their own homes or in
smaller institutions run by local government, voluntary associations or private companies. After 1981 the emphasis had
been placed increasingly on home or private care (see 6.2.4).
The Commission's report provided an authoritative summary
of the scale of need and the failure of policy effectively to meet
it.

Introduction
1. Nearly everybody at some stage of life is incapacitated to some
degree by illness or accident.... The form of the incapacity may be
physical with impaired mobility, sight or hearing; or it may even
involve a combination.... People with such incapacities are usually
divided into four 'client groups': elderly, mentally handicapped, mentally ill and physically handicapped people. The principal agencies
engaged in caring for these client groups are the National Health Service (NHS), local authorities (housing, personal social services and
education) and independent agencies in the private and the voluntary
sectors....

4. At any one time over a third of a million people from these client
groups are supported through public funds in 'residential care'....
These people are accommodated in a variety of settings, supported by
the health service (if in hospital), local authorities (either in residential
accommodation or in private or voluntary accommodation) or by
Supplementary Benefits (private or voluntary accommodation) as
shown in Table 1.

5. In addition there are probably in excess of a million people
receiving day care or domiciliary care funded through the NHS, social
services departments or social security attendance allowances. Three
quarters of these are elderly and the remainder are split between the
other client groups, as shown in Table 2.

Table 1: Pattern of residential care funded by the public sector, 1984

Number of Clients

	Elderly	Mentally Ill	Mentally Handicapped (inc. Juniors)	Younger Physically Handicapped	Total
Hospital In-Patient	54,100	70,700	40,600	1,400	166,800
Local Authority Staffed Homes	109,100	2,400	12,100	5,200	128,800
– Local Authority Supported	10,600	1,400	5,000	4,100	21,100
– Supplementary Benefit Supported	34,900	1,900	2,500	600	39,900
Totals	208,700	76,400	60,200	11,300	356,600

Table 2: Pattern of community care funded by the public sector, 1984

Number of Clients

	Elderly	Other Priority Groups
Day Hospital: daily attendances	7,000	15,000
LA Day Centre/Adult Training Centre: places	34,000	74,000
Home help: cases/week	453,000	33,000
Meals: recipients/week	218,000	—
Personal Aids: cases/year	302,000	106,000
Attendance Allowances	249,000	177,000

Note: Many people receive combinations of these services but national statistics do not permit any analysis of 'packages of care'.

1. Grounds for concern

19. During 1981 the Government stated in *Care in Action* ... that 'it has been a major policy objective for many years to foster and develop community care for the main client groups – elderly, mentally ill, mentally handicapped and disabled people and children – as well as for special and smaller groups such as alcoholics'. The study has sought evidence of the extent of the change in the balance of care; there should be an increasing proportion of people cared for by domiciliary and day care services in their own homes with a corresponding reduction in institutional services.

20. Unfortunately, however, progress towards community care has been slow. Analysis suggests that:

(a) Progress has been generally slower than would be needed to offset the rundown in NHS provision.

(b) The response across the country has been very uneven: the situation in some areas is much more serious than the national figures would suggest.

(c) Future prospects are unattractive....

Services for mentally handicapped people

22. In 1971, the Government published a White Paper ... which outlined the principle of community care, and provided guidance to local authorities and health authorities....

23. For mentally handicapped people the build-up of community services is actually ahead of the run-down of hospital places.... However, since 1971 concepts of what is possible have moved on, making the targets out-of-date.... Experience gained over the last 20 years has shown that mentally handicapped people are able to live much more independently than was envisaged in 1971. Furthermore some authorities are moving ahead very well. Hence others must be doing little or nothing at all for the average progress to be behind even the 1971 schedule....

Services for mentally ill people

24. In 1975 a White Paper ... was published setting a framework for the development of services for mentally ill people....

28. ... It must be a matter for grave concern that although there are 37,000 fewer mentally ill and mentally handicapped patients today than there were ten years ago, no-one knows what has happened to many of those who have been discharged. Some ... have died; others are likely to be in some form of residential care; the rest should be receiving support in the community. But no one has the necessary information to confirm whether or not this is in fact the case.... It is likely that a significant proportion of those discharged from NHS hospitals will have been before the Courts and will now be imprisoned; others will have become wanderers, left to their own devices with no support from community-based services....

Services for elderly people

30. Services for the elderly face different problems. There are no large hospitals specifically for the elderly.... But there are many long-stay wards in hospitals that could be replaced by community-based services to advantage; and many people in residential homes who do not need to be there....

31. ... While there has been a decrease in reliance on hospital beds

this has been more than offset through the growth in numbers of private residential homes....

32. ... Domiciliary services which allow people to remain in their own homes have been struggling to keep pace with demographic trends....

Unattractive prospects

46. In short, the community care initiative will largely have failed. Instead a new framework based on residential homes will have replaced hospital beds. While this will almost certainly provide an improvement in some areas, it will be unnecessarily expensive; it will be inappropriate for many people; and it will not provide the range of options for improving the quality of life....

47. ... Poor value for money results for the taxpayer because less effective and efficient forms of care persist ... more effective community services are not being adequately developed. Moreover other people may require more care which is currently not available, so that there is a mis-match between services and people.

48. The run-down of old long-stay hospitals and increase in numbers of elderly people both require major initiatives in service development over the next 15 years.

Making a Reality of Community Care: A Report by the Audit Commission, London, 1986, pp. 7–8, 15–19, 27.

6.1.3 The Thatcherite solution

Sir Roy Griffiths, who had inspired the managerial revolution in the NHS (see 3.3.2), was commissioned in 1986 to resolve the chaos identified by the Audit Commission. His solution was that local authorities, working to clear and properly funded government objectives, should take the lead in securing the optimum care for those in need regardless of whether the providers were public, voluntary or private. These proposals were so radical – not least because they appeared to enlarge the role of local government with which the Conservative government had become embattled – that their acceptance was delayed. They were finally incorporated into the 1990 NHS and Community Care Act, once the Cabinet had been persuaded that through oversight of local plans and the work of both the Audit Commission and the new Social Service Inspectorate, power would remain firmly within Whitehall.

9. There is a temptation against the background of the Audit Commission's work to tackle at the outset the matters highlighted, of funding on the one hand and, on the other, the complex network of relationships and responsibilities at the local level between the various authorities, voluntary groups, etc. I chose first to view the position at two extremes, of policy at the centre and consumer satisfaction in the field. At the centre, community care has been talked of for thirty years and in few areas can the gap between political rhetoric and policy on the one hand, or between policy and reality in the field on the other hand have been so great. To talk of policy in matters of care except in the context of available resources and timescales for action owes more to theology than to the purposeful delivery of a caring service. This is not an argument in itself for more resources: the imperative is that policy and resources should come into reasonable relationship, so that we are clear about what community care services are trying to achieve and so that leadership and direction to those providing service can be given. The problem is compounded by the responsibility for inputs to community care at the centre being divided ... – a feeling that community care is a poor relation; everybody's distant relative but nobody's baby.

10. At the other extreme one is immediately struck by differences between the arrangements for provision of medical and non-medical care. If a person is in need of medical care he knows that he has to contact his GP.... It would be too elaborate and indeed inappropriate for a similar system to be set up for non-medical care. What is surprising ... is that such a system involving the assignment of a person in need of support to an individual carer, so as to become his responsibility, is rarely made, even where it would be highly applicable....

11. ... The aim must be to provide structure and resources to support the initiatives, the innovation and the commitment at local level and to allow them to flourish.... To prescribe from the centre will be to shrivel the varied pattern of local activity....

Following his assessment of the problems, Sir Roy Griffiths then outlined what he described as the keystones of his recommendations.

22. At the centre a new focus for community care should be provided with a Minister clearly and publicly identified as responsible for community care. Funding of social services authorities should be by way of specific grant amounting to say 50 per cent of the costs of an approved programme.... Approval of the social services authority's programme is simply designed to ensure that plans are well thought through; that they represent value for money at local level and meet the needs of the locality; that adequate provision is being made for support of the voluntary groups and that they are participating in the preparation and implementation of the plan; that the role of the informal carer is appropriately supported; and finally that the commitment and contribution of the appropriate housing and health authorities have been secured as part of the plan....

24. At local level the role of social services authorities should be reorientated towards ensuring that the needs of individuals within the specified groups are identified, packages of care are devised and services co-ordinated; and where appropriate a specific care manager is assigned.... The onus ... should be on the social services authorities to show that the private sector is being fully stimulated and encouraged and that competitive tenders or other means of testing the market are being taken.

25. This is a key statement. The role of the public sector is essentially to ensure that care is provided. How it is provided is an important, but secondary consideration and local authorities must show that they are getting and providing real value....

27. I believe that the above will provide an acceptable framework. It substitutes for the discredited refuge of imploring collaboration and exhorting action a new requirement that collaboration and action are present normally as a condition for grant. It places responsibility for care clearly within the local community.... It will bolster experiment and innovation....

28. But any recommendations are made with a full appreciation that implementation will bring problems. There is no neat perfect solution waiting to be discovered....

39. ... There is a need to experiment with a whole variety of initiatives – social/health maintenance organisations, insurance/tax incentives, not simply for the individual, but for the individual in the family context.... More immediately there is no reason why, on a controlled basis, social services authorities should not experiment with vouchers or credits for particular levels of community care, allowing individu-

2

als to spend them on particular forms of domiciliary care and to choose between particular suppliers as they wish....

Community Care: Agenda for Action, A Report to the Secretary of State for Social Services by Sir Roy Griffiths, London, 1988, pp. iv–x.

6.1.4 New Labour's solution

New Labour's initial blueprint for the personal social services indicates that little progress was made after 1990. The 'third way' largely endorsed Griffiths's analysis and emphasis on service delivery; and, despite attacking the subsequent Conservative bias towards private care, it remained agnostic on *how* services should be delivered. This extract typically reveals a suspicion of the public sector professionals and a concern for regional equity which, by definition, only centralised policy could ensure.

Introduction
1.3 Social services ... do not just support a small number of 'social casualties'; they are an important part of the fabric of a caring society. It is a concern for everyone that social services should be providing the best possible service.
    1.4 That objective is not being met....

Protection
All too often children and vulnerable adults have been exposed to neglect and abuse by the very people who were supposed to care for them. There have not been effective safeguards, and the ones that did exist were frequently ignored....

Co-ordination
Sometimes various agencies put more effort into arguing with one another than looking after people in need. Frail elderly people can be sent home from hospital, and do not get the support which was promised.... Recent Audit Commission findings have also shown poor co-ordination between housing and social services....

Inflexibility
Although social services help many people to live fuller and more active lives, they sometimes provide what suits the service rather than

what suits the person needing care. Groups with specific needs, such as people from ethnic minorities, can be poorly served.... It can increase dependency and exclusion instead of alleviating them.

Clarity of role
Up to now, neither users, carers, the public, nor social services staff and managers have had a clear idea which services are or should be provided, or what standards can reasonably be expected.... This lack of clarity of objectives and standards means that on the one hand social services cannot easily be held to account, and on the other hand they can get blamed for anything that goes wrong.

Consistency
Social services are a local service, and vary from one part of the country to another.... This is inevitable – an inner city area such as Tower Hamlets will not have the same mix of social services needs as a rural area like Devon.... However, there must be national standards so that we can avoid some people not getting the level of quality of service that Parliament has said should be available everywhere....

Inefficiency
An important finding ... is that there is scope for many authorities to get more for what they spend on social services. The costs of services differ substantially from one authority to another, with often a 30 per cent difference in unit costs for the same service.... By running services more efficiently, some councils could save as much as £10 million, which could be used for better services....

1.7 The proposals in the White Paper look ... to the creation of modern social services. The last Government's devotion to the privatisation of care provision put dogma before users' interests, and threatened a fragmentation of vital services. But it is also true that the near-monopoly local authority provision that used to be a feature of social care led to a 'one size fits all' approach where users were expected to accommodate themselves to the services that existed. Our third way for social care moves the focus away from who provides the care, and places it firmly on the quality of services experienced by, and outcomes achieved for, individuals and their carers and families.

1.8 This third way ... is based on key principles....

(a) care should be provided to people in a way that supports their independence and respects their dignity....

(b) services should meet each individual's specific needs, pulling together social services, health, housing, education or any others needed. And people should have a say in what services they get and how they are delivered.

(c) care services should be organised, accessed, provided and financed in a fair, open and consistent way in every part of the country.

(d) children who ... need to be looked after by local authorities should get a decent start in life, with the same opportunities to make a success of their lives as any child. In particular they should be assured of a decent education.

(e) every person – child or adult – should be safeguarded against abuse, neglect or poor treatment whilst receiving care....

(f) people who receive social services should have an assurance that the staff they deal with are sufficiently trained and skilled for the work they are doing....

(g) and people should be able to have confidence in their local social services, knowing that they work to clear and acceptable standards.

Modernising Social Services, Cm 4169, 1998, pp. 5–9.

6.2 THE VOLUNTARY SECTOR

6.2.1 Defending voluntary provision

The creation of the welfare state was widely expected to diminish voluntary provision. With revenue likely to be cut as a result of higher personal taxation, organised charities would be even less able to deliver adequate services. Many in the labour movement also deeply resented 'the benevolent paternalism' of the past and questioned how new social 'rights' could be delivered by a patchwork of democratically unaccountable agencies. However, a debate in the House of Lords in 1949 on Beveridge's third report, *Voluntary Action,* prompted this famous defence of voluntarism by the Labour spokesman, Lord Pakenham (the later Lord Longford).

The noble Earl has asked me to repudiate the welfare State. I am forced back on the old question: what does one mean by the 'welfare state'? But certainly in the sense that I think the noble Earl has in mind, I am ready to repudiate it – namely, the State in which all welfare is to be provided by the State itself....

May I ... pass ... to a description of the Government's attitude to voluntary action? We consider the voluntary spirit is the very life-blood of democracy. We consider the individual volunteer, the man who is proud to serve the community for nothing, is he whose personal sense of mission inspires and elevates the whole democratic process of official Government effort. We are convinced that voluntary associations have rendered, are rendering, and must be encouraged to continue to render, great and indispensable service to the community....

We have moved far from the era of *laissez faire*. We have entered ... 'the era of the positive State'. But ... I want to make it plain, beyond any shadow of misunderstanding, that, in the view of the government, democracy without voluntary exertion and voluntary idealism loses its soul. All forms of democratic government are dependent on the same spirit, but the Socialist form most of all.... Voluntary social service organisations have a part to play as essential in the future as any they have played in the past.

Parliamentary Debates (Lords), 5, vol. 163, 22 June 1949, cols 119–20.

6.2.2 The Seebohm Report

> Responding to the revival of voluntarism in the 1960s, the Seebohm Report belatedly and with due caution provided a blueprint for co-operation – and constructive tension – between it and the statutory sector.

495. Voluntary organisations pioneered social service reform in the past and we see them playing a major role in developing citizen participation, in revealing new needs and in exposing shortcomings in services. In certain circumstances, voluntary organisations may act as direct agents of local authority in providing particular services, though such arrangements can present problems both to the local authority, which may be led to neglect its own responsibilities and to the voluntary organisation which may be prevented from developing its critical and pioneer role....

496. ... A really productive partnership between the local authority and voluntary organisations in the social service field will require

modifications in the ideas of both. The day when voluntary organisations could act as vehicles for upper and middle class philanthropy appropriate to the social structure of Victorian Britain is now past. Remnants of old practices and attitudes remain in the condescension and social exclusiveness of a few voluntary organisations and in the suspicion and mistrust of some local authorities. On the whole, however, established voluntary organisations are reviewing and assessing critically their policies, and new types of voluntary organisation are emerging, often around self-help groups, and increasingly characterised by the youthfulness of their members and the radical nature of their criticisms of the existing services. The local authority will need to tolerate and use the criticisms made by voluntary organisations and not expect the partnership to be without conflict. A certain level of mutual criticism between local authority and voluntary organisations may be essential if the needs of consumers are to be met more effectively and they are to be protected from the misuse of bureaucratic and professional power in either kind of organisation.

Report of the Committee on Local Authority and Allied Personal Social Services, The Seebohm Report, Cmnd 3703, 1968, pp. 152–3.

6.2.3 The 1978 Wolfenden Report

The privately funded Wolfenden Report drew together the views of the major participants in voluntary provision. It reviewed postwar developments; and, whilst endorsing Seebohm's objective of extending consumer choice, it illustrated how far the crisis of the mid-1970s had challenged the assumptions underlying that Report's recommendations by suggesting a very different balance between the public and voluntary sectors.

Summing up the changes over the past quarter of a century, it seems that today there are more voluntary organisations and that growth has been in the direction of organisations that are: (i) more specialised in their objectives and membership; (ii) based on mutual benefit rather than benevolent paternalism; (iii) concerned to influence the policies and practices of public authorities; and (iv) secular and materialist in outlook rather than inspired by the desire to rescue or evangelise....

Signposts

Earlier ... the hope was expressed that the trends towards increasing the scale of statutory services would be halted, if not reversed. Perhaps this was a covert way of saying 'small is beautiful'. It did not imply reservations about the desirability of social and environmental services or of extensions to them. Rather it was suggesting the need for a change of direction in the way they are provided. Such a change of direction suggests two more specific propositions about the future of voluntary organisations:

(i) There will be an important role for voluntary organisations that act as alternatives to statutory services. Alternatives are not viable in all services: hospitals are too capital-intensive to be replicated simply so as to offer a choice, and social security has to be provided on a uniform basis. But in a number of situations, notably in the residential, domiciliary and day-care fields, voluntary provision does already to some extent and could to greater extent in the future, offer clients or those acting on their behalf, a choice. This ... is ... a justification of voluntary provision where it extends the range of services available; where the voluntary sector possesses advantages by way of specialist knowledge and skills and flexibility; and as an encouragement to voluntary organisations to make well judged entries into those fields where ... a leavening of choice and variety could be introduced.

(ii) A reappraisal of attitudes to the extension of statutory provision is needed, both because of the problems of bureaucracy and scale already discussed and also because we cannot in future be so confident about the availability of resources. Instead of imposing new duties on public authorities whenever additional needs are recognised, a less automatic assumption of statutory responsibility can be envisaged. In some situations it may be more desirable to encourage the voluntary and informal sectors to remain or become major instruments of social service.

The Future of Voluntary Organisations, The Wolfenden Report, Joseph Rowntree Foundation, York, 1978, pp. 185–8.

6.2.4 The re-prioritisation of voluntary provision

The Conservative government's first major statement on policy towards the elderly confirmed the wisdom of the Wolfenden

Committee's assumption that a perceived scarcity of resources would dictate policy. The use of the word 'increasingly' in the final sentence reveals that, whatever the continuing postwar role of voluntarism, there was to be a distinct change in policy. The door was opened for the private as well as the voluntary sector.

Foreword

The Government's overall priority is to reduce and contain inflation.... We cannot indefinitely spend more than we earn. As the economy improves, elderly people will share in that improvement. In the meantime, we have to hold back public spending....

Nevertheless ... the Government has kept to its commitment to protect the real value of State retirement pensions over time. We have the needs of the growing numbers of elderly people – particularly the very old and frail – very much in mind in maintaining a high level of spending in the health and personal social services.

Money may be limited, but there is no lack of human resources. Nor is there a lack of goodwill. An immense contribution is already being made to the support and care of elderly people by families, friends and neighbours, and by a wide range of private, voluntary and religious organisations. We want to encourage these activities....

Chapter 1 Introduction

...

1.6 The cost of national insurance retirement and supplementary pensions for elderly people is at present over £11 billion a year, representing over 17 per cent of all public expenditure in the United Kingdom and over 5 per cent of the country's gross national product....

1.7 Moreover, the cost of pensions represents only a part of the taxpayers' and ratepayers' money which public authorities devote to the care and support of elderly people. Special housing; health care in the community and in hospital; social services and help in the home; and subsidies for fuel and travel are obvious examples. It is estimated that support for and services for elderly people now account for more than one-third of total expenditure on the main social programmes in the United Kingdom....

1.8 Substantial amounts of public expenditure are thus involved. The Government's policy is to contain the growth of public expenditure and of the public sector borrowing requirement, with a view to restoring economic growth. For the time being ... any additional resources devoted to elderly people can only come from other spending areas, or from taxpayers....

Community resources
1.9 Whatever level of public expenditure proves practicable, and however it is distributed, the primary sources of support and care for elderly people are informal and voluntary. These spring from the personal ties of kinship, friendship and neighbourhood. They are irreplaceable. It is the role of public authorities to sustain and, where necessary, develop – but never to displace – such support and care. Care *in* the community must increasingly mean care *by* the community....

Growing Older, Cmnd 8173, 1981, pp. iii, 2–3.

6.3 CHILDREN IN NEED

6.3.1 The Allen letter

Two events propelled vulnerable children to the top of the political agenda at the end of the Second World War. The first was a letter to *The Times* by Lady Allen, which provoked a deluge of similar letters, an all-party motion in the House of Commons and finally the appointment of the Curtis Committee on the Care of Children, which reported in 1946.

Sir, – Thoughtful consideration is being given to many fundamental problems, but in reconstruction plans one section of the community has, so far, been entirely forgotten.

I write of those children who, because of their family misfortune, find themselves under the guardianship of a Government department or one of the many charitable organisations. The public are ... unaware that many thousands of these children are being brought up under repressive conditions that are generations out of date and are unworthy of our traditional care for children. Many who are orphaned, destitute, or neglected still live under the chilly stigma of 'charity'; too often they form groups isolated from the main stream of life and education, and few of them know the comfort and security of individual affection....

212

A public inquiry, with full Government support, is urgently needed to explore this largely uncivilised territory. Its mandate should be to ascertain whether the public and charitable organisations are, in fact, enabling these children to lead full and happy lives and to make recommendations how the community can compensate them for the family life they have lost. In particular, the inquiry should investigate what arrangements can be made ... for the careful consideration of the individual children before they are finally placed with foster-parents or otherwise provided for; how the use of large residential homes can be avoided; how staff can be appropriately trained and ensured adequate salaries and suitable conditions of work, and how central administrative responsibility can best be secured so that standards can be set and can be maintained by adequate inspection.

The social upheaval caused by the war has not only increased this army of unhappy children but presents the opportunity for transforming their conditions....

Yours sincerely
MARJORY ALLEN of HURTWOOD

The Times, 15 July 1944.

6.3.2 The death of Dennis O'Neill

The second event was the death in foster care of a thirteen-year-old boy, here reported in *The Times*.

Underfed boy beaten with stick
Death after blows on chest and back
An inquest was held at Pontesbury, near Shrewsbury, yesterday on the body of DENNIS O'NEILL, aged 13, who had been sent to live at a lonely farm in a wild part of Shropshire, and who, a doctor said, died after being beaten on the back with a stick and struck violent blows on the chest. Dr A. J. Rhodes, pathologist at the Royal Salop Infirmary, Shrewsbury, said that the boy, whose parents live at Commercial Road, Newport, Mon., was under-nourished, thin, and wasted, and was well below normal weight. He had a number of septic ulcers on his feet and his legs were severely chapped. He appeared to have received little or no medical attention....

The jury returned a verdict that death was due to 'acute cardiac failure, following violence applied to the front of the chest and back while in a state of under-nourishment due to neglect'.

At Pontesbury on Saturday REGINALD GOUGH, 31, farmer ... was charged with the manslaughter of the boy....

His wife, ESTHER GOUGH, 29, was charged with having wilfully ill-treated, neglected, and exposed the boy in a manner likely to cause suffering and injury.

It was stated that O'Neill was sent to Bank Farm on the instruction of the Newport Education Committee on January 28 of last year.

The Times, 6 February 1945.

6.3.3 The 1948 Children Act

The recommendations of the Curtis Committee were translated into a Children Act, one of the five pieces of legislation which came into force on the Appointed Day in 1948. Its optimistic objectives, here summarised by officials in the Home Office for the guidance of ministers steering it through the House of Lords in February 1948, provide a chilling checklist for the achievements of the next fifty years. The educational aspirations voiced in para. 22, for example, were still being sought by New Labour in 1997 (see 6.1.4, para. 1.8); and the continuing absence of the guarantee sought in para. 37 for each child to have someone 'vitally interested in his welfare' was exposed by the testimony of children in care to the 1997 Utting inquiry (6.3.9).

1. Three years ago, following correspondence in the press ... public concern was aroused by the publication by Lady Allen Hurtwood of a pamphlet describing the gravely unsatisfactory conditions under which many children in the care of local authorities and voluntary organisations were living.... The need for investigation was grimly underlined by the tragedy of the boy Dennis O'Neill....

2. A committee on the care of children under the chairmanship of Miss Myra Curtis ... was appointed ... in March 1945 ... charged to inquire into the existing methods of providing for children who were deprived of a normal home life....

5. The recommendations ... fell broadly into three sections. The first concerned the centralisation of administration ... at the departmental level to secure comprehensive supervision and control; the second the centralisation of local authority administration to secure concentration of responsibility; the third the methods to be adopted to secure adequate care of the children. On the first issue ... the Government had decided that the central department for England and Wales would be the Home Office....

6. ... The Home Office has for many years had a protective function in regard to children.... It has for long been the responsibility of the Home Office to provide for the welfare and training of children found to be in need of care or protection or to have offended against the law, on the liberal view that it is commonly a matter of chance on which side of the fence the child falls. It is general experience that a child's environment is a primary factor leading to appearance before a court, whether as a case of neglect or delinquency....

7. ... The Bill provides that local authorities should exercise their functions through a Children's committee....

8. ... Clause 40 of the Bill contains a requirement that a Children's Officer should be appointed for the area of each local authority.... It is envisaged that the Children's Officer will often be a woman....

11. The duty proposed on local authorities ... is to receive into their care ... any child in their area under the age of 17 who is an orphan, or is abandoned or lost, or whose parents or guardians are unable by reason of incapacity or any other circumstances to provide for his proper accommodation, maintenance and upbringing.... Clause one of the Bill does not ... empower an authority to take a child away from his parents or guardian against their wishes....

15. ... A main duty placed on the authorities is to further the best interests of a child in their care and to afford him an opportunity for the proper development of his character and abilities....

22. It is intended that children in care should have the same opportunity of higher education and training as children living with their parents.... The intention is that the child in care should have access to all the educational benefits provided by the local authority for children in general, and that the local authority should meet all the child's other requirements in the way the parent of sufficient means would be expected to do....

23. Part IV of the Bill provides for the control of voluntary homes....

26. While there is nothing but praise for the fine work of the best of the voluntary organisations, it is necessary to ensure that a proper standard is maintained everywhere....

After a date to be appointed by the Secretary of State, a voluntary home may not be carried on unless registered by him....

27. Some of the smaller voluntary homes show an excellent perception of children's needs, but are hampered by lack of funds.... Power has accordingly been taken to make grants towards the expenses of voluntary organisations for special purposes connected with the improvement of voluntary homes....

32. The Bill empowers inspectors ... to visit children in care, and to inspect premises provided by local authorities ... as well as voluntary homes. The inspectors will be empowered also to visit children boarded out by local authorities and voluntary organisations, and children who are subject to supervision under the child life protection provisions....

37. ... Only by imaginative personal and individual care can a children's officer and her colleagues and the officers of the voluntary organisations ensure that every child has, in the words of the Curtis Report, 'someone to whom he can turn who is vitally interested in his welfare'.

Public Record Office, MH 102/1528, pp. 1–5, 7–8, 11–13, 15–16.

6.3.4 The 1960 Ingleby Report

The appointment of the Ingleby Committee as early as 1956 revealed concern about the 1948 Act and especially the lack of preventive powers for local government and the specialist treatment of children outside the context of broader social issues. Its call for further consideration of a family service led eventually to the appointment of the Seebohm Committee.

The community services available
19. In the child care service, as in other social services, the problem of preventing neglect of children in their own homes has received much attention in recent years, with growing emphasis on the need to treat the family as a unit and to help parents to remedy the conditions that lead to neglect or to avoidable separation of children from their

parents....

20. Local authorities have no power under the Children Act, 1948, to give help in cash or kind to the families of children in care or of children who may have to be received into care because of their home circumstances; and the extent to which they may properly employ staff in their children's departments ... to prevent the need for children to come into care, is doubtful....

Co-ordination of existing services

38. In dealing with the prevention of neglect in the home, it is ... essential to distinguish the following stages:

   (a) the detection of families at risk;

   (b) the investigation and diagnosis of the particular problem;

   (c) treatment: the provision of facilities and services to meet the families' needs and to reduce the stresses and dangers that they face....

40. Arrangements for the detection of families at risk should extend over the widest possible front. Many different sorts of agency and worker will function in this rôle. Neighbours, teachers, medical practitioners, ministers of religion, health visitors, district nurses, education welfare officers, probation officers, child care officers, housing officers, officers of the National Assistance Board and other social workers may all spot incipient signs of trouble....

43. The second stage – investigation and diagnosis – is the one which many of our witnesses seemed to overlook; they tended to confuse it with detection, and with treatment. We think it is most important that there should be early reference of cases to a unit within the local authority that can give skilled and objective diagnosis – a unit untrammelled by departmental loyalties, and with authority to decide the best means of providing for each family at risk....

44. In the larger local authority, one way of meeting this important stage might be through the creation of a special unit (a 'family advice centre' or 'family bureau'), which would be a central point of reference both for the various local authority services and for members of the public....

45. The third stage – treatment – should be in the hands of existing agencies both statutory and voluntary....

Additional powers and duties of local authorities

47. It may be that the long-term solution will be the reorganisation of the various services concerned with the family and their combination into a unified family service.... These are matters well outside our

terms of reference, but we urge the importance of their further study by the Government and by local interests concerned.

48. Meanwhile, the aim should be to improve co-ordination on the basis of the three-fold division of functions discussed in paragraphs 38–45. Departmental boundaries should not be a major consideration in the arrangements, which must be flexible enough to meet the variety of situations. To ensure maximum flexibility and an adequacy of power, we recommend that there should be a general duty laid upon local authorities ... to prevent or forestall the suffering of children through neglect of children in their own homes. In carrying out this duty local authorities should have powers ... to do preventive casework (either themselves or through the agency of a voluntary society) and to provide material needs that cannot be met from other sources....

49. We think it is a matter of first importance that there should be adequate arrangements to make known to the public the various services, including voluntary organisations, available to help them in time of need, and where to apply for advice....

50. ... We recommend that there should be a statutory obligation on local authorities ... to submit for ministerial approval schemes for the prevention of suffering of children though neglect in their own homes....

Report of the Committee on Children and Young Persons, The Ingleby Report, Cmnd 1191, 1960, pp. 10–20.

6.3.5 The death of Maria Colwell

The death of Maria Colwell in January 1973, so soon after the implementation of the Seebohm Report, appeared to confirm the widespread suspicion that both the machinery and method of social work remained deeply flawed. It left the new social services departments extremely vulnerable during the mid-1970s crisis. These press extracts illustrate the suspicion at both a popular and an informed level.

Social worker booed at Brighton inquiry
The social worker who supervised Maria Colwell, aged seven, until her death was booed and shouted at when she gave evidence at an

inquiry at Brighton yesterday.... The inquiry is investigating how local authorities and other agencies dealt with the child, who died on January 7 after a beating by William Kepple ... her stepfather, who is serving an eight-year prison sentence for her manslaughter.

Miss Lees, who was supervising the girl under the court order that returned her to her mother, explained why she and senior social workers supported the mother's application to have her daughter back. The child was the centre of a conflict in a family feud between Mrs Kepple, the mother and ... an aunt who had brought the child up for six years.

Any decision would have caused the child stress and trauma but a case conference agreed that in her long-term interests she should be gradually prepared for a return to her mother.

Miss Lees ... said she was dealing with 70 cases before the child's death. Fifty were children, four of them actively at physical risk.

She thought it essential for the child to see her natural mother, brothers and sisters.

'Even when a child expresses difficulty about seeing a parent, I still feel there is a feeling about the natural parent. I agree it is current thinking and it is supported by my experience', she said....

The Times, 6 November 1973.

Social workers wrong, QC tells inquiry into the death of Maria Colwell

The decision by social workers that sent Maria Colwell back to her natural mother's home ... was in line with current welfare thinking and training but it was a mistake, a QC suggested today.

The social workers' first mistake was not to oppose an application by Mrs Pauline Kepple to revoke the court order that placed the child in the custody of foster-parents ... QC counsel for the inquiry said.

He told the inquiry ... there was also a failure on the part of Miss Diane Lees, the supervising social worker, to retrieve the situation five months later when she investigated complaints that Maria was bruised and was being ill-treated.

The first mistake was not Miss Lees's responsibility, he said. The second mistake was 'virtually inevitable, having regard to current thinking that children should not be removed from the care of natural parents unless there is clear evidence they will suffer serious harm.

'The failure to retrieve the situation in April 1972, was due to a combination of the following facts. First, the allocation to Miss Lees of a caseload which in type and quantity no social worker could properly carry without some of the people involved being put at risk.

'There was an absence of powers which were needed if supervision was to be effective. There was also a failure to devise a system whereby Miss Lees was kept informed of what others knew concerning a child in her care. And there was a failure to make standard arrangements for suspected child abuse cases to be referred for expert medical advice'....

The Times, 8 November 1973.

6.3.6 The 1989 Children Act

> The 1989 Act was a major restatement of policy which, as this extract illustrates, reaffirmed the limited powers of local authorities as against the expressed wishes of children or parents.

20 (4) A local authority may provide accommodation for any child within their area ... if they consider that to do so would safeguard or promote the child's welfare....

(6) Before providing accommodation ... a local authority shall, so far as is reasonably practical and consistent with the child's welfare –

(a) ascertain the child's wishes regarding the provision of accommodation; and

(b) give due consideration (having regard to his age and understanding) to such wishes of the child as they have been able to ascertain.

(7) A local authority may not provide accommodation ... for any child if any person objects who (a) has parental responsibility for him; or (b) is willing and able to

(i) provide accommodation for him; or

(ii) arrange for accommodation to be provided for him.

(8) Any person who has parental responsibility for a child may at any time remove the child from accommodation provided by or on behalf of the local authority.

The Children Act, 1989 c 41, Part III.

6.3.7 New Labour and the 'crisis of child care'

Soon after taking office, New Labour was confronted with evidence of widespread abuse of children in both their families and care, as well as the continuing failure to take decisive action. Its instinctive reaction – summarised in this press report – was to extend the Conservative strategy of sending 'hit squads' to local authorities which (regardless of resource constraints) were assumed to be failing.

The government is ready to take new powers ... following a series of high-profile child-abuse cases.... These would include sending social care task forces into departments deemed to be failing. Ministers already have powers to send teams into failing local education authorities and the new social services powers – which would require legislation – would be modelled on this.

Evidence has emerged of a crisis in child care. Allegations of child abuse in residential care homes, heard at the North Wales tribunal, and a series of high-profile inquiries into the deaths of abused children have undermined public confidence in the care system.... But there is concern that the lessons of major inquiries into abuse are still not being learnt.

There have now been more than 30 large inquiries. The death in 1974 of Maria Colwell, the Frank Beck Inquiry in Leicestershire, Staffordshire Pindown, Cleveland and the Clyde report on Orkney. With more than a dozen police forces investigating abuse, further inquiries are likely.

In many cases the recommendations of published reports have a familiar ring, but have not always been universally adopted. Leading child-care lawyer, Allan Levy QC, who chaired the Pindown Inquiry in Staffordshire, said yesterday, 'There have been at least 30 significant inquiries in the last 20 years or so if not more. It is the same scenario over and over again and it has been going on for years. We are just not following up on these recommendations. When you look through the various reports you are reading the same material, the same recommendations, the same failings, and I find it very very disturbing.'

The Independent, 19 October 1997.

221

6.3.8 The 1997 Utting Report

> In response to public concern, a thorough review of residential
> care was commissioned which its chairman, Sir William
> Utting, described as 'a crash course in human (predominantly
> male) wickedness and in the fallibility of social institutions'.
> Rather than realising the hope in 1948 that all children in care
> would be provided with someone 'vitally interested' in their
> welfare, all too often care had provided someone interested in
> their systematic abuse. This press report summarises the
> catalogue of failure revealed by the report.

The report, *People Like Us*, says there needs to be a rethink on the
current strategy of residential care. [It] says that councils now spend
less on residential care than they did 10 years ago. 'We feel that residential child care as a national service has shrunk to below that which
provides a reasonable choice for children.'

Research had shown that 75 per cent of children leaving care have
no academic qualifications of any kind. More than half of them are
unemployed, and 38 per cent of young prisoners have been in care.
One in seven girls was also pregnant on leaving care aged 16 or 17.

On welfare of children in care the report says it received evidence
of high rates of ill health. 'Professor Jo Siebert told us that children
looked after by local authorities were the most deprived group of children he had met, with serious health needs requiring expert attention
from community paediatricians and psychiatrists. A submission to us
estimated that 75 per cent had mental health problems, some complex
and severe, and some with undiagnosed psychoses.'

On paedophiles in the care system, [it] says: 'Becoming associated
with residential work as an employee or volunteer provides the abuser
with a captive group of vulnerable children. Abusers may be good at
their jobs, winning respect, affection or fear from their colleagues and
admiration from the parents whose children they corrupt.'

The report goes on: 'Persistent sexual abusers are a scourge of
childhood. Each one who adopts the lifetime career of abusing children sexually will amass a library of hundreds of victims. All of these
will be damaged, many will be caused unspeakable psychological and
physical harm. People who prey upon children in this way are sexual
terrorists.'

The Independent, 20 November 1997.

222

6.3.9 Home truths

> Given the increased emphasis since the 1980s on 'consumer empowerment', the Utting Committee sought the opinion of children in residential care. Their testimony revealed how the hopes of Lady Allen and the Curtis Committee had been consistently disappointed and still went unrealised even in areas of perceived 'best practice' such as Camden.

7.3 Entering the care system causes bewilderment, displacement and loss. The new entrant is peculiarly vulnerable at that point to bad influence by predatory adults and delinquent peers. What is needed then and thereafter is a trusted adult who knows the system, answers questions, listens to anxieties, cracks problems, guides and supports. Children lose control over what happens to them....

7.4 With experience they acquire cynicism about whether things can go well for them. Inertia takes over because it is too difficult to change things. *'Young people felt they were not routinely listened to or involved in planning and decision making.'* ...

7.5 The danger most often referred to was that from other children: particularly bullying, physical abuse and theft....

7.6 Less was said about danger to personal safety from staff....

7.7 Confidence in the complaints procedure is low....

7.8 The small group of Camden children knew why they were being looked after and what their care history was. They were familiar with their care plans and with complaints procedures. They understood what 'feeling safe' meant and how to share fears for their safety with a responsible adult. What upset them most was the sense of crisis and emergency that surrounded changes of placement....

7.11 The common theme to our discussions with young people was their very reasonable desire to be treated as people and as individuals – which is what the Children Act intended – and the reality that local authorities needed much more than avowed good intentions to achieve this. The inadvertently oppressive nature of professional systems was exposed by the Camden child who said, very simply, *'I don't like people making decisions about me and they think they know what's best for me just by reading my file'.*

Department of Health, *People Like Us*, London, 1997, pp. 76–7.

Guide to further reading

There is a mass of secondary literature on postwar welfare, written by a wide range of academic and non-academic authors. At times it appears to represent a tower of Babel, especially when specialist language is used. More commonly, however, it provides a stimulating mix of information, ideas and interpretations.

The mix of authors is well illustrated by the three standard histories, which are written respectively by a historian, a social policy expert and a journalist. They are R. Lowe, *The Welfare State in Britain since 1945*, Basingstoke, 2nd edn, 1999; H. Glennerster, *British Social Policy since 1945*, Oxford, 2nd edn, 2000; and N. Timmins, *The Five Giants*, London, 1995. They can be supplemented by the comprehensive range of short essays in P. Alcock et al., *The Student's Companion to Social Policy*, Oxford, 1998, and two more conventional collections of essays: D. Gladstone (ed.), *British Social Welfare*, London, 1995, and R.M. Page and R. Silburn, *British Social Welfare in the Twentieth Century*, Basingstoke, 1999. An economic historian's interpretation is provided by P. Johnson in R. Floud and D. McCloskey (eds), *The Economic History of Britain since 1700*, vol. 3, Cambridge, 1994, whilst a wider historical perspective is employed in D. Gladstone, *The Twentieth-Century Welfare State*, Basingstoke, 1999.

The model analysis of the output and outcomes of the core policies since 1970 is H. Glennerster and J. Hills, *The State of Welfare*, Oxford, 2nd edn, 1998. Analysis is broadened in N. Ellison and C. Pierson, *Developments in British Social Policy*, Basingstoke, 1998. Key issues confronting New Labour are presented with great clarity in H. Glennerster, *Paying for Welfare*, London, 3rd edn, 1997, and J. Hills, *The Future of Welfare*, York, 1997. Its response is evaluated in M. Powell, *New Labour, New Welfare State?*, Bristol, 1999, and P. Toynbee and D. Walker, *Did Things Get Better?*, London, 2001.

The best statistical guide to policy outcomes is A.H. Halsey and J. Webb, *Twentieth-Century British Social Trends*, Basingstoke, 2000, while the best guides to regional variations in policy are J.G. Kellas, *The Scottish Political System*, Cambridge, 4th edn, 1989, and D. Birrell and A. Murie, *Policy and Government in Northern Ireland*, Dublin, 1980. K. Young and N. Rao provide a good guide to local policy implementation in *Local Government since 1945*, Oxford, 1997.

The political debate

A good introduction is V. George and P. Wilding, *Ideology and Social Welfare*, London, 1985. This can be supplemented by C. Pierson, *Beyond the Welfare State*, Cambridge, 2nd edn, 1998, and F. Williams, *Social Policy*, Cambridge, 1989. Also useful is V. George and R. Page (eds), *Modern Thinkers on Welfare*, London, 1995, whilst N. Barr, *The Economics of the Welfare State*, Oxford, 2nd edn, 1994, is comprehensive and contains non-technical summaries. An excellent collection of key texts is C. Pierson and F.G. Castles (eds), *The Welfare State Reader*, Cambridge, 2000.

Social security

There is no comprehensive history of social security, although M. Hill, *Social Security Policy in Britain*, Aldershot, 1990, provides a good introduction. Jose Harris has written the classic biography *William Beveridge*, Oxford, 2nd edn, 1997, and examined his legacy, in the light of New Right attacks, in 'Enterprise and welfare states: a comparative perspective', *Transactions of the Royal Historical Society*, 40, 1990, pp. 175–95. A selection of Beveridge's writings appears in K. and J. Williams, *A Beveridge Reader*, London, 1987, and his legacy is further analysed in J. Hills et al., *Beveridge and Social Security*, Oxford, 1994. A stimulating introduction to policy in the 1960s is K.G. Banting, *Poverty, Politics and Policy*, London, 1979, whilst a comparative framework for policy until 1975 is provided by P. Baldwin, *The Politics of Social Solidarity*, Cambridge, 1990. The poor themselves are well covered by K. Coates and R. Silburn, *Poverty: The Forgotten Englishmen*, London, 1970, and P. Townsend, *Poverty in the United Kingdom*, Harmondsworth, 1979. K. Kiernan

Guide to further reading

et al., *Lone Motherhood in the Twentieth Century*, Oxford, 1998, provides an excellent introduction to an increasingly politicised group of claimants.

Health care

A brief, expert summary of the relevant literature is provided by V. Berridge, *Health and Society in Britain since 1939*, Cambridge, 1999. Foremost amongst the citations are R. Klein, *The New Politics of the NHS*, London, 3rd edn, 1995, and C. Ham, *Health Policy in Britain*, Basingstoke, 3rd edn, 1992, both of which can be supplemented by the exhaustive two-volume official history, C. Webster, *The Health Services since the War*, London, 1988–96. Excellent comparative analysis is provided by C. Ham, *Health Check*, London, 1990, and M. Moran, *Governing the Health Care State*, Manchester, 1999.

Education

Two excellent collections of documents, as mentioned in Chapter 4, are J.S. Maclure, *Educational Documents*, London, 5th edn, 1986, and H. Silver, *Equal Opportunity in Education*, London, 1973. They can best be contextualised by B. Simon, *Education and the Social Order, 1940–1990*, London, 1991, and by two books by Roy Lowe, *Education in the Postwar Years*, London, 1988, and *Schooling and Social Change, 1964–1990*, London, 1997. Research in one particular area of controversy is well summarised in M. Sanderson, *Education and Economic Decline, 1870s to 1990s*, Cambridge, 1998.

Housing

A good modern introduction is P. Malpass and A. Murie, *Housing Policy and Practice*, Basingstoke, 5th edn, 1998, whilst an older text puts Britain's experience into an excellent comparative perspective: D. Donnison and C. Ungerson, *Housing Policy*, Basingstoke, 1982. K.G. Banting, *Poverty, Politics and Policy*, London, 1979, is again an excellent introduction to the problems of the 1960s, whilst P. Dunleavy, *The Politics of Mass Housing, 1945–1975*, Oxford, 1981, provides a classic exposure of high-rise building. An equally

227

definitive analysis of planning is provided by A. Cox, *Adversary Politics and Land*, Cambridge, 1984. The peculiar Scottish experience is well summarised by A. Gibb, 'Policy and politics in Scottish housing since 1945' in R. Rodger (ed.), *Scottish Housing in the Twentieth Century*, Leicester, 1989.

Personal social services

Two good documentary collections are B. Watkin, *Documents on Health and Social Services: 1834 to the Present Day*, London, 1975, and J. Packman, *The Child's Generation: Child Care Policy from Curtis to Houghton*, London, 1975. Two of the main client groups are well covered by H. Hendrick, *Child Welfare*, London, 1994, and by R. Means and R. Smith, *Poor Law to Community Care: The Development of Welfare Services for the Elderly, 1939–1971*, Bristol, 1998. The evolving relationship between government and voluntary agencies is documented in G. Finlayson, 'A moving frontier', *Twentieth Century British History*, 1, 1990, pp. 183–206, and in J. Lewis, *The Voluntary Sector, the State and Social Work in Britain*, Cheltenham, 1995. The solution reached in the 1990s is criticised in J. Lewis and H. Glennerster, *Implementing Community Care*, Milton Keynes, 1996. Finally, important policy variations are noted in J. Murphy, *British Social Services: The Scottish Dimension*, Edinburgh, 1992.

Index

This book covers a large number of people and issues. This index only lists those mentioned more than once.